W9-DCU-474

WITHDRAWN

Transport and Environment

TRANSPORT ECONOMICS, MANAGEMENT AND POLICY

General Editor: Kenneth Button, *Professor of Public Policy, School of Public Policy, George Mason University, USA*

Transport is a critical input for economic development and for optimizing social and political interaction. Recent years have seen significant new developments in the way that transport is perceived by private industry and governments, and in the way academics look at it.

The aim of this series is to provide original material and up-to-date synthesis of the state of modern transport analysis. The coverage embraces all conventional modes of transport but also includes contributions from important related fields such as urban and regional planning and telecommunications where they interface with transport. The books draw from many disciplines and some cross-disciplinary boundaries. They are concerned with economics, planning, sociology, geography, management science, psychology and public policy. They are intended to help improve the understanding of transport, the policy needs to the most economically advanced countries and the problems of resource-poor developing economies. The authors come from around the world and will represent some of the outstanding young scholars as well as established names.

Titles in the series include:

Air Transport Networks
Theory and Policy Implications
Kenneth Button and Roger Stough

Analytical Transport Economics
An International Perspective
Edited by Jacob B. Polak and Arnold Heertje

Transport and Environment
In Search of Sustainable Solutions
Edited by Eran Feitelson and Erik T. Verhoef

MONTGOMERY COLLEGE
ROCKVILLE CAMPUS LIBRARY
ROCKVILLE, MARYLAND

Transport and Environment

In Search of Sustainable Solutions

Edited by

Eran Feitelson

Senior Lecturer, Department of Geography, Hebrew University of Jerusalem, Israel

Erik T. Verhoef

Researcher, Department of Spatial Economics, Free University Amsterdam, The Netherlands

TRANSPORT ECONOMICS, MANAGEMENT AND POLICY

Edward Elgar
Cheltenham, UK • Northampton, MA, USA

2671Y1

JUN 12 2002

© Eran Feitelson and Erik T. Verhoef 2001

All rights reserved. No part of this publication may be reproduced, stored in a retrieval system or transmitted in any form or by any means, electronic, mechanical or photocopying, recording, or otherwise without the prior permission of the publisher.

Published by
Edward Elgar Publishing Limited
Glensanda House
Montpellier Parade
Cheltenham
Glos GL50 1UA
UK

Edward Elgar Publishing, Inc.
136 West Street
Suite 202
Northampton
Massachusetts 01060
USA

A catalogue record for this book
is available from the British Library

Library of Congress Cataloguing in Publication Data

Transport and environment: in search of sustainable solutions/edited by Eran Feitelson, Erik T. Verhoef.
    p. cm.—(Transport economics, management, and policy)
    Includes index.
    1. Transportation—Environmental aspects. 2. Sustainable development. I. Feitelson, Eran, 1956– II. Verhoef, E. T. III. Series.
TD195.T7 T728 2001
363.73′1—dc21   00–067345

ISBN 1 84064 105 3

Printed and bound in Great Britain by Biddles Ltd, *www.biddles.co.uk*

Contents

Figures

Tables

Contributors

Piet H.L. Bovy   Faculty of Civil Engineering and Geosciences and The Netherlands Research School for Transport, Infrastructure and Logistics (TRAIL), The Netherlands.

Kenneth J. Button   Institute of Public Policy, George Mason University, Fairfax, USA.

Galit Cohen   Department of Spatial Economics, Free University Amsterdam, The Netherlands.

Eran Feitelson   Department of Geography, Hebrew University of Jerusalem, Israel.

Harry Geerlings   The Netherlands Research School for Transport, Infrastructure and Logistics (TRAIL), Erasmus University Rotterdam, The Netherlands.

René Kemp   Maastricht Research Institute on Innovation and Technology (MERIT), of Maastricht University, The Netherlands, and STEP, Oslo, Norway.

Wim Korver   Department of Transport, The Netherlands Organization for Applied Scientific Research (TNO), Delft, The Netherlands.

Kees Maat   OTB Research Institute for Urban, Housing and Mobility Studies, Delft University of Technology, The Netherlands.

Stephen Marshall   Bartlett School of Planning, University College London, UK.

Peter Nijkamp   Department of Spatial Economics, Free University Amsterdam, The Netherlands.

Ilan Salomon   Department of Geography, Hebrew University of Jerusalem, Israel.

Benoît Simon   Centre for European Evaluation Expertise (C3E) – Mouterde Consultants, Issy les Moulineaux, France.

Patricia G.J. Twaalfhoven   PPK Environment & Infrastructure Pty Ltd, Australia.

Arjan J. van Binsbergen   Faculty of Civil Engineering and Geosciences and The Netherlands Research School for Transport, Infrastructure and Logistics (TRAIL), The Netherlands.

Toon van der Hoorn   Transportation Research Centre (AVV), Ministry of Transport, Rotterdam, The Netherlands and Faculty of Economics and Econometrics, University of Amsterdam, The Netherlands.

Hans C. van Ham   Faculty of Technology, Policy and Management, Delft University of Technology, The Netherlands.

Daniëlle B. van Veen-Groot   Department of Spatial Economics, Free University Amsterdam, The Netherlands.

Bert van Wee   National Institute of Public Health and the Environment (RIVM), Bilthoven, The Netherlands and Faculty of Geographical Sciences, Utrecht University, The Netherlands.

Erik T. Verhoef   Department of Spatial Economics, Free University Amsterdam, The Netherlands.

Johan G.S.N. Visser   The Netherlands Research School for Transport, Infrastructure and Logistics (TRAIL), Delft University of Technology, The Netherlands.

Preface

The environmental aspect of transport has been one of the dominant issues on the political agendas for many countries and for a growing number of years. Likewise, it has received ample attention in the transport-orientated literature. Cynical pessimists may point out that the slow pace at which scientific progress seems to be made matches that of policy achievements. Optimists would point at successful policies, technologies and spatial planning concepts, which may not have led to a world-wide sustainable transport system – however defined – but at least give hope for the future.

This book aims to bring together contributions from various disciplines to the study of the broad field of 'Transport and Environment'. The general questions involved in this field appear time and time again to be complex and multifaceted. Any strictly mono-disciplinary approach is therefore likely to miss out on important other factors that may eventually determine a certain solution's or approach's viability. Nevertheless, researchers in this field still often have some natural tendency to stick to their origins, and transdisciplinary communication and cooperation is witnessed less often than probably desirable. With this book, we hope to contribute to a more intensive communication across the boundaries of traditional sciences, by offering contributions from a policy analysis, economic, spatial analytical and technological background.

The infrastructure offered by the 'Network on European Communications and Transport Activities Research' (NECTAR) has proved to offer an excellent means for realizing our goal. The various contributions have been presented at one of the meetings of NECTAR's 'Transport and Environment' cluster. Without NECTAR, this book would not have existed.

We thank the contributors and reviewers for the valuable time and effort they have put in this undertaking, which may not always have run as smoothly as originally envisaged due to our personal shortcomings. We hope that the readers and contributors, after reading this book, will agree that it was worthwhile waiting.

Eran Feitelson, Jerusalem
Erik Verhoef, Amsterdam
July 2000

PART I

Policy Aspects

1. Transport and environment: from policy measures to sustainability notions and back

Eran Feitelson and Erik T. Verhoef

INTRODUCTION

Transportation is essential for human development. At the same time transport systems give rise to a wide set of externalities, many of them environmental. One facet of the transformation of most Western societies to post-materialist value systems, to use Inglehart's (1977) terms, is the greater awareness of and readiness to act on environmental issues. As a result there has been a major transformation in the way environmental effects of transport are viewed and dealt with over the last thirty years.

The shift in the policy arena cannot be described as resulting from any single event. Rather, it has been a process. As awareness of the environmental implications of transport has risen during the last thirty years, the policy discourse has changed too. From a discourse that centered first on growth and later on equity issues it gradually widened to include the environmental effects of transport and the possible ways to address them (Masser et al., 1992). Consequently, it evolved into a multifaceted discussion of the ways and rationales for intervention, and of the role of environmental goals relative to other goals. However, the need for concrete action has remained.

In recent years the importance of transportation-induced environmental externalities has increased. This is due in part to the relative success of developed countries to bring an increasing array of emissions from point sources under control, and in part to the increase of transport-induced emissions resulting primarily from the rapid rise in the number of vehicles and km-vehicles driven. This, in turn, is an outcome of the rising need for flexible mobility and haulage in post-industrial societies (Bell and Feitelson, 1991) and of the demographic trends toward smaller older households and spatial deconcentration (ECMT, 1995). Yet, as the number of actors in the policy field increases, in part an outcome of the rising public awareness of environmental issues, transaction costs of enacting specific policy measures has been rising too. The resulting picture, therefore, is one where the potential benefits of actions designed to reduce transportation's environmental externalities and the costs of such actions are rising concurrently (though not necessarily at the same rate). As a result the question what actions can actually be taken to address the environmental implications of transport is becoming ever more compelling.

The purpose of this book is to present some recent contributions to the analysis of actual measures, options and policies within increasingly complicated settings. However, to set the stage for this discussion and provide a framework, a brief review of the evolution of the discourse of policies geared to address transport's effects is useful. After this very brief review the current set of policy options and analyses of such options is presented, followed by a description of the book's structure.

FROM IMPACT ASSESSMENT TO SUSTAINABILITY NOTIONS

The environmental effects of transport have long been recognized. However, until the 1970s only a few policies or actions were enacted to address these effects. Moreover, the actions enacted were for the most part of very limited scope. Hence, with only few exceptions (such as the 1963 Buchanan Report) it cannot be said that they amounted to an overall policy or strategy to address the environmental effects of transport.

The early 1970s were undoubtedly a watershed in the environmental policy field, as they marked the first comprehensive attempts to address wide-ranging environmental issues. Yet, the emphasis during that era was on the identification of the most deleterious effects and their mitigation. Consequently, many of the policy actions that were enacted to address the environmental effects of transport in the 1970s focused on specific effects and measures. In North America, and later in Western Europe, they were often advanced in response to the findings of environmental impact statements or analyses. Indeed the determination of such effects and their policy implications were the focal point of discussions in this field in the mid-1970s (Johanning and Talvitie, 1976; Larwin and Stuart, 1976). In West Europe much attention was given to planning measures, yet these were also developed in a piecemeal manner at various locales, and not as part of overall strategies (OECD, 1979).

While transport was viewed as an important source of pollution it was not at the focal point of environmental policies enacted in the 1970s. However, as developed countries have increasingly been successful in bringing the pollution emanating from other sources (particularly point sources) under control, while the emissions from transport continue to rise, the relative importance of transport from the perspective of overall environmental policies has been rising. This is manifest in the increasing attention transport receives in the ongoing discussions of implementing Agenda 21 in Europe (O'Riordan and Voisey, 1998).

Concurrently, the importance attached to environmental goals in the transport policy field has also been rising. This can be seen in the views of transportation analysts (Masser et al., 1992), as well as in the increasing array of rules and regulations targeting various elements of the transport systems. Moreover, the range of transport issues addressed within this context has also increased.

The policy actions advanced, and ultimately enacted, are a function of the way problems are framed (Dery, 1984). In the 1970s the problems were usually defined as the physical deleterious effects of transport, such as air pollution, noise, vibrations, visual blight and energy consumption (Sharp and Jennings, 1976, for example). Therefore, it is not surprising that the policies advanced were piecemeal measures designed to mitigate these effects. These included, for example, noise barriers to reduce noise effects along busy routes and more stringent emission standards.

The most significant change in recent years has been in the overall discourse. Essentially, two closely related changes can be observed, culminating in what Weale (1992) termed the 'new environmental politics'. The first is the questioning of the essential policy approach. In particular, economists have increasingly stressed that the crux of the problem is market failures, which should be addressed by market-based instruments, as these have potentially significant efficiency and effectiveness gains (Button, 1993; Verhoef, 1994). The second is the widening of the discourse to include longer time frames, the crossing of boundaries and a wider array of goals. This shift is subsumed under the advent of sustainable development notions, which have come to dominate much of the environmental policy discourse in recent years. The main criticism of this shift focuses on its vagueness and hence the difficulty in translating it into concrete agreed-upon policies (Dryzek, 1997). Actually, the multiple definitions of sustainable development allow a very wide variety of policy measures to be proclaimed sustainable by their proponents, thus making the concept less useful in the policy discourse than would seem from the wide reference to it in policy documents and academic papers.

Sustainable development and sustainable transport have indeed become the most common buzzwords in all discussions of the policies geared to address the environmental implications of transport. Yet, they are no better defined in this field than in other fields. Thus, questions regarding the practical implications are today at the forefront of the policy discourse regarding the transport–environment interface. Essentially, the search is for practical solutions that can advance the sustainability notions. This is the focus of the book.

THE CURRENT AGENDA: EFFECTIVE, ACCEPTABLE POLICY MEASURES

Policy measures are enacted in order to induce change. The need for such change is driven by societal agreement on the desirability of certain goals, as these address issues seen as problematic. In order to meet those goals, targets have to be specified. This process is presented schematically for the case of transport in the central part of Figure 1.1. Essentially, the environmental problems lead to the identification of goals, such as the reduction of emissions. However, to achieve those goals, certain changes need to be effected with regard to specific transport variables (ECMT, 1995). For example, in order to reduce CO emissions, either the emission factor or the total vehicle-km driven should be reduced. These can be achieved if the vehicle fleet is modernized and cars without a catalytic converter are taken off the road, for example, or people shift from the private car to public transport, high-occupancy vehicles or non-motorized modes.

There are many measures that can help achieve the desired changes. These can be grouped in many ways. Much of the discourse in recent years has

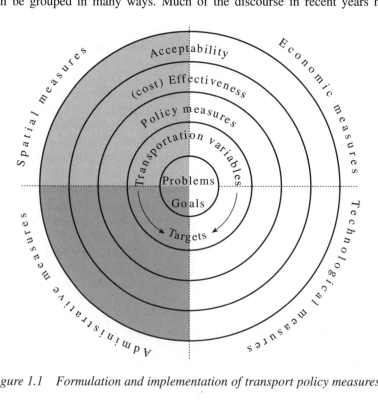

Figure 1.1   Formulation and implementation of transport policy measures

focused on the possibilities for shifting the emphasis from regulative measures to greater use of economic tools. Another notable strand of recent discussions focuses on the implications of urban form for the transport–environment–energy nexus (Anderson et al., 1996; Banister, 1992). Yet, control of urban form is but one possibility for affecting this nexus through planning. As the chapters in this volume indicate, the range is much wider, and its benefits need not be limited to the reduction of CO_2 emissions. Perhaps the greatest potential for addressing the environmental effects of transport lies with the fourth group of measures noted in Figure 1.1 – the technological measures – as several of them can reduce emissions substantially at source. Technological measures have been consistently considered and discussed, at least in the more technically orientated literature. However, the focus of such discussions has tended to be narrow, often not addressing the main impediments to the utilization of technological options – the conditions under which they are likely to be adopted.

The question of policy adoption ranges however beyond the technological measures. Actually, it is pertinent for all measures. This question can be divided into two, featured by the two exterior circles in Figure 1.1. The first is, what is the likely effectiveness of each measure. To address this question the assumptions underlying the proposition of the measure discussed have to be specified and scrutinized. In reviewing this issue for the case of rail, Salomon et al. (1997), for example, found that many of the purported benefits are based on assumptions that are unlikely to be met, at least in the Israeli case.

However, even when a measure is potentially highly effective it will not necessarily be adopted. As the policy enactment process is ultimately a political process, it is necessary that the proposed measures be politically acceptable. Economists have shown time and again that economic instruments are potentially cost-effective (Button, 1993). Yet, such instruments have only rarely been used (Levinson, 1998). Thus, in recent years several studies have analysed the factors that affect the political acceptability of such measures, focusing on their distribution implications (Verhoef et al., 1997; Rienstra et al., 1999; Rietveld, 1997). The question of political acceptability and the distribution aspect of policies is not limited to economic instruments. Rather, it is pertinent to all types of measures, and central to discussions of policies in the context of sustainable development or sustainable transport notions (Plaut and Shmueli, 2000).

The attractiveness of sustainability notions and their widespread acceptance stems to a large degree from their inclusiveness. Essentially, they imply that growth and equity goals should be addressed in a manner that does not harm future generations. Thus, it potentially addresses concerns of economic interests, minorities or other groups concerned with equity issues and of environmentalists. To achieve these multifaceted and essentially contradictory goals, the measures used have to be seen as cost-effective and just from a distribution perspective. Hence, sustainability notions cannot be advanced without addressing these aspects. Moreover, it is unlikely that any single set of measures would be sufficient to advance such notions. Thus, in order to advance the sustainability notions at this point it is necessary to indulge again in detailed policy analyses, focusing, however, on a wider array of issues. This is the purpose of the book.

THIS BOOK

The implementation of sustainable transport concepts implies that all facets of transport be addressed as part of long-term strategies at various spatial levels. That is, while most of the transport policy literature focuses on the mitigation of the effects of private vehicles, usually focusing on a very limited set of measures that are enacted in one time period at one spatial level (national, regional, metropolitan or local), a truly sustainable transport perspective suggests that the scope of action should be broadened. In particular, it should include additional elements of the transport sector, such as freight transport, aviation and maritime transport, and transcend the usual time and space constraints. Moreover, such a strategy has to address economic and equity concerns in addition to the environmental targets it is often designed to meet.

The first part of the book focuses on the type of studies that are necessary to advance such broad concepts. Yet, as is manifest throughout the book, the studies themselves are well targeted at specific issues that have to be addressed before comprehensive sustainable transport strategies can indeed be formulated and implemented. The primary requisite of all the background studies is that policy issues be analysed. Yet, such analyses are not always conducted in a sufficiently careful manner. Therefore, in Chapter 2, Twaalfhoven and van Ham evaluate a policy analysis study of the sustainable freight transport policies in the Netherlands.

The enactment of single policy measures at one point in time does not amount to a sustainable transport strategy. In order to formulate a strategy that transcends a one-generation time horizon and addresses the range of concerns raised within the sustainable development discourse, such measures have to be assembled into policy packages. Yet, the question how such policies should be packaged has not received much attention to date. In Chapter 3, the options for such packaging are identified by Feitelson, Salomon and Cohen.

One of the transport sectors that has not been well integrated into the sustainable transport discourse, but whose importance in the post-industrial economy is growing, is aviation. In Chapter 4, Button asks whether current air transport policies are sustainable. One of the main issues he looks at is the efficiency of such policies.

As noted above, much of the discourse in recent years has focused on regulative and economic tools. Therefore, these issues were not emphasized in this volume. Rather, emphasis is placed on the two types of measures that received perhaps less attention in recent years – technology measures and spatial (or planning) policies.

Technological options, and particularly a shift away from the internal combustion engine, have undoubtedly great potential for reducing the deleterious environmental effects of transport. The main question in this regard concerns the potential of alternative fuel systems, and particularly electric vehicles. This is the topic of the first two chapters in Part II. Wim Korver analyses four drive concepts (internal combustion engines, electric vehicles, hybrid vehicles and fuel cells) under four scenarios. He finds that hybrid vehicles are the most likely to replace the internal combustion engine, and that electric vehicles may play a significant role only under a growth scenario, and then only with significant government support. In Chapter 6, Kemp and Simon also examine the future of electric vehicles, using a co-evolutionary sociotechnical scenario method, focusing on the interaction between technological factors and society. They too find that hybrid vehicles are likely to provide the best interim step, with battery-based electric vehicles or fuel cells providing a long-term option. Yet such options will only materialize if significant societal changes in the way cars are used take place.

The remaining chapters in Part II focus on a relatively under-researched issue: the potential of urban underground freight transport. In Chapter 7, Visser and Geerlings present a conceptual stepwise framework for the development and implementation of so-called 'mega-technological innovations'. The concrete example they consider is underground freight transport. Although they acknowledge that there are currently large uncertainties on the costs and benefits of underground transport, they conclude that there is certainly potential for underground freight transport in a sustainable transport system. This conclusion is shared by van Binsbergen and Bovy in Chapter 8, who in their contribution pay specific attention to the implications of underground freight transport for logistic concepts.

Part III of the book focuses on the different facets of the planning measures that can be used for addressing transport's environmental effects. These measures can pertain to different spatial levels. This part is structured in a sequence leading from the local level to the international level. In Chapter 9, Stephen Marshall looks at urban design issues from a public transport perspective. In doing so, he discusses the total urban area, the area along transit routes and local design features around transit nodes, arguing that all these features have to be addressed if public transport is to become more attractive. In

Chapter 10, Kees Maat analyses the much vaunted premise that compact cities can be important for reducing transport's energy consumption, focusing on the Dutch experience. Based on two case studies he concludes that the actual benefits are more modest than usually purported. Then, in Chapter 11, van Wee and van der Hoorn move to the next spatial level, by analysing scenario studies of the Randsad in the Netherlands. In the final chapter, van Veen-Groot and Nijkamp move up to the international level, setting up a scenario-based study of the interactions between globalization processes, international transport and CO_2 emissions.

Overall, the different chapters in this volume use different disciplinary backgrounds and different methodologies for advancing, discussing and evaluating a wide variety of seemingly unrelated policy measures. Yet, it is only by critically examining a very wide variety of possible measures and actions that sustainable development notions can be further advanced, as only such studies conducted in the light of the sustainability notions advanced in recent years can help transform sustainable development and sustainable transport notions into practical strategies.

REFERENCES

Anderson, W.P., P.S. Kanaroglou and E.J. Miller (1996), 'Urban form, energy and the environment: a review of issues, evidence and policy', *Urban Studies*, **33**, 7–35.

Banister, D. (1992), 'Energy use, transport and settlement patterns', in M.J. Breheny (ed.), *Sustainable Development and Urban Form*, London: Pion, pp. 160–81.

Bell, M. and E. Feitelson (1991), 'Economic restructuring and the demand for transportation services', *Transportation Quarterly*, **45**, 517–38.

Button, K.J. (1993), *Transport, the Environment and Ecnomic Policy*, Aldershot: Edward Elgar.

Dery, D. (1984), *Problem Definition in Policy Analysis*, Lawrence, KS: University Press of Kansas.

Dryzek, J.S. (1997), *The Politics of the Earth: Environmental Discourses*, Oxford: Oxford University Press.

European Conference of Ministers of Transport (ECMT) (1995), *Urban Travel and Sustainable Development*, Paris: OECD.

Inglehart, R. (1977), *The Silent Revolution*, Princeton, NJ: Princeton University Press.

Johanning, J. and A. Talvetie (1976), 'State of the art and EISs in transportation', *Transportation Research Record*, **603**, 25–30.

Larwin, T.F. and D.G. Stuart (1976), 'Issue-oriented approach to environmental impact analysis', *Transportation Research Record*, **583**, 1–14.

Levinson, D. (1998), 'Road pricing in practice', in K.J. Button and E.T. Verhoef (eds), *Road Pricing Traffic Congestion and the Environment: Issues of Efficiency and Social Feasibility*, Cheltenham: Edward Elgar, pp. 14–38.

Masser, I., O. Sviden and M. Wegener (1992), 'From growth to equity and sustainability: paradigm shift in transport planning?', *Futures*, **24**, 539–58.

O'Riordan, T. and H. Voisey (eds) (1998), *The Transition to Sustainability: The Politics of Agenda 21 in Europe*, London: Earthscan.

Organization for Economic Cooperation and Development (OECD) (1979), *Urban Transport and the Environment*, 4 vols, Paris: OECD.

Plaut, P.O. and D.F. Shmueli (2000), 'Sustainable Transport – a Comparative Analysis of Israel, the Netherlands and the United Kingdom,' *World Transport Policy and Practice*.

Rienstra, S.A., P. Rietveld and E.T. Verhoef (1999), 'The social support for policy measures in passenger transport: a statistical analysis for the Netherlands', *Transportation Research*, D 4, 181–200.

Rietveld, P. (1997), 'Political economy issues of environmentally friendly transport Policies', *International Journal of Environment and Pollution*, **7**, 398–416.

Salomon, I., E. Feitelson and G. Cohen (1997), 'The rail solution: promise and limitations', *Riveon Lekalkala*, **44**, 663–99 (in Hebrew).

Sharp C. and T. Jennings (1976), *Transport and the Environment*, Leicester: Leicester University Press.

Verhoef, E. (1994), *The Economics of Regulating Road Transport*, Cheltenham, UK: Edward Elgar.

Verhoef, E.T., P. Nijkamp and P. Rietveld (1997), 'The social feasibility of road pricing: a case study of the Randstad area', *Journal of Transport Economics and Policy*, **31**, 255–76.

Weale, A. (1992), *The New Politics of Pollution*, Manchester: Manchester University Press.

2. Sustainable freight transport for the Netherlands: an evaluation of a policy analysis study

Patricia G.J. Twaalfhoven and Hans C. van Ham

INTRODUCTION

Many studies are carried out in the area of transportation and infrastructure within the Netherlands to assist policy makers to improve the basis to exercise their judgment on transportation issues. This chapter includes a report on an evaluation of the success and role of a policy analysis study, FORWARD, in the policy process. The FORWARD study was focused on sustainable freight transport for the Netherlands. The success of such a policy analysis study is difficult to define and measure, partly because different actors have different goals and perspectives. Each actor related to the study views the role, success, and usefulness of the study from its own perspective. First, the policy context and background of the FORWARD study is described. This is followed by a brief description of the research approach, the policy options examined, the performance measures used, and the results of the study. The second part of the chapter is focused on how different actors that were related to the study perceive the success and/or failures of the FORWARD study.

TRANSPORT POLICY IN THE NETHERLANDS

Analyses carried out at the end of the 1980s indicated that, similar to other European countries, there would be a large number of problems facing the Dutch transport system over the years to come. In 1990, ahead of its time (OECD, 1994), the Dutch government published a policy statement on transport, *Tweede Structuurschema Verkeer en Vervoer* (SVV II), in English, the Second Transport Structure Plan (Ministerie van Verkeer en Waterstaat, 1990). The overall purpose of the transport policy described in SVV II is to ensure accessibility; however, as economic growth had brought about even more rapid increases in road transport, the accessibility of industrial and commercial centers was threatened. Moreover, the competitive position of the transport sector was, and is, endangered by congestion problems, which is a 'hot' issue for the Netherlands, where international transport and distribution plays an important role in the economy. Other than causing congestion problems, road transport damages the environment in at least four ways: depletion of energy sources, air pollution, noise nuisance and fragmentation of the countryside. A decline in road safety is another of the resulting problems. The difficulty that Dutch society was, and still is, facing is that solutions, which will allow economic growth, do not fit into the context of a sustainable society. A sustainable society typically implies setting limits on the environmental effects of the transport system, which may conflict with economic growth. Facing these conflicting goals, the Dutch government decided in 1990 that action needed to be taken and described the policy to be followed to design a sustainable transport system in the SVV II document.

In the SVV II document, various targets are defined with respect to (i) environment and amenity, for example, by 2010 emissions of NO_x and unburned hydrocarbons emitted by road vehicles must be 75 per cent lower than in 1986; the total area disturbed by high noise levels, that is, larger than 55dB(A), should not be greater than in 1986; (ii) managing and restraining mobility, for example, major residential developments will be served by public transport; and (iii) accessibility, for example, the capacity of the public transport system in the main corridors will be doubled compared to 1986; high-quality rail links will be established between the main seaport areas and their hinterland for freight transport.

In the SVV II document a large number of policy measures were formulated in order to achieve the defined aims. The formulated policy measures were grouped into four categories: (i) environment and amenity, (ii) managing and restraining mobility, (iii) accessibility, and (iv) support measures (see Figure 2.1).

The government constantly reviews the progress made to monitor the actual developments and move step by step along the desired route. The government has reported on this annually since 1993[1] in the Beleidseffecten Rapportages (BERs), in English, the Policy Assessment Reports. These formal policy assessments and additional analyses of the developments in transport showed, on average, poor performance on environmental indicators and good results in relation to the economy and accessibility (Ministerie van Verkeer en Waterstaat, 1997).

The Policy Assessment Report 1996 (ibid.), for example, showed a more or less stable pattern of NO_x emissions (see Figure 2.2). Without intensifying and taking new policy measures, the aim of a 75 per cent reduction of the NO_x emissions in 2010 will not be achieved.

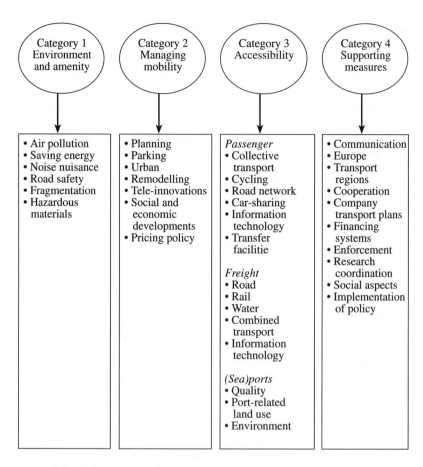

Figure 2.1   Policy categories

Despite the fact that SVV II is fairly comprehensive in its policy recommendations, there had been a continued debate about the importance, and the effects, of specific policy options. Part of the continuing public debate was focused on the alternatives for dealing with freight transport. Little attention was given to freight transport policy in SVV II, not many policy statements were included about freight transport in particular. Only 13 of the 170 pages of the document were dedicated specifically to freight transport. In these pages it was briefly stated that the various targets defined with respect to environment and amenity, managing and restraining mobility, and accessibility also hold for freight transport (Ministerie van Verkeer en Waterstaat, 1990). Most attention was given to policy options to increase, or at least retain, the economic benefits of freight transportation by road, rail and water,

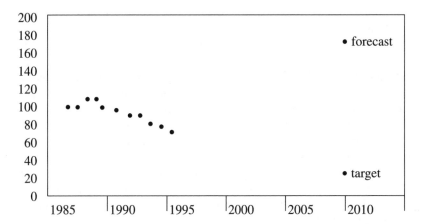

Figure 2.2 NO_x emissions by road traffic (index 1986 = 100; 2010 = 25)

by enlarging its strong international market position. Furthermore, attention was given to logistics, improving and expanding the infrastructure, and increasing the transport efficiency. Various parties argued that there could be more attractive alternatives to a number of the policy options suggested in SVV II.

The continuing public debate about the importance of freight transport to the Dutch economy and about the environmental consequences of freight transport motivated the Ministry of Transport, Public Works and Water Management, hereinafter the Ministry, to commission a broad study of freight policy options and their impacts and costs.

THE FORWARD PROJECT

FORWARD (Freight Options for Road, Water, and Rail for the Dutch) is a freight policy analysis study, which was carried out by RAND Europe (formerly the European-American Center for Policy Analysis), which is part of the California-based RAND Corporation. The study was carried out over a two-year period from the end of 1992 to the end of 1994.

The problem originally posed to the analysis team was to find the best ways to shift freight off the highways and on to other transport modes. However, this was soon realized to be too narrow a problem definition and more of a solution statement than a problem statement. Asking the ministry why freight should be shifted off the highway revealed a desire to reduce the negative effects of road freight transport. There are other ways of dealing with the negative effects of road freight transport besides shifting it off the highways, such as making better use of the existing infrastructure and truck fleet, or employing cleaner diesel engines.

It was also realized that there were likely to be many optional policy actions for coping with the negative impacts of road freight transport, and that preferences among these actions would depend on the relative importance placed on their effects. People concerned about environmental effects are likely to evaluate policy options differently from people concerned about economic effects. A major component of the problem was how to provide some rationale for choosing among a large number of policy options and making tradeoffs among many measures of effectiveness.

The goal of the research was eventually defined as (European-American Center for Policy Analysis, 1996a p. 10): 'Find the best strategies to mitigate the negative impacts of the growth of freight transport while retaining the economic benefits'.

With the support, and active participation, of the ministry staff members, a set of policy analysis tools were designed and built to assess the impacts of various policy options, called tactics, identify promising tactics, and design promising combinations of tactics, called strategies, to help achieve various policy goals. The study examined as many policy options as possible and evaluated each policy option's effects on a broad range of performance measures, including emissions, noise, safety, congestion, costs, added value to the economy and employment. This was done for three alternative economic scenarios for the year 2015. A spreadsheet model called Policy Analytic Computational Environment for FORWARD (PACE-FORWARD) was developed to assess the impact of the possible changes in the transport system (Carillo et al., 1996). A second model, called the Cost-Effectiveness Model (CEM), was developed to rank the tactics based on their cost-effectiveness. The CEM and other tools and information were used to design possible strategies.

The research approach used in the study is depicted in Figure 2.3 (European-American Center for Policy Analysis, 1996b). A short description of the steps in the process and the study's main conclusions follow.

Scenarios, Tactics and Impacts

Freight demand scenarios for the year 1990, that is, the 'current' situation, and for three scenarios for the year 2015 were developed, based on freight demand data developed by the Dutch research institute (NEA).

The performance measures considered in the FORWARD study were divided into six categories: emissions, noise, safety, congestion, costs and the national economy. The emissions category consisted of six types of emissions: CO_2, NO_x, C_mH_n, CO, SO_2 and aerosols. The effects on the noise

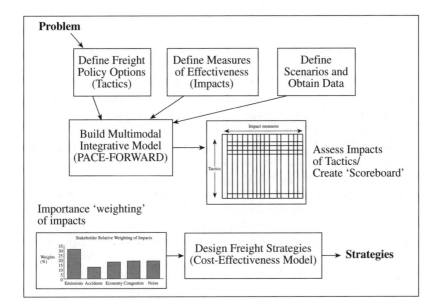

Figure 2.3   Research approach

nuisance were measured by the average distance from the highways to the 55 dB(A) noise contour. To measure safety, the impacts on the number of truck-involved accidents, injuries, fatalities and accidents related to the transport of hazardous goods were estimated. Total congestion severity, that is, number of incidents × average length of backup × average duration of incident, was taken as a measure of congestion on the Netherlands highways. The net incremental cost of a tactic, that is, its net additional cost over all stakeholders, was taken as a measure for the cost. For the macroeconomic impacts, the changes in employment and value added for the transport and production sectors were estimated.

The tactics evaluated fell into three main categories (European-American Center for Policy Analysis, 1996c): (i) *Direct Mitigation Tactics*, which seek specifically to reduce one or more of the negative impacts at their source, for example, the use of soot filters, cleaner engines, low-noise tires and electric vans; (ii) *Transport Efficiency Tactics*, which seek to use the truck fleet and transport infrastructure more efficiently, for example, the use of city distribution centers and larger trucks; (iii) *Mode Shift Tactics*, which were specifically designed to stimulate the shift of freight off the roads and on to other modes of transport, for example, using a regional dispatching system at ports and having the railroads give priority to freight transport over passenger transport, building multimodal centers.

The PACE-FORWARD Model

A microcomputer-based spreadsheet model called PACE-FORWARD was developed to assess the impacts of the tactics. It was planned to use existing analytic tools to estimate the effects. It turned out, however, that no existing model or combination of models could satisfy the broad set of requirements of the project. As a result, PACE-FORWARD was developed, which uses data, factors and relationships from existing Dutch transportation models and databases.

PACE-FORWARD allows the user to choose one of the modelled tactics and one of the scenarios: the current situation (1990) or one of the future scenarios, that is, for the year 2015. The model then calculates the impacts on air pollution, noise pollution, safety, congestion, costs and the national economy. The user chooses the impacts to be displayed and how they are displayed. The results can be given as absolute numbers or in percentage changes from a base case. Alternative formats for displaying the results include maps, graphs, and scorecards. Figure 2.4 shows the user interface of PACE-FORWARD and gives an example of a graphical display of the results generated by the model (European-American Center for Policy Analysis, 1996b).

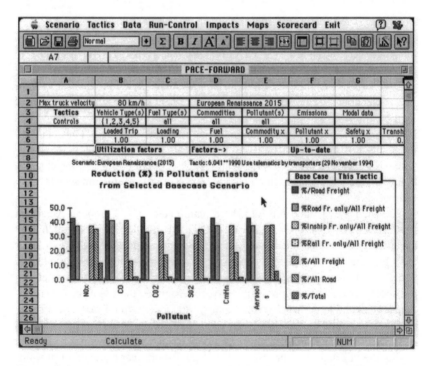

Figure 2.4   User interface and sample display from PACE-FORWARD

Strategy Design

A strategy was defined as a combination of promising tactics designed to achieve a certain goal, where promising means that the tactic is beneficial relative to the costs. In the FORWARD study, an approach was developed to design strategies. The approach was based on a CEM that uses a scorecard for a particular scenario and a given set of weights on the impacts to rank the tactics based on their cost-effectiveness. The outcome of this approach was a set of strategies and strategy design tables that can be used by policy makers to design their own strategies based on their own goals, constraints and weights.

In all, 12 illustrative strategies were designed. The CEM was used to determine the effects and to produce graphs of the cumulative effectiveness and the cumulative costs of the set of tactics that form a strategy.

Results

The main conclusions of the FORWARD study were stated as follows (European-American Center for Policy Analysis, 1996a).

Transport efficiency tactics are disproportionately represented at the top of all lists of cost-effective tactics for a very broad range of weights. They improve many impact measures, for example, reducing the amount of truck movements affects all impact measures, and by their nature they tend to save money because of their efficiencies. In other words, if you can reduce the number of kilometers traveled, many negative impacts are reduced, and you also save money, because of a reduction in the investment and operational costs, including labor cost. Furthermore, the transport efficiency tactics can be implemented in the near term since many of them do not rely on future technological developments. The political feasibility of certain regulatory changes, however, may imply a longer-term change for some. Finally, these tactics call for the involvement of many stakeholders, so the burden of implementation does not fall on a single agency or group.

Certain direct mitigation tactics are cost-effective and either produce net reductions in the overall cost of freight transport, or only small increases. Two examples of such tactics are to *use quieter tires* and to *use electric vans in urban areas*. These tactics, although sometimes showing dramatic improvements for the measures on which they focus, generally rank lower in cost-effectiveness than the transport efficiency tactics, because they focus on only a few impacts and they have net positive costs. The importance of these tactics is that they can 'fill in' for gaps in improvement by focusing on particular impacts not provided by the transport efficiency tactics.

Because direct mitigation tactics focus on particular negative impacts, whether they are promising or not depends to a great extent on the importance weighting of the impact measures. For example, someone who cares only about NO_x emissions would favor the clean engine tactic, while someone who cares only about CO_2 emissions would not. Furthermore, although direct mitigation tactics tend to cost more than the transport efficiency tactics, the costs might be manageable by targeting the largest contributors to an impact. For example, they could be selectively implemented to target urban vehicles, national or international trucking, and even selectively implemented in certain regions for haulers of specific commodities.

Mode shift tactics tend to be inferior in both absolute effectiveness and cost-effectiveness to the combination of transport efficiency and direct mitigation tactics. A reason for this is that waterway and rail improvements are relatively expensive, and they do not realize very much mode shift for a number of reasons. First, there is only limited opportunity for mode shift. The average distance traveled by national freight is less than 50 kilometers, so it is unlikely that rail or waterway transport, which usually also require pre- and after-road transport and transshipment, will be attractive to forwarders for national freight movement. Second, the quantity of longer haul, international trucking is much smaller than the quantity of national trucking, whether measured in terms of tonnes or tonne-kilometers. Thus, the quantity of road haulage that can be affected by mode shift tactics tends to be smaller than that affected by other tactics. Mode shift tactics that attempt to focus on the international movement of freight between specific regions affect even a smaller quantity of transported goods, because these goods are already shipped mostly by water.

EVALUATION OF THE SUCCESS AND ROLE OF FORWARD IN THE POLICY PROCESS

Many studies are carried out in the area of transportation and infrastructure, within the Netherlands and within Europe, to assist policy makers to improve the basis to exercise their judgment on transportation issues. The natural question that emerges is: what makes the FORWARD study successful and what role does it play in the decision-making processes?

Success is a problematic concept in the sense that one does not have to agree upon success criteria. Various actors may perceive differently the success and failure of the policy analysis study to which they were related. After all, success is usually defined as the achievement of something desired, planned or attempted (Anonymous, 1979; Hornby, 1982). Such requirements may differ per actor, as a result of their different roles and interests with respect to the policy analysis study and the surrounding problem situation

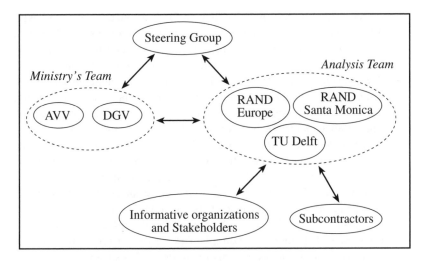

Figure 2.5   Actors involved in the FORWARD project

(Miser and Quade, 1988). Consequently, the elements on the basis of which different actors consider a study successful, and the relative values of these elements, may differ. In line with this thought, the success of a policy analysis study is in the eye of the beholder and different actors may define and assess the success of a study differently (Goeller, 1988).

Figure 2.5 shows the actors who played a role in one way or the other and to a greater or lesser extent in the FORWARD study, and, as such, were related to the study. The arrows indicate the mutual relationships in terms of the formal communication patterns. The characteristics of the actors are described below.

- *The analysis team* carried out the policy analysis study. The team was composed of researchers from RAND Europe, RAND Corporation, and the school of Systems Engineering, Policy Analysis and Management (SEPA) of the Delft University of Technology.
- *Subcontractors* made substantial contributions to the study, despite the fact they were brought in on a temporary basis. The Nederlands Economisch Instituut (NEI), in English, the Netherlands Economic Institute, developed a model to estimate macroeconomic impacts, and the research organization NEA was the source of the freight transport demand data.
- *The ministry's project team* interacted directly with the analysis team to review the study's status, identify the next steps to be taken, assign responsibilities for the next steps, and liaise with the policy makers. The

team provided support and coordination for data collection and work with other contractors, and provided tactical guidance for the study. The team was composed of members of the Directorate General for Freight of the Ministry (DGV) and of the associated Transport Research Centre (AVV).

- *The steering group* provided guidance on the scope and emphasis of the research. The group was composed of representatives from industry, other government ministries, and various offices within the ministry. The policy conclusions were presented to the steering group.

- *Informative organizations and stakeholders* were consulted by the analysis team and the ministry's team as part of the process of understanding the problems related to the freight transport system, policy options that might be taken to mitigate those problems, and ways of estimating the consequences of these options. In addition to receiving information about the study and its results, the informative organizations and stakeholders, for example, RIVM, TNO, Bureau Binnenvaart, provided state-of-the-art information to the analysis team.

From a systematic review of the literature and research in evaluation of policy analysis studies it appeared that a wide variety of elements are focused on evaluating policy analysis studies and/or similar activities. Different aspects are generally considered, including content and process-related aspects, direct results of the study, what is being done with these results, whether the problem situation was improved, and the like (Thissen and Twaalfhoven, 2001).

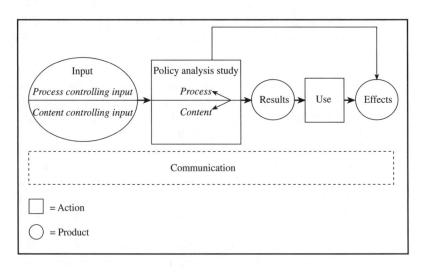

Figure 2.6   Conceptual structure for classification of success elements

On the basis of this observation, a conceptual structure was developed to take into account the broad set of aspects that are used, or can be used, as a basis for evaluating policy analysis studies. The structure was used to categorize the various elements that different actors focus on, or might consider, when evaluating the success and failure of policy analysis studies. The conceptual structure is illustrated in Figure 2.6 (Twaalfhoven, 1999).

A policy analysis study is viewed as an action, or a series of actions, controlled by particular inputs, leading to specific products or results, for example, a report and/or a model. Two primary dimensions of a policy analysis study are distinguished: content and process. The results of the policy analysis study might be entirely or partly used by different actors, leading to various effects. A policy analysis study may also lead to some effects without having produced any results, as yet. Throughout the series of actions and resulting products, communication takes place among the various actors who are related to the study and the surrounding policy process.

The following categorization of success elements is introduced in the conceptual structure:

- *Input*: these are elements that relate to what preceded the policy analysis study, for example, who initiated the study and why the analysis was initiated.
- *Content*: these are elements that relate to the content of the study, for example, the subject on which the analysis focuses, the research approach, the validity of the analysis methods used, and the variety of alternatives and criteria considered in the study.
- *Process*: these are elements that relate to the analysis process and its organization, for example, the transparency of the organization of the process, the cooperation among and/or involvement of various actors, and the use of resources, time and money.
- *Results*: these are elements that relate to the products of the policy analysis study, for example, the findings of the study, including the presentation, relevance, availability and validity of the study's results.
- *Use*: these are elements that relate to who uses which elements of the study and for what purpose.
- *Effects*: these are elements that relate to the possible effects of the policy analysis study, for example, feeding the policy discussion, affecting the policy process, affecting the decisions taken, increasing the insights into the problem and possible solutions, improving the problem situation, and/or shifting the balance of power and responsibilities among the actors involved in the problem situation.
- *Communication*: these are elements that relate to the communication among the actors during the whole sequence of activities and products,

for example, internal and external communication during the study, and changes in communication patterns among the actors as a result of the study.

Representatives of the various actors were interviewed to get insight into the different success perceptions with respect to the FORWARD study. Per actor, two to three individuals were interviewed. Open interviews were used to identify the set of success elements that the actors focus on when evaluating the study's success. After the open part of the interview, a more structured approach was used to touch on various aspects that the interviewee might have forgotten to mention. This structure followed from the conceptual structure depicted in Figure 2.6. Different questions were asked, pointing at various aspects to trigger the interviewees to indicate all elements that they considered to be important in evaluating the FORWARD study.

When asking the actors what elements they focus on when evaluating the FORWARD study, most of them mentioned effects of the study in terms of implemented policy options, formulated policies and freshly generated follow-up projects, which were significantly influenced by the FORWARD study. This *outcome success* is discussed in the next subsection.

The additional success elements that the actors mentioned during the interviews are outlined in the following subsection, structured in accordance with the conceptual structure given in Figure 2.6. A summary of the variety of success elements mentioned by the different actors is given at the end of this section in Table 2.1.

Outcome Success of FORWARD

As it became obvious that road transport was not going to meet its environmental targets, the Ministry established a joint project group (IMAGO) with government officials and representatives from the transport industry, consignors and consignees (Ministerie vanVerkeer en Waterstaat, 1994). The FORWARD study indicated that improving efficiency in road transport could be very effective; however, in the SVV II document, policy actions in the field of mitigation and modal shift prevailed over efficiency measures. As a direct result of the FORWARD study, the instruction for the IMAGO project group was to look for additional policy actions with an emphasis on efficiency measures.

The follow-up of IMAGO, the TRANSACTIE program, provided a framework for actions to be taken at the organizational level, which aim at higher occupancy rates in road transport. Efficiency scans, for example, played an important role in this program. As part of the TRANSACTIE program, companies were screened on an individual basis in terms of their transport needs, possible actions to increase efficiency, and the (positive) environmental and financial effects of these actions. Optimization of transport as part of a company's logistical chain also played an important role in the TRANSACTIE program. In this case, the companies were screened at a more general level. The approach proved to be very fruitful: at the time of the interviews, approximately 100 companies had volunteered to be examined at a general level, in the next few years.

Analysis of the developments in freight transport showed a good performance with respect to the economic targets but a poor performance with respect to the environmental indicators. Therefore, in addition to new policy measures, intensifying the existing transport policy was needed, resulting in a focus on environmental policy measures, which would not damage the economic performance of freight transport. The adjusted policy was described in two reports: (1) *Samenwerken aan Bereikbaarheid* (SWAB), in English, Working Together towards Accessibility, focusing on passenger transport and infrastructure (Ministerie van Verkeer en Waterstaat, 1996a) and (2) *Transport in Balans* (TIB), in English, Transport in Balance, focusing on freight transport (Ministerie van Verkeer en Waterstaat, 1996b).

Various actors saw the FORWARD study as one of the factors leading to more and special attention within the ministry for freight transport, and, partly due to the FORWARD study, for the first time a separate policy document was published on freight transport! Furthermore, the FORWARD study provided an important input for the TIB document in terms of promising policy measures and its recommendations. The TIB document contains, besides new efficiency measures, common policy actions such as stimulating intermodal transport, more competition in rail and inland waterway transport and innovative city distribution centers. Based upon high expectations of innovations, technology gained priority, and this was approved by parliament in the budget of 1996.

In summary, many actors mentioned the following two criteria to evaluate the success of the FORWARD study: (i) implemented alternatives improve the problem situation, and (ii) the selection of the alternatives was influenced significantly by the analysis. The emphasis put on efficiency measures in the TIB document was mentioned as proof for the second criterion. At the time of the interviews, implementation of these measures had already started, and the first results showed a significant reduction in vehicle kilometers and air pollution (Ministerie van Verkeer en Waterstaat, 1996b). Due to the enthusiasm of companies wanting to participate in the TRANSACTIE program, a further improvement in the current situation was expected. In this sense the first criterion of success would also be met.

Additional Success Perceptions with Regard to the FORWARD study

It appeared from the interviews that the actors considered many other success elements to determine the extent of success of the FORWARD study and its role in the policy process. The additional success perceptions outlined below are structured in accordance with the conceptual structure given in Figure 2.6.

Input

The ministry asked RAND Europe to carry out the FORWARD study. Competing research organizations especially looked quite suspiciously and skeptically at the newly established European-American company, in particular at the help they received from the ministry in their establishment, and at the study they were carrying out. Therefore, for the competing research organizations, elements related to who initiated the FORWARD study and the reason why the analysis was initiated played a major role in their, sometimes biased, perception of the success of the study.

Content

The ministry's team and the steering group spoke appreciatively of the content of the FORWARD study. The broad and integrative policy analysis approach was particularly highly valued. In the FORWARD study, a broad perspective was taken in terms of the policy actions investigated and the impacts of those actions. As many tactics as possible were considered and their impacts were reflected against the measures of interest of the broad spectrum of stakeholders. In its breadth, the FORWARD study was also multimodal, in that it considered the interactions among modes, the elasticities of demand for the various modes, and actual intermodal freight transport. Furthermore, another reason why various actors considered the FORWARD study to be successful is the fact that the study was integrative. The study was integrative in two ways: (i) it attempted to bring together multiple tactics to provide robust strategies that would mitigate all negative impacts of freight transport, and (ii) it used and integrated existing Dutch research and existing Dutch models. As one of the members of the ministry's team put it: 'Because of FORWARD we know what we know and what we don't know, and that helps us in setting up a new research agenda and steering new research projects'.

In addition to the positively valued aspects, members of the ministry's team and the steering group also mentioned some aspects that they valued negatively. The effects of speed and driving behavior were not worked out well in the study. Furthermore, the cost aspects of policy options and the impacts and cost aspects of combinations of policy options should have been given more attention.

Process

The research and the final results were developed through iterations with the stakeholders and the ministry's team. From the perspective of the analysts and the team, these interactions provided important inputs and more assurance that the conclusions and recommendations would be understood and accepted. The actors involved in carrying out and steering the analysis especially appreciated the openness of the research process, that is, the willingness to take other people's visions and knowledge into account. As one of the actors said: 'this is an important factor for providing a useful product at the end of the study'. Another aspect that formed a basis for the ministry to value the success of the FORWARD study positively is that the steering group showed their strong and enthusiastic support throughout the study.

Not all process-related aspects were highly valued: 'In terms of budgetary aspects, FORWARD was not a success' is a statement made by members from both the analysis team and the ministry's team. The same holds for the duration of the study: the FORWARD study took much more time than originally planned. In this sense, 'money and time were not used efficiently'. The reasons for this, as some actors pointed out, were to be found in the cultural differences and in the physical distances: RAND Europe is an American research organization that had little experience within the Dutch research culture and direct communication between RAND Corporation in Santa Monica and the people in Delft, Rotterdam and The Hague, was limited because of time differences. Notwithstanding the above, the informal communication, the work climate among the actors in the Netherlands and in the United States, and the secondary aspects such as trips between the two countries and working outings, were highly valued and mentioned as success elements.

Results

The results of the FORWARD study, reflected in a final report, three supporting volumes, an intermediate report, and the model PACE-FORWARD, were well received by the ministry's project team and the steering group. Members of the analysis team mentioned this as an indicator for success. The reports were clear, readable, and presented in time to the ministry's project team and the steering group. The distribution and presentation of the documents to the outside world, however, was greatly delayed. The fact that it took more than two years after finishing the study to distribute the reports widely was mentioned, and valued negatively, by all actors interviewed. As a member of the steering group said: 'Because of the delay in distributing the reports and a poor follow up, momentum was lost, particularly within the research world'.

Use

The analysis team and the ministry's team considered the FORWARD study a success, because the insights the study gave were used in formulating policy, implementing policy measures in the form of pilot studies, and initiating new programs. The model that was developed during the study, that is, the PACE-FORWARD model, was valued differently by the various actors. The ministry's team was very enthusiastic about the model, because of its *potential* use. Given appropriate support and data, the model and its architecture provided, and still provide, the ministry with a capability to reevaluate the policy actions investigated in the FORWARD study as more information on tactics emerges or changes in scenario projections of demand occur. The model can be used to investigate changes in the relative emphasis applied to the various impact measures, and it can be used to evaluate new tactics and strategies once they are fully defined and implemented in the model and data structure. Others actors, informative organizations in particular, however, showed their skepticism because, at the time of the interviews (1998), the model had not been used structurally in policy formulation and related processes. 'It is a very expensive toy for a limited number of policy makers'.

The way the results of the FORWARD study were used in various important policy documents was valued differently by the actors interviewed. Some actors, that is, the analysis team and the ministry's team, considered the fact that the study's results were expressed in policy documents as a success element. Others, informative organizations in particular, pointed out that the policy documents refer incorrectly to the results of the FORWARD study, or even misuse the results.

Effects

Various interviewees also mentioned some other effects of the FORWARD study, in addition to the effects discussed above, as indicators of success. First, the study provided many stakeholders with insights into the problems in the field of freight transportation and into promising policy options that can be taken to solve these problems. The FORWARD study increased the awareness of the problems related to freight transportation, particularly within the ministry. Second, the FORWARD study gave direction to political discussions and to policy to be formulated. It had given policy makers a basis to exercise their judgment on transportation issues. The insights gained through the FORWARD study were said to lead potentially to a more efficient use of time during the policy process. Another success element, mentioned by the steering group, was that the study was a way for them to show other parties with interests in freight transportation that the ministry was looking very seriously at the problems. 'If we had not shown that we are taking the freight transportation problems seriously, we would be in trouble with the other parties that have interests.'

Table 2.1   Success elements mentioned by actors relating to FORWARD

	Analysis team	Sub-contractors	Ministry's team	Steering group	Information organizations and stakeholders
Input		– Expertise analysis team – Setting up process study			
Content	+ Broad and integrative approach		+ Broad and integrative approach + Identification of knowledge gaps	+ Broad and integrative approach – Some aspects require more attention	
Process	+ Openness ± Physical distances – Budget – Length of study	+ Openness	+ Openness + Support of steering group + Secondary aspects ± Physical distances – Budget – Length of study	+ Openness – Budget – Length of study	+ Openness
Results	+ Approval of client – Delayed distribution		+ Clear, readable – Delayed distribution	+ Clear, readable – Delayed distribution	– Delayed distribution

Table 2.1 (cont.)

	Analysis team	Sub-contractors	Ministry's team	Steering group	Information organizations and stakeholders
Use	+ Insights used in policy process		+ Insights used in policy process + Potential use model – Use model not institutionalized		– Model is an 'expensive toy'
Effects	+ New programs + Referred to in policy document		+ New programs + Referred to in policy + Insights in problems and solutions	+ New programs + Policy document + Insights in problems and solutions + Show problems is taken seriously	+ Insights in problems and solutions – Referred to in policy documents
Communication	+ Informal communication		+ Joint effect ministerial departments + Potentially improve external communication		

Note: – indicates a negatively valued element; + indicates a positively valued element; ± indicates an element that is positively and negatively valued.

30

Communication

Members of DGV and AVV participated in the ministry's project team, and because of this joint participation both parties learned much from each other. For example, members of DGV mentioned having gained insights into carrying out such a policy analysis study: 'A research project as complicated as FORWARD is no piece of cake!'. Members of AVV realized that the question 'How do you present information to policy makers?' is not easily answered. These mutual insights were seen as an indicator of the success of the FORWARD study. Furthermore, both parties mentioned that the PACE-FORWARD model has the potential to improve the communication between the ministry and external parties: by using the model, results can be shown and discussed, and data provided by external parties can easily be integrated into the model and used in its calculations.

CONCLUDING REMARKS

In this chapter, the success and role of a policy analysis study on sustainable freight transport for the Netherlands, that is, the FORWARD study, was evaluated from the perspective of various actors. It was illustrated that different actors related to the FORWARD study perceive the success and role of the study differently. Some actors consider whether, and how, the FORWARD study influenced implemented policy options, formulated policy and new projects being set up, while other actors consider the validity of the model developed and the consistency of the results, when valuing the study's success. In other words, 'the success is in the eye of the beholder'.

The conceptual structure that was introduced in this chapter (see Figure 2.6) appeared generally to be exhaustive for identifying and classifying the different elements that actors consider when evaluating the success of a policy analysis study. The structure reflects the broad set of aspects that can be used as a basis for evaluating policy analysis studies. A distinction was made among the following seven categories of elements: input, content, process, results, use, effects and communication.

Many actors mentioned valuing the success of the FORWARD study by assessing its effects on transport policy and the problem situation, that is, by its outcome success. At the time the study was carried out, the transport policy needed an upgrade. In that sense, the time was ready for such a study. The FORWARD study served as an eye-opener by indicating that improved efficiency in road transport could be very effective. This idea was worked out and implemented in the adjusted transport policy as described in the TIB document, and in the IMAGO program and its follow-up. According to various interviewees, the FORWARD study was a success from this perspective.

Looking at other (categories of) success elements, a richer picture emerges. The content of the study was highly appreciated, albeit that some aspects should have been given more attention. The FORWARD study provided many actors with insight into the freight transport problems and directions in policy making. With respect to the open research process, members of DGV and AVV greatly appreciated working closely together and, as a result, learned much from each other. Another success element that was pointed out by the analysts and the ministry's team concerned the commitment of the steering group, which lasted the whole study, even though the study took longer and was more expensive than anticipated. The results, issued in various reports, received a warm welcome from the inner circle, that is, the ministry's team, the steering group and the analysts, but were distributed to the outside world with a two-year delay. According to some actors this was typical for the follow-up of the FORWARD study in terms of scientific exposure and limited use of the PACE-FORWARD model: the study lost momentum.

Little attention has been paid so far in the literature to systematic evaluation of the success of policy analysis studies and to learning about the conditions under which some approaches may be expected to be more successful than others. This chapter is a first attempt to provide an empirical basis towards broad, evaluative and comparative research for advancing the field of policy analysis. Insights into how different actors perceive the success of a policy analysis study can be particularly used in setting up and carrying out a policy analysis study. Analysts have many opportunities in designing and carrying out a policy analysis study to increase the probability of the study's success from a particular perspective. From evaluating the FORWARD study, it appeard that the broadness of a study, the presentation and distribution of its results, its match with the policy process and needs, and communication particularly require special attention in setting up a policy analysis study.

NOTE

1.   The first formal Policy Assessment Report was published in 1993, and it contains a report on the progress made in 1992. In 1992 a prototype Policy Assessment Report was published reporting on the developments in 1991.

REFERENCES

Anonymous (1979), *Webster's New Twentieth Century Dictionary*, New York: Simon & Schuster.

Carillo, C. et al. (1996), *PACE-FORWARD: Policy Analytic and Computational Environment for Dutch Freight Transport*, MR-732-EAC/VW, Santa Monica, CA: RAND.

European–American Center for Policy Analysis (1996a), *FORWARD-Freight Options for Road, Water, and Rail for the Dutch, Executive Summary*, MR-739-EAC/VW, Santa Monica, CA: RAND.

European–American Center for Policy Analysis (1996b), *FORWARD-Freight Options for Road, Water, and Rail for the Dutch, Final Report*, MR-736-EAC/VW, Santa Monica, CA: RAND.

European–American Center for Policy Analysis (1996c), *FORWARD-Freight Options for Road, Water, and Rail for the Dutch: Tactic Definitions*, DRU-1385-EAC/VW, Santa Monica, CA: RAND.

Goeller, B.F. (1988), 'A framework for evaluating success in systems analysis', in H.J. Miser and E.S. Quade (eds), *Handbook of Systems Analysis: Craft Issues and Procedural Choices*, Chichester: John Wiley & Sons Ltd, pp. 567–618.

Hornby, A.S. (1982), *Oxford Student's Dictionary of Current English*, New York: Oxford University Press.

Ministerie van Verkeer en Waterstaat (1990), *Tweede Structuurschema Verkeer en Vervoer, Deel d: Regeringsbeslissing*, Tweede Kamer, Vergaderjaar 1989–1990, 20 922, nos 15–16, 's Gravenhage, the Netherlands: SDU Uitgeverij.

Ministerie van Verkeer en Waterstaat (1994), *Notitie Goederenvervoer* (Policy Memo on Freight Transportation), Den Haag, the Netherlands.

Ministerie van Verkeer en Waterstaat (1996a), *Samenwerken aan Bereikbaarheid*, Den Haag, the Netherlands.

Ministerie van Verkeer en Waterstaat (1996b), *Transport in Balans*, Den Haag, the Netherlands.

Ministerie van Verkeer en Waterstaat (1997), *Beleidseffectrapportage 1996*, Den Haag, the Netherlands.

Miser, H.J. and E.S. Quade (eds) (1988), *Handbook of Systems Analysis; Craft Issues and Procedural Choices*, Chichester: John Wiley & Sons Ltd.

Organization for Economic Cooperation and Development (OECD) (1994), *Internalising the Social Costs of Transport*, European Conference of Ministers of Transport, Paris: OECD.

Thissen, W. and P. Twaalfhoven (2001), 'Towards a conceptual structure for evaluating policy analytic activities', *European Journal for Operational Research*. (forthcoming)

Twaalfhoven, P. (1999), *The Success of Policy Analysis Studies: An Actor Perspective*, Delft, the Netherlands: to be published by Eburon (dissertation).

3. From policy measures to policy packages: a spatially, temporally and institutionally differentiated approach

Eran Feitelson, Ilan Salomon and Galit Cohen*

INTRODUCTION

A wide array of measures have been advanced to address transport's environmental externalities. Nevertheless, the trends continue to be negative from the environmental perspective (Nijkamp, 1994; Pucher and Lefevre, 1996). One of the reasons for this is the wide variety and extent of externalities of transportation systems and the tradeoffs involved in any attempt to address these externalities. These tradeoffs are apparent across spatial levels, between externalities and between the measures advanced to address the different externalities. For example, measures improving the local environment by diverting traffic from residential zones, or promoting traffic-free areas in city centers, may have adverse environmental effects on a wider spatial scale – as congestion and local air pollutant concentrations along main thoroughfares may rise, and trip distribution may shift toward nodes with ample parking, subsequently encouraging the development of suburban centers, which in turn promotes vehicular traffic.

Such tradeoffs are well known. Nevertheless, many of the proposals for 'sustainable transport' focus on improving a very limited set of indices – the most common in recent years being the reduction of air pollution and CO_2 emissions – and discuss a very limited set of measures as the means to attain limited targets. However, many of the studies taking such a limited approach reach the conclusion that a single measure is insufficient even when trying to reach a limited set of objectives (see Barton, 1992, for an example). A very common conclusion of many studies is that policy measures have to be

* This study was funded by the Israeli Ministry of Environment and the German–Israeli Foundation for Scientific Research and Development. The authors would like to thank Valerie Brachya for inititiating the study, as well as for insightful comments. However, responsibility for the views expressed herein, as well as any remaining errors, rests solely with the authors.

combined into policy packages (Wegener, 1996, for example). Indeed, the cases where success is reported are largely those where policy packages have been implemented (Pucher and Lefevre, 1996; Rabinovitch and Leitman, 1996).

The need to combine policies stems from the multiple interactions among policy tools (ECMT, 1995). These interactions are not limited to the tradeoffs noted above. Policies can also reinforce one another. Such reinforcement can be due to a similarity in the goals or targets addressed by the policy measures, or to the fact that one policy addresses the negative implications of a second set of policies. For example, a combination of restraint measures and improved public transport may help increase the effectiveness of transit improvements and make the impact on car drivers more palatable. However, the success of such a combination is not assured, as it is highly dependent on local circumstances and the actual measures used (Wachs, 1993).

One of the important potential implications in the rising interest in sustainable transport and sustainable development notions is the emphasis such notions can place on addressing the full scope of environmental issues, as well as analysing them within a wider perspective – including equity and growth issues (Greene and Wegener, 1997; Nijkamp, 1994). Regrettably, many of the sustainable transport programs still focus on a limited set of indices, ignoring potentially important interactions. Transport segments of sustainable development programs and sustainable transport strategies usually include a wide set of measures intended to address an array of goals or targets. However, these programs often seem like a 'laundry list' of policy tools. In many cases it is unclear to what extent the multiple interactions among the policy tools have been considered in the preparation of such lists. Moreover, as the European Conference of Ministers of Transport's (1995, p. 81) study notes 'all too often individual policies are introduced without reference to other policies which are currently in operation'.

The purpose of this chapter is to propose an approach for combining policy measures into a coherent policy package, taking into account the differences in issues, timing and spatial scale of the different measures, as well as the institutional aspects. This proposition is made on the basis of the Israeli case. However, its principles are likely to be applicable elsewhere, too.

THE ISRAELI SCENE: INCIDENTAL TOOLS, DISJOINTED APPLICATION

Environmental considerations were introduced into the Israeli policy scene in the early 1970s, mainly as a result of a diffusion processes within several epistemic communities (Feitelson, 1986). Transportation and physical planners introduced the traffic cell concept on the basis of the British Buchanan Report. Pedestrian schemes and land-use planning guidelines for promoting public transport were introduced into the planning discourse within the Ministry of Transportation (MOT). Noise issues were introduced into land-use delibera- tions around the Ben Gurion and Sde Dov airports. Planning capacities at the metropolitan level were enhanced by the establishment of metropolitan trans- portation planning teams, which advanced many bypass roads thus reducing through-traffic in residential areas.

In addition to the planning innovations considered at the time, the MOT enacted emission testing as part of the annual car test requirements. As Israel is too small a market to affect transportation technologies, this measure was seen as the most readily applicable means to reduce emissions at the source of old and new cars.

During the 1980s the emphasis in Israeli environmental policies shifted toward the use of environmental impact assessment as a result of the growing power of the Environmental Protection Service (the predecessor of the Ministry of Environment), especially within the regulative planning system (Brachya, 1993; Feitelson, 1998a). In 1982, environmental impact statements (EISs) were institutionalized as a by-law of the Planning and Building Law. Within a few years, transportation projects became the focal point of EISs. Approximately 20 per cent of all EISs prepared in Israel between 1982 and 1994 pertained to roads. Within the transport field, traffic management concepts were introduced, as a result of the growing attention such measures received within the professional transportation planning community. However, as a result of changes within the MOT, which led to the decline of the Economics and Planning wing and the dismantling of the office of chief scientist, the capacity of the MOT to introduce innovative concepts, with regard to transport planning in general, and the environment in particular, was reduced.

As a result of increasing environmental awareness and subsequent public opposition to road schemes, environmental issues have obtained increasing prominence in the transportation planning discourse since the mid-1980s. However, until recently this discourse focused on the project level. Consequently, road agencies (in particular the Public Works Department, which is responsible for interurban roads) gained increasing proficiency in addressing the visual and noise implications of new roads as part of the project. During the last decade, noise barriers and landscaping thus became a common feature along roads.

The last few years, since 1990, are an era during which the Israeli planning agenda in general and the environmental planning agenda in particular have been transformed (Feitelson, 1998b; Shachar, 1998). As a result of these trans- formations, concentrated deconcentration notions have been incorporated in a series of plans, rail development has been promoted, and environmental concerns have been ingrained as an integral part of several regional and national master plans. However, despite the introduction of sustainability notions into the planning discourse and the realization that land-use and environmental policies should have an economic facet, economic instruments have not been used in Israel. This is primarily due to the fact that the authority over all tax and subsidy issues rests within the Treasury, which does not consider environmental issues as part of its mandate (Cohen, 1998).

The situation that emerges from this very brief history is that of piecemeal implementation of measures chosen according to lines of authority. However, the overall transportation policy is largely a 'residual policy' (ibid.). That is, most of the measures affecting transport policy goals are enacted by agencies that have another agenda, and thus the actual transport policy is determined 'by the way' (Dery, 1999). This can be seen in Table 3.1. Many of the tools that can be used to address transport's environmental effects are not enacted due to their transportation or environmental implications, but rather according to the agenda of the agencies having the power to enact those measures. As a result, any attempt to formulate a comprehensive transport policy, or to internalize transport's negative externalities, has to be conducted in liaison with a large number of agencies. Lacking an overriding incentive or pressure for agencies to cooperate, this reduces the likelihood that a meaningful comprehensive policy will be adopted and implemented.

Rising traffic congestion, safety concerns and conflicts over transport facilities have led to the rise of transport issues in the public agenda. In 1992 they were, for the first time, part of the public discourse in the national elections, that is mostly dominated by national security issues. The need for a comprehensive transport strategy was called for by environmental non-governmental organizations (NGOs) as part of their struggle against the proposed cross-Israel highway. Against this background, the Ministry of Environment (MOE) requested that a comprehensive policy strategy be prepared to address the environmental implications of land transportation, as a basis for discussion with other agencies.

GOALS, TARGETS AND POSSIBLE MEASURES

Israel is a small very densely populated country, whose population has been growing faster than that of other developed countries, mainly due to immigration (Mazor, 1993). Hence, the main environmental concerns in Israel, with relation to transport, have been air pollution (particularly CO, NO_x and particulates), noise and open spaces. In contrast, CO_2 emissions and effects on watercourses have not been of interest, due to Israel's relatively small contribution to

Table 3.1   The authority and main considerations in enacting selected measures in Israel

Measure	Authority	Main considerations
Gasoline taxes	Treasury	Fiscal
Public transport subsidies	Treasury	Fiscal
Vehicle taxes	Treasury	Fiscal
Parking policies	Ministry of Transport and local jurisdictions	Level of service to drivers
Land-use policies	Planning Commissions and Ministry of Interior	Environmental, open space and coordination of development
Environmental impact statements	Ministry of Environment and Planning Commissions	Environment
Traffic management	Ministry of Transport and local jurisdictions	Level of service, safety, environment
Vehicle standards	Ministry of Transport	Safety
Vehicle tests	Ministry of Transport	Safety, environment
Introduction of alternative fuels	Ministry of National Infrastructure (Energy) and Ministry of Transport	National energy strategies; fiscal; environment
Promotion of pedestrian and bicycle paths	Local jurisdictions and the Ministry of Housing	Quality of life; urban regeneration; environment
Road construction policies:		
• metropolitan	Ministry of Transport and local jurisdictions	Level of service of drivers; safety
• inter-city	Public Works Department (Ministry of National Infrastructure)	
Rail construction or improvement policies	Ministry of National Infrastructure	Level of service; safety

global CO_2 emissions and lack of high-quality surface water. Therefore, the policy focus was on the three issues seen as most important locally. As can be seen in Table 3.2, each of the main policy focus areas is affected by a number of transport parameters. Each of these can be a focal point for intervention, and thus a potential policy target.

Any actual policy proposal, however, is likely to use some manipulation of

Table 3.2 Parameters that affect the main policy areas

Policy focus (problem area)	Parameters
Air quality	Vehicle fleet; vehicle maintenance; number of trips (especially cold starts); modal split; trip distribution; vehicle-km driven; emission factors; driving conditions; fuel characteristics
Noise	Vehicle fleet; number of vehicle trips; trip distribution; modal split; driving conditions; infrastructure attributes; land use
Open space	Infrastructure attributes and standards; number of vehicles; trip distribution; modal split

these potential targets to advance a more general target that can be addressed by multiple measures. In the case of air pollution in Israel, for example, an explicit target of increasing the ratio between person-km traveled to vehicle-km driven was stated (Salomon et al., 1996). This can be achieved by a variety of measures, such as measures that increase public transport's modal split, car pooling, tools that raise the cost of driving (such as gasoline taxes) and planning measures allowing for greater use of non-motorized modes. However, this target, as well as any other target, is not likely to be commensurate with some other targets or goals. If, for example, the reduction in the ratio is achieved by an increase in trips made in noisy buses, the overall noise exposure may actually worsen.

The measures advanced to address policy concerns are usually divided into several groups. Typical typologies differentiate between technological measures, traffic management, demand management, infrastructure development and land-use planning, or between regulative measures and economic measures. In practice, however, many of the measures do not fall neatly into any of the categories, regardless of typology. Parking limitations, for example, can be considered both as economic tools (if parking fees are used as a second-best congestion tax or pollution taxes) and regulative tools (if parking availability is restricted). Similarly, they can be viewed as demand management measures, traffic management tools and part of land-use plans. From a policy perspective, however, this is not important. The real question is which measures should be used in conjunction with which other measures, rather than which group of measures is preferable. In other words, the actual measures should be the focus of discussion and analysis, rather than the policy type to which they are assigned according to some typology. This is not to say that typologies are not useful (and indeed they are used later on in this chapter) – only that the discussion of policy types as such may miss the main points that have to be considered when trying to formulate policy packages.

In order to choose which measures may be most useful for achieving a stated target, they have to be analysed individually. The questions that can be asked regarding each measure are multitude:

- How effective is it in achieving its stated goals?
- How cost-effective is it?
- What are its macroeconomic implications, if any?
- What are its social and distributional implications?
- What are its environmental effects (both direct and indirect)?
- Is it acceptable publicly and politically? And by whom?
- What are the prerequisites for implementing it?
- What is the time frame within which it can be implemented and lead to results?
- At what spatial and administrative level can it be enacted in order to be effective?
- Who has the authority to implement it?
- What are the likely behavioral responses to it?

Answering these questions for each measure would clearly require substantial research over a long period. In many cases the resources necessary to conduct such research may not be available. Therefore, it is usually necessary to rely heavily on literature reviews of the actual experience with regard to each measure. However, even comprehensive literature reviews may not yield answers to all of these questions for many specific instruments, as the experience with regard to a significant number of measures is limited, and often not well recorded or analysed. Moreover, the lessons reported in the literature may be determined by the local context within which they were derived, and hence not be pertinent to the case at hand. Consequently, almost invariably policy packaging has to be conducted under a significant degree of uncertainty.

The aforementioned questions are important for formulating comprehensive policy package that will be effective, efficient and acceptable. However, in practice it may often be infeasible to formulate such packages within the political time constraints. Hence, it is often necessary to advance partial suggestions. These would still be an improvement over the current approach whereby measures are advanced separately in a piecemeal manner. In this study we suggest that the most important questions that have to be answered can be limited to four:

- What are the main effects of the measure?
- What is the time frame within which the measure can be enacted and have an effect?
- What is the spatial level at which it is effective?
- Under which conditions can the measure be expected to be effective?

These questions can usually be answered in a relatively straightforward manner. However, they merit a brief discussion.

Most policy measures can be differentiated into direct and indirect effects. The direct environmental effects are usually taken into consideration. For example, the main environmental effects discussed in the context of rail schemes are the externalities generated by the railway (noise, vibrations and so on) and the extent to which they may affect modal split (Feitelson, 1994). They may, however, also have indirect effects due to induced demand, shift of funds from bus subsidies, and land-use effects. As Wachs (1993) has observed, railway systems may thus have deleterious equity effects. The potential and disadvantages of any measure can be assessed, therefore, only if both the direct and indirect effects are identified. However, some of the indirect effects may be difficult to anticipate at the time the measure is discussed.

The time frame for considering the use of any measure is actually composed of three elements: the time needed to enact the measure, the time needed for the implementation of the measure once it has been decreed, and the time needed for the relevant market segments to react to the measure.

The time needed to enact a measure is a function of the legal processes that have to be undertaken before a measure is promulgated. In some cases a simple administrative decision may suffice. In many cases the enactment of a measure is contingent upon the completion and ratification of plans. In other cases, by-laws or existing legislation have to be modified, requiring the approval of legislatures. More rarely, new major legislation would have to be adopted. Obviously, procedures requiring legislation can be expected to take a substantially longer period of time to be enacted than those that can be adopted under existing procedures and rules. Clearly, the time such procedures would actually take will be affected by the extent and power of interests promoting and opposing the adoption of the specific measure.

For some measures the time needed to implement them, once they have been adopted, can be very short. Raising gasoline tax rates is an example of such a case. However, in many other cases the time period can be substantial. In certain cases, such as when a new rail system is decided upon, this period may last for many years. Overall, it is expected to be a function of transaction costs, which in turn are a function of the interagency coordination required,[1] the extent to which new infrastructure is needed, the level of funds needed and the ability of the agency promoting the measure to secure these funds. This, in turn, is a function of the importance of this issue in the national agenda, and the extent to which there is opposition to the implementation of the proposed measure (something that is affected by the measure's distributional effects).

Many measures are intended to affect behavior. Therefore, the actual effects of these measures would not be felt immediately after their enactment. Rather, the extent to which these effects would be felt is likely to be a function of the time allowed for the relevant actors to react. In some cases, such as the opening of a new road or service, this reaction may occur quite rapidly. In cases where relative prices are changed (due to some tax or subsidy scheme) adaptations may take longer. One such case is the effect of changes in vehicle tax structure (Cohen, 1998).

From a spatial perspective it is important to recognize that many of the measures proposed are relevant only in limited areas. Metro services, for example, are pertinent only in dense core areas of large cities, and are largely irrelevant for rural areas. Therefore, the use of policy tools has to define for which area or spatial extent each type of policy is pertinent.

In the Israeli case the spatial dimension was differentiated into three levels: the urban areas, the metropolitan level and the national level. In larger countries it may be possible to differentiate between the national level and peripheral or remote areas which have particular transport-related environmental problems.

In the urban areas, the main problems stem from the close proximity of emission sources to receptors. Hence the measures needed to address these problems are those that either affect emissions at the source or affect the local environment by reducing direct exposure and enhancing quality of life at the micro level.

At the metropolitan level, it is possible to affect travel patterns at a wider dimension. These include the most substantial traffic flows. At this level it is possible to propose comprehensive public transport, infrastructure and land-use plans. At this level it is also possible to establish road-pricing schemes and truck routes. In other words, the metropolitan level allows for the use of measures whose scope is beyond the city level, but are relevant only where traffic flows are substantial.

Some of the measures affect the whole economy, as they cannot be differentiated by place, at least in small countries such as Israel. An example for this case are gasoline taxes and vehicle standards.

Finally, it has to be realized that the utility and implementability of many measures is contingent upon certain prerequisites being met. For example, the introduction of alternative fuels or electric vehicles is contingent upon the availability of a sufficient array of appropriate fueling stations, or battery recharge points. These prerequisites are not limited, however, to technology. The introduction of truck routes, for example, requires that all the functions that need truck services be located in places that can be served by such routes. This necessitates an appropriate and effective land-use planning mechanism, which can prevent market failures due to lack of coordination between the transportation planning agencies and land-use decisions.

In Table 3.3 different policy measures are summarized according to the four questions discussed above. While these measures are grouped according to the usual typologies, they are analysed separately and thus the typology is merely for convenience of presentation and not an issue in itself.

The entries in Table 3.3 are sensitive to local circumstances, and hence reflect the Israeli situation. This is particularly true for the time it is estimated that it would take for the measure to have an effect. As many of the measures have not been tried in any specific circumstances, this column is thus an educated guess, rather than a true estimate. The entries in the time column in the table represent thus our guesstimates for the Israeli situation, taking into account the Israeli decision-making structures, prior experience with each measure (including the time it takes consumers to react), the rates of changes in vehicle fleets (of private and public transport means) and the rate of physical development. Naturally, it can be expected that other analysts would come up with somewhat different estimates, and that these estimates would be different for other countries. Still, from a methodological perspective a similar table would have to be filled for any specific set of circumstances.

A SPATIALLY AND TEMPORALLY DIFFERENTIATED FRAMEWORK

Any sustainable transport strategy that is to be considered would at the very least have to present a comprehensive policy package. Comprehensiveness can be defined along several dimensions. At the minimum it should include three dimensions: the issues addressed, time and space. A comprehensive policy package should include measures that would have effects at different time spans. That is, it should not focus exclusively on immediate or short-term improvements, thus disregarding measures that have long-term effects but do not provide any short-term benefits. Nor can it focus exclusively on the long term, even if the most effective measures may be implemented only in the long term (which is the case for many of the potentially most promising technological options). Similarly, it is necessary that such a package would address issues and options at various spatial levels. It is insufficient to address a single issue, such as global warming or noise, or even a set of issues and policies whose effects are purely global, or local. Rather there is a need for a mix of measures that would include short- and long-term measures that address a wide variety of issues that are pertinent at different spatial levels.

Table 3.3 Main attributes of selected policy measures

Measure	Main effect	Spatial level	Total time for effect	Main targets
Technological Measures				
Electric vehicles	Reduce emissions at source	Urban	25 years +	2nd and 3rd cars in family, for intra-urban trips
Change of fuels in buses	Reduce emissions at source	Mainly urban	Approximately 5 years	Intraurban bus lines
Improved private vehicle technology	Reduce emissions at source	National	5–15 years (depending on availability on world market)	New car buyers
Improved car maintenance	Reduce emissions at source	National	1–2 years	Owners of old cars
Improved infrastructure:				
• quiet pavements	Reduce noise	Mainly urban	5–10 years	Roads near residential areas
• porous pavements	Reduce runoff	Urban or interurban	5 years +	Water sensitive areas
• improved rail	Reduce noise and improve performance	National	5 years +	
Traffic management				
Traffic calming	Reduce through traffic and improve safety in residential areas	Urban	Within 5 years	Residential areas
Coordination of public transport services	Increase public transport attractiveness	National and/or metropolitan	5–10 years	Potential public transport users
Park and ride	Increase public transport attractiveness	Metropolitan	Within 5 years	Commuters on radial routes
Parking adjusted to public transport supply	Increase attractiveness of public transport	Mainly central cities	Approximately 5 years	Commuters to central business district

Table 3.3 (cont.)

Measure	Main effect	Spatial level	Total time for effect	Main targets
Coordination of traffic lights	Reduce 'stop and go' traffic	Urban	Within 5 years	Drivers on main thoroughfares
Closure of city center to private vehicles	Reduce emissions and increase public transport's attractiveness	Urban (city center)	5–10 years	Employees and visitors in city centers
Pedestrianization schemes	Encourage non-motorized transport	Urban (city center)	5–10 years	Businesses, customers and visitors to city
Truck routes	Reduce exposure (mainly noise and particulates)	Metropolitan	Within 5 years	Heavy trucks (above 4 tons)
Demand management				
Raising of gasoline taxes	Reduce vehicle-km	National	Immediate	All car users
Road pricing	Reduce congestion	Metropolitan	10–15 years	Car users
Vehicle taxes	Slow rise in motorization rate	National	Immediate (within a year)	Current and potential car owners
Pollution taxes	Disincentive for use of high-pollution modes and vehicles	National (possibly metropolitan)	5–10 years	Current and potential car users, particularly of older cars
Differential parking fees	Reduce car use to city centers	Urban or metropolitan	Immediate (within a year)	Commuters to city centers
Car and van pooling	Reduce vehicle trips	Metropolitan or urban	Within 2 years	Commuters to large employment centers
Tax of company vehicles	Reduce vehicle trips and vehicle-km driven	National	Within 2 years	Company car users
Administrative controls on vehicle ownership or use	Reduce vehicle trips	National or metropolitan	Within 5 years	Depends on specifics of limitation
Information	Improve vehicle flows and thus lower emissions	Metropolitan	Within 2 years	Mainly commuters

Table 3.3 (cont.)

Infrastructure and land-use planning

Measure	Main effect	Spatial level	Total time for effect	Main targets
Control of urban form	Increase attractiveness of public transport and non-motorized transport, reduce vehicle-km	Metropolitan	20+ years	All segments of the metropolitan population and businesses
Increase mixed uses	Support non-motorized travel, reduce vehicle-km	Urban and metropolitan	10–20 years	Urban population
Cycling paths	Encourage cycling	Urban	Within 5 years	Short-range travelers
Bus lanes	Change modal split in favor of public transport	Urban and metropolitan	Within 5 years	Mainly on radial lines
Light rail	Change modal split in favor of public transport	Urban and metropolitan (inner rings)	5–15 years	Commuters to central business district
Metro	Change modal split in favor of public transport	Metropolitan core	15+ years	Commuters within metropolitan area
Suburban rail	Change modal split in favor of public transport	Metropolitan	1–5 years	Commuters to the central city
Noise-sensitive planning	Reduce noise exposure	Urban	5–10 years	Residential areas near main routes
Lower standards for roads and parking	Reduce loss of open space and visual amenities	Urban (parking) and interurban (road standards)	10 years +	Areas with inadequate open spaces and highly visible areas
Coordination of densities parking and public transport	Change modal split in favor of public transport	Metropolitan	20 years +	Commuters to central city and businesses

In Table 3.4, such a comprehensive framework is presented, on the basis of the specification of the features of the different measures that is presented in Table 3.3. The entries in Table 3.4 appear, by necessity, in a highly abbreviated form. They do not reflect, therefore, the many nuances that have to be taken into consideration when they are actually implemented. In reality many of the measures should appear in more than one category, depending on the exact nuance considered. For example, it is indeed possible to improve the information provided to users of most transport systems within a very short time span. However, the implementation of automated highway as part of an intelligent vehicle technology and highway system (IVHS) would probably take well over a decade (Sperling, 1995). Moreover, the actual effects of any instrument used would also be a function of the variant of the measure that is adopted in practice.

Table 3.4 does not show the effectiveness or limitations of each instrument.

Table 3.4   A spatially and temporally differentiated framework

Spatial level	Within a year or two	Between 1 and 5 years	Between 5 and 15 years	Over 15 years
Urban areas	Parking fees	Shift of buses to alternative fuel; traffic calming; cycling paths; reduced parking standards	Quiet pavements; closure of city centers to cars and pedestrian schemes; noise sensitive planning; increase in mixed uses	Electric cars
Metropolitan areas	Car and bus pooling; improved information systems	Truck routes; suburban rail; bus lanes; coordination of parking and public transport policies	Coordination of public transport systems; light rail	Changes in urban form; coordination of densities and public transport supply; metro
National level	Gasoline taxes; company cars tax; emission testing	Emission-based limitations on car imports	Better vehicle technologies; pollution taxes; lower standards for sensitive interurban roads; improved interurban rail	Introduction of new fuels to private cars

However, in an actual application they would most probably be spelled out, as was the case in the report actually submitted to the Israeli Ministry of Environment (Feitelson et al., 1998). Finally, it is important to reiterate that Table 3.4 reflects the Israeli circumstances. Thus, it is likely that certain attributes of many measures would vary according to setting. This is most likely to be true with regard to the time it would take the measure to be adopted and have an effect. Still, the table provides a comprehensive framework for adopting and implementing different measures in a way that would ensure that the policies would have an effect over a substantial time period and at different spatial levels.

Table 3.4 does not include two sets of instruments. The first are measures that foster the use of telecommunications in lieu of movement. The reason these are omitted is the inordinate ineffectiveness of these instruments, an issue debated at length elsewhere (Salomon, 1986; Mokhtarian, 1998). The second set are measures intended to affect attitudes and positions, mainly through education. In essence, these instruments can be used as part of any policy package, regardless of time frame. Thus, they can be added to any of the packages that may be advanced.

Perhaps the most readily available instrument is an increase in gasoline tax. In Israel, such a decision can be taken almost overnight. While such an increase is unlikely to affect the vehicle-km driven significantly, it may contribute eventually to greater fuel efficiency (Crawford and Smith, 1995). This may have a beneficial effect for greenhouse gases, but a more limited effect on local air pollutants or noise. To have an effect within the urban areas it may be possible to use parking fees and policies within a relatively short time. This instrument may, thus, complement a rise in gasoline taxes. However, as both increase motoring costs they are likely to draw significant opposition from very powerful interests (in particular the car and road lobby). The most effective measure in the short range may be better emission-testing routines, as a relatively small number of high emitters are often responsible for a very high percentage of emissions (Wachs, 1993).

Once the time frame is widened, but still limited to the short term (up to five years) the number of options available increases substantially. Within urban areas it is possible to reduce through-traffic in residential areas and implement traffic-calming measures. It is also possible to promote non-motorized transport by implementing pedestrianization schemes and building cycling paths. However, to prevent a decline of city centers following pedestrianization schemes, complementary parking policies and public transport enhancements have to be undertaken. The public transport schemes are likely to be at the metropolitan level. In Israel, a continuous bus-lane system and suburban rail can be operated within this time frame along existing rights of way. If, however, such complementary measures cannot be implemented within the same time frame as the pedestrianization schemes, the pedestrianization program should be postponed until the complementary measures are in place. Otherwise the loss of business in the central city may offset the purported gains.

Traffic management measures (such as coordinated traffic signals) can be implemented within this time frame to reduce emissions, though their effects are limited (Hall, 1995). It is also possible to introduce quiet pavements to a sufficient percentage of city streets (as a function of urban resurfacing budgets). Within five years it may also be possible to consider road pricing. Technically, this would primarily be a function of the rate at which the technology necessary for electronic road pricing could be introduced. However, the main impediment to the introduction of road pricing is likely to be the question of political feasibility (TRB, 1994). Ultimately, therefore, political factors are likely to determine whether and when this measure is adopted. As in Israel road pricing has been introduced to the policy discourse only recently, this measure appears in Table 3.4 only in the 5–15 years column.

At the national level, car and van pooling can be enhanced. As organized employee bus services are relatively well established in Israel, such measures can be implemented with relative ease. While increased vehicle taxes, or administrative limitations on vehicle imports, can be implemented within five years, they would lead to an aging of the vehicle fleet, something that may have detrimental results overall. Thus, while these options are available, they have to be scrutinized with care.

To address environmental issues at the intermediate time range, of between five and fifteen years, it is possible to adopt measures that require infrastructure investments, but are not based on structural changes. It is also possible to adopt technologies that are readily available, but will take time to penetrate and have an overall impact on the environment.

Within the urban areas it is possible to implement within this time frame a coordinated parking, public transport, pedestrianization and cycling scheme. It is also possible to introduce light rail (which does not exist at present in Israel), and/or to introduce alternative fuels to the bus fleet. As this fleet is centrally controlled, the infrastructure necessary to introduce alternative fuels can be made available at relatively few operation centers, thus reducing the overall transaction costs of such a transformation. This time scale is also commensurate with the fleet changeover rate of the main bus companies in Israel. It should be noted, however, that privatization may make this process somewhat more complex, if control and coordination are decentralized. At the metropolitan level this scheme can be complemented by a timed transfer public transport system, and the construction of 'park and ride' centers in the outer rings of the metropolitan areas (Feitelson, 1995). Such a system may allow public transport to be more competitive in circumferal trips, a market share it hardly competes for today.

Emissions factors are likely to decline within this time frame, due to vehicle fleet turnover and the lower emission rates of new vehicles. As in many small countries, Israel does not have an impact on vehicle technology. However, the availability of lower-emitting vehicles with internal combustion engines provides even small countries such as Israel with options to reduce emission factors by setting stricter standards for imported cars.

One set of measures that can be introduced within this time frame, and is widely supported by much of the contemporary literature, are road-pricing and pollution taxes. Pollution taxes should be differentiated from road pricing (discussed above) as they are levied on the pollution directly. Thus, the ability to levy them is also dependent on technology, as it is necessary to measure pollution easily without impeding traffic. Where such technologies have been tested, they have shown that emission testing is inaccurate (Glazer et al., 1995). Still, questions of the acceptability of all such tax schemes remain (Rietveld, 1997).

At the long term, over 15 years, it is possible to have an effect on urban form and perhaps adopt new technologies. There is an ongoing debate on the importance of urban form, and the contribution of different urban forms (Anderson et al., 1996; Banister, 1992; Breheny, 1992). On one hand, compact city forms may be conducive for public transport and non-motorized transport. On the other hand, they may lead to greater exposure of population. There is, however, also some agreement – that dispersed urban forms are detrimental for public transport and non-motorized transport. Thus, some control over land use to enhance densities and coordinate development patterns and public transport systems seems to be agreed upon by most observers.

In the long run it may be possible also to adopt new technologies, if they become economically feasible in the interim, or to construct rail-based systems that require heavy investments (such as metro systems). While at present there is considerable skepticism regarding the potential of rail options (Feitelson, 1994; Wachs, 1993), considering their limited success so far (Gomez-Ibanez, 1985; Pickrell, 1992), several new vehicle technologies can provide a basis for hope (Sperling, 1995). Within the next three decades, electric vehicles, fuel cells and various hybrids may become commercially viable. Still, as Sperling (1995) rightly notes, this would come about only if an active set of policies would provide an incentive for the development and adoption of such technologies during the interim period.

DISCUSSION AND CONCLUSIONS

The framework described in this chapter was structured for the Israeli case. Thus, it is more than likely that the place of specific measures within this framework would shift if it is considered elsewhere. It is also likely that the attractiveness of the various measures would change as experience in their use, and especially in combined use of several instruments, accumulates. Still, the framework provides an approach for formulating a strategy that would address multiple environmental externalities from transport at different spatial levels over a substantial period. While the need for such frameworks is intuitively clear they have not been spelled out in most cases.

The framework advanced here, however, has several structural limitations that would have to be addressed in the future. The first is the question of authority. As is shown in Table 3.1, the authority to enact the different measures is divided among various agencies. For most of these agencies the environmental effects of transport are at best a minor concern. Thus, it would be necessary to accompany the analysis of which measures should be used at each stage and spatial level with an implementation strategy. This strategy would have to propose ways for convincing the different agencies to implement the measures, or to shift the authority for implementation to agencies which do view treatment of transport's environmental externalities as part of their mandate. Naturally, this second option is likely to lead to interagency strife, something that is not necessarily conducive from an environmental perspective (though in some cases inevitable).

A second limitation of the framework as depicted here is its disregard of the question of acceptability. In certain cases it is highly likely that a measure that is technically feasible may be seen as unacceptable for a certain interest group (Salomon and Mokhtarian, 1997). In such cases, unless the opposition is identified and addressed, the implementation of the measure may be delayed or defrayed. One approach that may help address this problem is the addition of measures that are desired by the opposing group into the package. If the adoption of the desired measures is made contingent upon the adoption of the whole package, this approach may help bring the opposition around. To this end, however, there is a need to widen the analysis of measures so it includes the degree to which they are acceptable to different groups, and hence to identify which groups or concerns have to be addressed as prerequisites for the adoption of the measure.

A third, technical, limitation of the approach is that it does not address directly the effectiveness of the policy measures, and the synergetic effects among them. To address these issues it would be necessary to model the overall effects of such interactions, and consumer reactions to them.

Currently a study attempting to address the second and third limitations is underway. However, this study too will not assure that the resulting package is indeed commensurate with sustainable development notions. To do so, it would be necessary to widen the scope of goals and targets for which measures are sought to include intrageneration equity issues. In particular it would be

necessary to address the equity implications of the different measures introduced to address environmental problems. While such an addition is quite
feasible, it remains for future research.

NOTE

1. A concrete example of this point is presented in Feitelson and Papay's (1999) discussion of
    the factors that affect the sharing of rights of way.

REFERENCES

Anderson, W.P., P.S. Kanaroglou and E.J. Miller (1996), 'Urban form energy and the
    environment: a review of issues, evidence and policy', *Urban Studies*, **33**, 7–35.
Banister, D. (1992), 'Energy use, transport and settlement patterns', in M.J. Breheny
    (ed.), *Sustainable Development and Urban Form*, London: Pion, pp. 160–81.
Barton, H. (1992), 'City transport: strategies for sustainability', in M.J. Breheny (ed.),
    Sustainable Development and Urban Form, London: Pion, pp. 197–216.
Brachya, V. (1993), 'Environmental assessment in land use planning in Israel',
    Landscape and Urban Planning, **23**, 167–81.
Breheny, M.J. (1992), 'The contradictions of the compact cities: a review', in M.J.
    Breheny (ed.), *Sustainable Development and Urban Form*, London: Pion, pp.
    138–159.
Cohen, G. (1998), 'Transport policy as a residual policy: the impact of the Ministry of
    Finance on ownership and use of private vehicles', Unpublished MA Thesis,
    Hebrew University of Jerusalem (in Hebrew).
Crawford, I. and S. Smith (1995), 'Fiscal instruments for air pollution abatement in
    road transport', *Journal of Transport Economics and Policy*, **29**, 85–92.
Dery, D. (1999), 'Policy "By the way": or when policy is incidental to making other
    policies', *Journal of Public Policy*, **18**, 163–76.
European Conference of Ministers of Transport (ECMT) (1995), *Urban Travel and
    Sustainable Development*, Paris: OECD.
Feitelson, E. (1986), 'Transport and environmental quality in Israel: a developmental
    survey', *Biosphera*, **15** (6), 9–15 (in Hebrew).
Feitelson, E. (1994), 'The potential of rail as an environmental solution: setting the
    agenda', *Transportation Research A*, **28A**, 209–21.
Feitelson, E. (1995), *Concepts for the Operation and Layout of Public Transport Lines
    in Metropolitan Areas with Ramifications for the Tel Aviv Metropolitan Area*, Report
    No. 188, Israeli Institute for Transport Research and Planning, Tel Aviv (in
    Hebrew).
Feitelson, E. (1998a), 'Environmental planning in Israel: a technocratic tale', Paper
    presented at an international conference on 50 Years of Planning in Israel, The
    Technion, Haifa, 20–21 December.
Feitelson, E. (1998b), 'Muddling toward sustainability: the transformation of environ-
    mental planning in Israel', *Progress in Planning*, **49**, 1–53.
Feitelson, E. and N. Papay (1999), 'Sharing rights of way along inter-urban corridors:
    a spatial temporal and institutional analysis', *Transportation Research D*, **4**,
    217–40.

Feitelson, E., I. Salomon and G. Cohen (1998), *Transport Policy for Environmental Protection*, Jerusalem: Ministry of Environment (in Hebrew).

Glazer, A., D.B. Klein and C. Lane (1995), 'Clean on paper dirty on the road: troubles with California's smog check', *Journal of Transport Economics and Policy*, **29**, 85–92.

Gomez-Ibanez, J.A. (1985), 'A dark side to light rail: the experience of three new rail systems', *Journal of the American Planning Association*, **58**, 337–51.

Greene, D.L. and M. Wegener (1997), 'Sustainable transport', *Journal of Transport Geography*, **5**, 177–90.

Hall, J. (1995), 'The role of transport control measures in jointly reducing congestion and air pollution', *Journal of Transport Economics and Policy*, **29**, 93–104.

Mazor, A. (1993), 'The land resource in spatial planning', in *Israel 2020: Master Plan for Israel in the 21st Century*, Stage A, vol. 2.

Mokhtarian P. (1998), 'A synthetic approach to estimating the impacts of telecommuting on travel', *Urban Studies*, **35**, 215–41.

Nijkamp, P. (1994), 'Roads toward environmentally sustainable transport', *Transportation Research A*, **28A**, 261–71.

Pickrell, D.H. (1992), 'A desire named streetcar: fantasy and fact in rail transit planning', *Journal of the American Planning Association*, **58**, 158–76.

Pucher, J. and C. Lefevre (1996), *The Urban Transport Crisis in Europe and North America*, London: Macmillan.

Rabinovitch, J. and J. Leitman (1996), 'Urban planning in Curitiba', *Scientific American*, **274** (3), 26–33.

Rietveld, P. (1997), 'Political economy issues of environmentally friendly transport policies', *International Journal of Environment and Pollution*, **7**, 398–416.

Salomon, I. (1986), 'Telecommunications and travel relationships: a review', *Transportation Research A*, **20A**, 223–38.

Salomon, I., Y. Gur and E. Feitelson (1996), *Transportation and Telematics*, Israel 2020 Strategic Plan, Haifa (in Hebrew).

Salomon, I. and P. Mokhtarian (1997), 'Coping with congestion: understanding the gap between policy assumptions and behavior', *Transportation Research D*, **2**, 107–23.

Shachar, A. (1998), 'Reshaping the map of Israel: a new national planning doctrine', *Annals of the American Academy of Political and Social Science*, **155**, 209–18.

Sperling, D. (1995), *Future Drive: Electric Vehicles and Sustainable Transport*, Washington, DC: Island Press.

Transportation Research Board (TRB) (1994), *Curbing Gridlock: Peak-period Fees to Reduce Traffic Congestion*, National Research Council, Washington, DC: National Academy Press.

Wachs, M. (1993), 'Learning from Los Angeles: transport, urban form and air quality', *Transportation*, **20**, 329–54.

Wegener, M. (1996), 'Reducing CO_2 emissions of transport by reorganisation of urban activities', in Y. Hayashi and J. Roy (eds), *Transport, Land-Use and the Environment*, Dordrecht, Boston and London: Kluwer, pp. 103–24.

4. Are current air transport policies consistent with a sustainable environment?

Kenneth J. Button

INTRODUCTION

Transport has been an important element in the economic development of virtually all countries. It is not, however, without its problems. The state of the natural environment is a continuing public concern in most countries and the impact of transport in general on the environment has received particular attention in recent years (Button, 1993). Transport has been the subject of major pieces of legislation at local, state, national and international levels as policy makers and those supplying transport services have acted to respond to this public concern. Much of this legislation has focused on immediate environmental impacts of transport, such as lead emissions, but the debate has more recently moved forward to the consideration of wider and longer-term effects within the context of a sustainable development framework.

Transport is not the only sector with major environmental implications. The underlying difficulty that is leading to public debates is that, because of a number of intrinsic features that are associated with transport, it is seen to lead to particular environmental policy problems. These features include.[1]

- it is a major sector in its own right (accounting for approaching 20 per cent of private expenditure in some countries);
- it is a growth sector;
- it is highly visible;
- transport is demanded where people are and this is becoming more common as urbanization expands;
- it is a mobile source of pollution (in the widest sense);
- it generates a diverse range of environmentally intrusive effects that extend from local noise issues to the emission of global warming gases;

- it is a major contributor to some particular forms of environmental damage (for instance, some 20 per cent of CO_2 emissions); and
- transport is widely 'traded' internationally, making it difficult to devise common policy strategies.

All transport modes combine these features although to differing degrees. Air transport is no exception. It is an important and growing transport sector. In 1994, for example, the aviation sector operated some 15 thousand aircraft serving more than 10 thousand airports. It employed about 3.3 million people (some 1.4 million in the United States) and carried 1.2 billion people and 23 million tonnes of freight.

Aviation has traditionally been one of the most heavily regulated of transport modes although in terms of economic regulations governing pricing and market entry, controls are rapidly being relaxed. In comparison with many other forms of transport, however, air transport has been left largely outside of many of the recent mainstream environmental debates. Where there has been concern and a policy reaction, it has mainly been in relation to issues of local importance and generally with regard to infrastructure matters (most notably aircraft noise around airports and fears concerning safety for those under flight paths).

The situation is, however, now changing. Air transport is clearly growing in importance as a mode of transport. Existing markets are expanding and new ones are emerging. Air transport is also becoming more visible than in the past, especially as ever increasing urban sprawl leads to encroachment on airports.[2] Increased use of airports also means more surface traffic to service them and to provide users with access.

The forecasts provided by commercial organizations such as Boeing (1998) and by international agencies, such as the International Civil Aviation Organization, also indicate that this growth pattern is likely to continue into the foreseeable future.

The traffic growth in air traffic is also taking place within a much less regulated market than in the past (Button et al., 1997). These changes were initiated by the passing of the 1978 Airline Deregulation Act in the US and more recently epitomized by the three packages of reforms that have liberalized European Union air transport. The trend is towards the liberalization of economic regulation and the privatization of airlines and air transport infrastructure. The results are that markets are driven more by commercial considerations. This has raised public concern about how the wider social interests are to be represented in decision making.

Aviation needs significant amounts of surface infrastructure to function effectively but many airports are now congested. For example, as long ago as 1988, a special task force of the International Air Transport Association identified the problems of seven European airports as critical. There are also mounting land access problems at some. Adding new airports or expanding existing ones imposes a variety of environmental costs on those living nearby but these may be costs that have to be borne if growth in air transport is to take place. There is, as a result, amounting conflict between those living near airports and those who use them (Button, 1998).

The perception of trends in environmental problems is often compounded because although many of the adverse effects of air transport, and especially noise round airports, have been reduced for individual flights and the noise envelopes for many airports are now consequently smaller, people's expectations have risen. In part this is because of rising living standards and concomitantly higher expectations, but whatever the cause, the public are becoming increasingly vocal in their environmental objections (GRA Incorporated, 1998).

Additionally, many of the public concerns about the environmental degradation that are generally associated with surface modes of transport have been addressed (albeit with varying degrees of success) and one can perceive a feeling that there is now the need to move on and to look at other forms of transport. Technology has considerably improved the fuel efficiency of the automobile, taxation and regulation has removed much of the lead pollution associated with gasoline use and catalytic converters have helped cut acid rain gas emissions. Such obvious interventions have not been observed regarding air transport.

This short chapter initially sets out to outline the main environmental implications of modern air travel. In particular it seeks to set this in the more general context of environmental concerns. It then moves on to offer a brief consideration of how one can look at the underlying reasons why air transport does create these difficulties. It pays particular attention to the way economists tend to look at these types of problem rather than being driven by pure engineering considerations. It is too brief to be comprehensive but does cover a number of emerging issues.

Finally, it pays attention to the policy tools that may be deployed to confront the worst of the difficulties. In tackling this last task, the aim is rather to look at the options that are available than to be prescriptive. This is for no other reasons than that the choices are often difficult and, in many respects, we still have limited knowledge concerning key parameters that underlie the adoption of a viable policy package. There is also the wider issue that air transport interacts with other transport modes and there is a need to review policy options in a broader context. This latter issue is outside of our remit.

AIR TRANSPORT AND THE ENVIRONMENT

Globally, air passenger traffic since 1960 has grown world-wide at an average yearly rate of 9 per cent and freight and mail traffic by some 11 and 7 per cent, respectively. In 1995, for example, some 1.3 billion passengers were carried by the world's airlines. Civil aviation has become a major service industry contributing to both domestic and international transport systems. It facilitates wider business communications and is a key component in the growth of tourism, now one of the world's major employment sectors. In addition to passenger transport, aviation is an important form of freight transport, with some estimates suggesting it carries up to 60 per cent of world trade by value (although of course not by volume) and forecast to rise to 80 per cent by 2014. In physical terms it is responsible for over 75 billion tonne-kilometers of traffic a year.

It is fairly safe to say that as a sector, aviation will continue expanding into the foreseeable future, albeit at differential rates in various geographical submarkets. A number of international agencies, aircraft manufacturers and airlines regularly produce forecasts of aviation traffic. While forecasting remains an art rather than a science, it seems likely that passenger traffic will grow at a rate between 5 and 7 per cent into the foreseeable future, much of it in the Asian-Pacific region (up to 9 per cent a year). Forecasts have also foreseen slower growth in the more mature US and European markets. Within these general trends there will inevitably be short-term fluctuations as the sector responds to variations in the international trade cycle and reactions to one-off shocks in the global international market – both reflections of the derived nature of demand for most air transport services.

This economic success, however, has been accompanied by increasing concerns about the longer term and the wider implications of air transport for society. While environmental matters have not been at the forefront of air transport policy concerns in the past, they are now attracting increasing attention.

While most people concur that environmental preservation is important, what constitutes an environmental concern is not always agreed upon. At the macro level, notions of sustainability and sustainable development have gained a widespread general acceptance following the publication of the Brundtland Report in 1987 (World Commission on Environment and Development, 1987).

While the notion that current generations should leave as a legacy a natural resource base for future generations comparable with the one it inherited itself has an intuitive appeal, operationalizing this at a global level has proved problematic. The concept is a general, global one and was not originally intended to imply rigidity in terms of the resources deployed in individual sectors or industries. At the level of individual sectors such as transport it is even more difficult to define a meaningful notion of sustainability and this becomes even more so at the level of the individual industry (see papers in Banister and Button, 1993). There are simply too many possible tradeoffs that could potentially lead to a sustainable path. There are also wider issues of social and political sustainability separate, but related, to that of the environmental concerns of the Brundtland Report (Button and Nijkamp, 1997). The notion of 'sustainable transport' is an attractive popular concept but a slippery one to put into practice.[3]

More traditional approaches to looking at environmental protection focus upon micro concerns, on particular issues and on individual environmental problems. These approaches, while less holistic in their basis, do provide a framework of analysis that is more consistent with normal policy making. Thus, while not intellectually ideal they offer tractable tools of immediate use in such areas as project appraisal, regulation and pricing.

In this context, aviation can be seen to have environmental effects at various levels. Some of these are local and concern such things as noise, land-take and soil contamination at airports and emissions of pollutants into the air by aircraft while at airports or during the landing and take-off cycle. Among these emissions are those of volatile organic compounds (VOC) due to fueling of aircraft and fuel handling in general, and CO emissions of aircraft due to incomplete combustion while being in the idle and taxi mode. For these pollutants the shares emitted at altitudes lower than 1.5 kilometers are dominant (from 50 to 80 per cent).

At a larger spatial scale the emissions stemming from climbing, approaching and cruising take the form of CO_2, NO_x, SO_2, CO, CH and VOC. At a global scale emissions that take place in the stratosphere (that is, the layer above 12 kilometers where the ozone layer is located are important). Since many aircraft cruise at about 10 to 12 kilometers, a non-negligible part of the aircraft effluent is emitted in the stratosphere.

While the partial equilibrium approach to environmental matters has on many occasions not found favor with ecologists who point, quite rightly, to the importance of systems in ensuring the long-term balance of the environment (see papers in Turner et al., 1999), this approach to a sustainable environment can often be divorced from social and political reality. Not only are there practical problems in treating sectors in isolation and, in so doing, ignoring intersector tradeoffs, but it may be difficult to communicate the importance of wider environmental matters and to gain the acceptance required for policy actions. Ultimately, a sustainable environment will only be possible if the political and social structure in which it sits is sustainable. In more concrete terms, this implies a more gradual approach to handling aviation-related environmental impacts and in providing policies to handle more immediate and transparent problems.

THE ENVIRONMENTAL COSTS

In terms of what is actually taking place regarding empirical and applied research, the traditional approach to environmental issues has mainly manifested itself in studies concerned with noise and pollution at airports and with certain aspects of safety.[4] A recent small-scale survey by Morrissette (1996) looking at the activities of US consultancy firms specializing in environmental work in relation to airports, for example, found that issues concerning wetland damage were of most importance followed by air quality, noise and storm water run-off pollution.

A considerable amount of work by academic and government economists has been done on the social costs of noise nuisance associated with air transport. A variety of techniques have been developed in order to place a monetary valuation of such nuisances at airports so that they may be traded off against the more narrowly defined economic benefits of air transport. Generally, this has involved efforts to express noise nuisance in terms of the financial implications of living near a major noise source, such as an airport, on house prices – for example, see Table 4.1 (taken from Johnson and Button,

Table 4.1   Estimates of the implications of noise nuisance effects on property values (percentage change per decibel increase)

Study	Year	% of house price	Country	Data
Abelson	1979	0.45	Australia	Disaggregate
Collins and Evans	1994	0.45	UK	Disaggregate
De Vany	1976	0.80	USA	Aggregate
Dygert	1973	0.60	USA	Aggregate
Emerson	1969	0.57	USA	Disaggregate
Gautrin	1975	0.35	UK	Disaggregate
Levesque	1994	1.30	Canada	Disaggregate
Maser	1977	0.62	USA	Aggregate
McMillan	1978	0.50	Canada	Disaggregate
McMillan	1980	0.87	Canada	Disaggregate
Mieszkowski	1978	0.40	Canada	Disaggregate
Nelson	1979	1.10	USA	Aggregate
O'Byrne et al.	1985	0.52	USA	Aggregate
O'Byrne et al.	1985	0.57	USA	Disaggregate
Paik	1972	0.65	USA	Disaggregate
Pennington et al.	1990	0.60	UK	Disaggregate
Price	1974	0.83	USA	Aggregate
Uyeno et al.	1993	1.13	Canada	Disaggregate

Source: Johnson and Button, 1997. Full citation of studies are contained in this paper.

1997) for a summary of some of these values derived from hedonic studies of house price differentials.[5]

These indirect approaches looking at noise-related markets suffer from several limitations, not the least of which is the need to allow for all other factors other than noise that affect house prices. Recently, researchers have concerned themselves with trying to gain more direct valuations through sophisticated questioning of those affected. Technically, these two approaches are referred to by economists as the revealed preference and the stated preference methodologies. Studies of the latter type indicate that noise nuisance costs may have been underestimated in earlier revealed preference work. Feitelson et al.'s (1996) work implies the valuation per decibel to be up to 4.1 per cent of property values.

In terms of atmospheric pollution, air transport also imposes adverse effects. The evidence on this, and in particular the particular implications of individual pollutants, however, is still not always solid. It does contribute NO_x to the atmosphere and is, thus, contributing to acid rain, but the evidence indicates this contribution is very small. At altitudes between 1 and 12 kilometers, aircraft emissions would seem to impact on the creation of global warming gases and at higher altitudes (where there is supersonic flight) to ozone depletion.

As a mode of passenger transport, air transport is slightly less fuel efficient than the auto but offers significant benefits in terms of time savings over longer distances (see column 2 of Table 4.2, although care must be exercised in the way this type of data is handled). In aggregate, air transport is responsible for about 5 per cent of the world oil consumption and 12 per cent of that consumed by the transport sector. The International Civil Aviation Organization estimates that civil aviation consumed about 138 million tonnes of aviation fuel in 1990 and that this will rise, given existing policies but allowing for improved technology, to about 220 million tonnes by 2020.

While one can always question these types of calculation, translating this into damaging emissions, the Air Transport Action Group in Geneva finds that

Table 4.2   Relative fuel consumption of air transport

	Energy per pkm (MJ/pkm)	Average speed (km/hour)	Energy use per travel hour (MJ/hour)
Aviation	2.2	500	1100
HSR	0.7	150	106
Intercity train	0.7	80	56
Car	1.5	50	75

air transport contributes only about 2–3 per cent of CO_2 emissions that are, in turn, responsible for about 1 per cent of any global warming effect. Stanners and Bourdeau (1995), focusing on the European Union, find air transport accounts for about 10 per cent of all transport energy consumption and is responsible for about 15 per cent of CO_2 emissions. Even more tentative are the estimates of the monetary costs of air pollution. A US study by Hansson estimated this to be about 1.08 cents per passenger ton kilometer, Kagerson's work in Scandinavia puts it at 0.70 cents while German analysis by IWW/INFRA offers a range between 0.18 and 1.09 cents.

There have also been efforts to place a larger set of values on the social costs of air transport and, in particular, to set these costs in the context of alternative modes. These studies rely on a combination of syntheses of previous work with new findings. The results of one recent study by Levinson et al. (1998) generated the estimates found in Table 4.3. The difficulties with such work are numerous and the findings, although helpful in a general sense, should be treated with some care.

While considerable effort has been put into measuring some impact of air transport, measuring many other environmental effects, let alone attempting to place a monetary value on them, is even more difficult than with items such as noise and air pollution. Airports, for example, despite often innovative design are not normally seen as visible delights. There are problems of drainage at and near airports as water courses are diverted and fuel seepage from storage tanks can take place.

Table 4.3   Comparison of long-run average social costs of passenger transport

Cost category	Air system ($/pkt)	Highways ($/pkt)
Noise	0.0043	0.00045
Air pollution		
CO	0.0000018	0.000033
VOC	0.0001530	0.002600
NO_x	0.0001700	0.000670
SO_2	–	0.000210
PM10	–	0.000057
Carbon	0.0005800	0.000170
Accidents	0.0005	0.0200
Congestion	0.0017	0.0069

THE ECONOMIC ISSUES

Economists have long had an interest in the environment, although the concerns for their thinking and their approach have changed over time as new issues have evolved and new policy debates have taken the stage. Thomas Malthus at the beginning of the nineteenth century, for example, focused on population growth, W.S. Jevons on the depletion of coal reserves and, more recently, Kenneth Boulding on the global resource base.

The classic microeconomic perspective is that at the margin, any additional activity should generate benefits at least as great as the costs that are imposed. In standard accounting terms this would just mean weighing up the financial pros and cons of options. The welfare economic view that underlies public policy making takes a much broader perspective and embraces a full range of social costs. There is a tradeoff between the different effects of any action that is multidimensional in its nature and this should be allowed for. What it does not mean, however, is that all environmental degradation is intrinsically undesirable; if the benefits to society exceed the costs then they are justified.

At the most basic level, economists view the underlying problem of excessive environmental degradation and deviations from a sustainable environmental path in terms of there being a market failure. In the very strictest terms this stems from the lack of adequate 'property right' allocations. In other words, there is no clear ownership of environmental attributes and, as a consequence, there is excessive consumption of them.[6] They are called 'commons' in the environmental economics literature. They are not used efficiently because of the lack of any market mechanism and are hence overexploited.

The environmental attributes are, therefore, external to the market process and to ensure their appropriate and efficient use they need to be brought within the market. As obvious as this may seem, it was not really until the work of the Nobel Prize winner Ronald Coase in the 1960s that this became generally accepted. Previous interest had mainly been in terms of most efficiently attaining some externally determined level of environmental resource exploitation.

If every environmental attribute were owned then there would be a market for them and they would be used efficiently but, of course, there may be good reasons why property rights are not allocated. It may be difficult to define exactly what they are and to police a market system – the transaction costs may be burdensome. There may be wider social reasons why the market process may prove inefficient (for example, due to monopoly elements) or be socially undesirable for income distribution reasons. It is difficult to think of practical ways in which property rights to future resource utilization, of the kind required to meet sustainability needs, can be allocated. Nevertheless, a lack of property right allocation is the underlying cause of excessive environmental degradation.

As a result of these problems and intellectual concerns, the Coasian approach is seldom seen as viable, although there have been some efforts at quasi-property right allocation policies in the guise of marketable permits for such things as lead additives for gasoline. One simple way of looking at the more pragmatic economic approach to environmental matters favored by practitioners rather than pure theoreticians, be it to do with air transport or some other activity, is to think in terms of a chain effect. Figure 4.1 provides a very simple outline of what is meant by this.

The long-standing standard microeconomic position is that 'Pigouvian taxes' can be imposed on those generating the adverse environmental externality to bring it more nearly to the socially desirable level. Those causing the environmental damage are, in this framework, charged by the authorities for so doing. This is not, however, strictly a market measure but rather a method for attaining a particular environmental standard – it is rather a fiscal instrument. Whether such taxes, or indeed subsidies in some cases, are preferable to other measures such as regulations on emissions has long been debated.

Ideally, within this framework, techniques such as cost–benefit analysis, therefore, include the environmental costs of activities as well as those immediately evident from the market. This is not, however, always straightforward to put into practice. There are, for instance, problems of valuation; it may not be possible for practical or political reasons to pursue some policy approaches and there are normally knock-on effects elsewhere in the system that are difficult to foresee.

In any case, the underlying economic issue is one of externalities. However, these externalities manifest themselves in the way air transport is provided (Link 2 in Figure 4.1). If the full costs of air transport are not made transparent

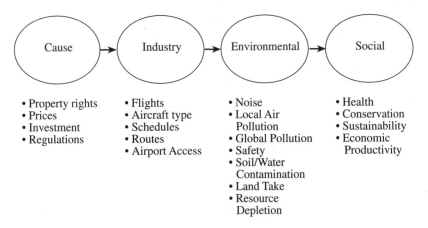

Figure 4.1   The stages of the environmental chain

to suppliers of air transport services then the suppliers will make decisions that are environmentally detrimental.

If the social costs of noise imposed on people around airports is not taken into account then there will be excessive aircraft movements and their timing will not allow for possible differing temporal sensitivities of local people to noise. Inadequate allowance for the atmospheric pollution effects of air travel will influence the fleet composition of carriers and their route choices. On the ground, traffic to and from airports causes a particular set of environmental problems and if this is not reflected in the prices that are paid for surface transport use then airport planning will fall short of environmental requirements.

These distortions to the air transport market then have effects for the environment (Link 3). In general, the existence of negative environmental activities in transport leads to an excess in the total supply of transport services; there is no exception to this in air transport. It also leads to suboptimal modal splits with excessive traffic being carried by modes that exhibit the highest relative external costs. The overall impact of these, and other industrial distortions, are the atmospheric, noise, land-use take and other environmental costs that cause social concern.

The final link in the chain is the impact of environmental degradation on society. After all, it is generally the social well-being of this and future generations that is the concern of people. An excessively degraded environment has immediate health implications (for example, high levels of noise causes stress) and can reduce traditional economic output: again, noise can affect sleep and this is reflected in lower levels of labor productivity (see papers in McMichael and Fletcher, 1997). In many cases there is the simple loss of welfare in knowing that the environment has been damaged and irreplaceable resources have been lost.

In the longer term, there are the much wider questions concerning sustainability and whether it is possible for the global ecosystem to provide the resources necessary for future generations if current levels of utilization continue. This can be extended to the consideration of whether current political, social and institutional structures can be sustained as the resource base is reduced.

POLICY APPROACHES

The Commercial Incentive

It is often taken for granted that there are few private sector reasons for taking account of environmental costs in decision making other than that government policy requires this or that. Government action will follow if private sector management does not act itself. This is not always the situation in practice, however. Airline managers may well have incentives to take at least some account of their actions on the environment when making commercial decisions.

One slightly different way of looking at air transport and environmental policy is to consider it in terms of incentives that influence the actions of those providing air transport services. We continue to focus on the airlines but parallel arguments are applicable to airports and other key actors in the game.

Essentially, the function takes the form:

$$S = f(E, G, I) + \varepsilon$$

where:

S reflects the environmental standard level adopted by an airline;
E reflects the private economic incentive to adopt an environmentally sensitive approach (for example, retention of reputation);
G represents government environmental codes and policies (for example, aircraft design features, maintenance standards taxation); and
I represents air transport infrastructure considerations (for example, airport design and air traffic control priorities).

There is an additional random element in the function ε, indicating the risk of something else that can unexpectedly influence the environmental attitude of an airline (for example, a war).

The equation is set out in this way to emphasize that airlines themselves sometimes have an incentive to contain the environmental costs of their activities. At one level, there is the pure public relations side. The public is not insensitive to what airlines do regarding the environment even if individuals are not immediately impacted by the actions of carriers. This is reflected in some of the action taken by carriers. The largest UK carrier, British Airways, for example, has a senior official responsible for environmental matters and regularly produces an environmental report setting out the actions of the airline.

In other cases the market itself acts to rein in some environmental costs. Fuel use is, for example, highly correlated with many elements of atmospheric pollution but it is also a major cost of supplying airline services. There is a natural commercial incentive to seek more fuel-efficient technologies in a competitive, market-driven airline industry. There is also pressure by the airlines for air traffic control systems to be improved and for airports to be designed so as to minimize routings and to limit congestion over airports.

The recent trend towards more liberal economic regulation and privatization of air transport may, on the one hand, be seen as removing it from public scrutiny but, on the other, may increase the private stimulus to be more socially conscious. Unlike state-owned concerns, for example, private airlines need to be sensitive to customer perceptions and if a good environmental image is what customers seek this can have implications at the margin. Given the operating margins airlines often operate with, this may prove important. Commercial undertakings are also more sensitive to the costs of such inputs as fuel, the consumption of which is also related to environmental impacts.

Government Interventions

When there is the need for official action, policy makers have a variety of instruments that may be used. Some have been put into practice, others are under consideration but many are still within the realms of academic debate.

In broad terms, policy interventions can be made at any of the four stages of the chain set out earlier in Figure 4.1. The government also has a wide portfolio of potential policy instruments at its disposal that can be applied at the various stages. The various policy tools can also have different uses, some being more suited to particular types of environmental considerations than others.

Table 4.4 offers a taxonomy of some of the possible portfolio of measures that are available to policy makers. While a number of different categorizations are possible, the dividing lines are drawn according to whether the instrument acts directly on the environmental source or is of a less direct nature (for example, affect overall demand for air transport services). Detailed consideration of all the alternatives is beyond the scope of this chapter, but some brief comments on the main categories of government interventions can be made.

- *Coasian approaches* Ideally, but also probably unrealistically, from an economic perspective property right allocations could be made more comprehensive, but failing that other remedial problems relating to pricing or directly regulating the use of environmental resources could be initiated. In fact, there are effective ways of making use of some of the features inherent in property rights. The use of tradable permits, whereby actors are allocated rights to make use of a predetermined quantity from their allocations has proved effective in related areas such as the reduction of lead in gasoline. It has also been experimented with to a limited extent at Denver Airport, where airlines can trade noise allowances between themselves.
- *Pigouvian charges* Government interventions can come through a variety of other direct channels (Button, 1994). Since full property right allocation is difficult, many economists favor the use of pollution charges of various kinds as mechanisms for reducing the environmental

Table 4.4 Taxonomy of policy instruments

	Market-based incentives		Command-and-control regulations	
	Direct	Indirect	Direct	Indirect
Plane	Emission fees Tax allowances	Tradable permits Feebates	Emissions standards	Inspection and maintenance Compulsory scrappage
Fuel		Fuel taxation	Fuel composition	Fuel economy standards Flying speeds
Traffic	Airport access pricing	Slot pricing Timing pricing	Routing limitations Aircraft type Airport design Noise insulation	Flight limitations

intrusion of air transport – essentially Pigouvian taxes. Manchester Airport in the UK, for example, has in the past charged higher landing/take-off fees for noisier categories of commercial aircraft. Emission charges are seen, because of their flexibility and because they equalize the marginal costs of abatement, as being the best way of attaining an administratively established level of pollution. They equalize the marginal costs of abatement.

Besides the need to have a fairly good idea of how sensitive users are to various levels of charge, there is the political difficulty that without some form of pay-back, these charges extract revenue from the sector in a way that fully allocated property rights would not. They essentially take resources from airlines and give them to government. A property right structure, in contrast, involves trade between airlines and those adversely affected with the automatic outcome that there are measures of compensation for those who are still adversely affected and penalties for those who continue to inflict damage on the environment. Further, it yields an optimal level of abatement rather than simply resulting in some level that has been deemed appropriate (albeit often with expert advice) by the authorities.

* *Command-and-control measures*   Equally, environmental regulations can also be deployed to meet a predefined environmental standard. The need to conform with noise restrictions (for example, the requirement to use Stage II aircraft) is a widespread form of regulation. Such policies are often seen as more easily enforced than charges and more transparent in their impact.

At the second stage seen in Figure 4.1, the way the industry operates and its scale can be controlled, again to reduce the environmental intrusion of air transport if this is felt to be excessive. In practice this is often the chosen approach of policy makers as a means of limiting problems around airports with many having flight limitations and night curfews. Instruments of direct regulation, therefore, abound. In addition to airport curfews and slot constraints, they embrace designated flight paths around airports, safety regulations, rules governing aircraft type, airport planning requirements, and regulations over destinations served (for example, the Perimeter Rules in the US). Fuel taxation may also be seen as important in this context as a fiscal device, as can overall airport charging regimes.

The problem with acting at this stage in the chain is that air transport policy itself has more than an environmental dimension to it. Acting indirectly on the environmental problems by influencing market conditions can potentially adversely affect the competitive environment in which air services are provided. While this may be done in a purely incidental way, there is always the underlying danger that actions purporting to be environmentally desirable in their orientation can be driven by secondary considerations to favor a particular carrier or airport.

- *Protecting the afflicted*   At the third stage is direct remedial action on environmental damage. In terms of noise, reductions in environmental intrusion are often achieved by insulating certain aspects of the environment (for example, the construction of noise barriers) or by fitting aircraft with mufflers. The global warming problems associated with CO_2 emission can be mitigated by remedial measures such as the creation of 'carbon sinks'. Essentially, the air transport sector is left to its own devices but government takes measures to adapt the environment to it.

Beside the fact that such policies often are only partially effective, the oft-heard objections to this type of strategy are mainly to do with distribution considerations. The problem is that the costs of insulating the environment are not directly borne by the air transport industry. There are also questions of effectiveness. Most of these types of measure only partially reduce the adverse effects and may themselves have secondary outcomes that are undesirable (for example, most noise barriers are not aesthetically pleasing).

Finally, society could 'treat' itself to overcome the adverse environmental effects of air transport. This may be in the form of compensation or it may be more direct, for example better medical care for those affected by noice-induced stress or for the effects of VOC on chest ailments. While theoretically this is a possible option it is generally treated very much as a last resort. The full social cost of many forms of environmental pollution is not known and many treatments for those that are understood are far from satisfactory.

A SUSTAINABLE ENVIRONMENT

What we can see from this brief outline is that there is a portfolio of policy tools that can be used to handle many of the individual environmental issues thrown up by the air transport sector. They can be deployed at different points in the environmental chain. From the perspective of a sustainable environment, the questions that need addressing become ones of whether the array of instruments are sufficient to meet the necessary criteria to attain such a state and, if so, whether they are currently being employed appropriately or, if not, whether there are the institutions available to ensure they will be in the future.

The first question is relatively simple to answer: the tool kit should in theory be able to meet the needs of a policy aimed at transport meeting the needs of a sustainable environmental policy. There is a large portfolio of instruments that can be drawn upon, the problems are really ones of understanding in more detail how they work and then in using them optimally.

To the second question, it is unlikely that at present they are being effectively employed to that end. A definitive answer is virtually impossible because without optimal strategies in other sectors, and with a lack of full information regarding cross-parameters with other sectors, it is difficult to know exactly what the degree of environmental resource allocation in aviation should be. Transport is a derived demand and there are alternatives both to transport and within the transport sector itself. Optimal use of any one mode depends upon optimal utilization of alternatives of all types.

There are also broad international issues to be considered when dealing with a global industry that has global environmental implications. International cooperation and coordination is important but difficult to attain.[7] The United Nations' International Civil Aviation Organization (ICAO) has a coordinating role in international air transport but equality in voting rights poses problems in reaching any meaningful policy strategy. The move towards a global air transport policy also assumes at a higher order still that the optimal macro path for an overall sustainable environment can be defined; it is not altogether clear that it can be!

What can be said is that there are serious and rising environmental costs associated with air transport that seem not to be fully internalized and are thus excessive in terms of what may be anticipated if a sustainable environment is to be attained. Bringing these items more fully into decision making is difficult and made particularly so because of the international nature of a large part of the air transport sector. Countries often have different incentive levels in terms of meeting various environmental targets.

CONCLUSIONS

Air transport is a major growth sector in the global economy. It brings with it not only improved communication for those in business but has opened up a whole range of leisure possibilities. At the same time it is bringing with it increased concern about the implications that this rise in air transport activity may have on the environment.

The sector has, to date, been reactive in a number of ways to meet these concerns, some of the reactions the result of market pressures and others the outcome of policy initiatives by governments. Compared to surface modes of transport, however, the environmental debate has been relatively subdued regarding aviation. This may continue to be the case, but even if this is so there is still a social need to ensure that air transport does not cause excessive environmental damage.

Policy makers have a variety of policy instruments that can be used to help ensure that air transport conforms to the longer-term needs of sustainable development, but there are problems. Information on the monetary equivalent costs of many forms of environmental damage is still scant and this makes comparisons of policy instruments difficult. There is still relatively little information concerning the effectiveness of many of the policy instruments. A problem here is not only that individual instruments are often still largely untried, but also in practice policies have a multidimensional nature involving a number of tools applied simultaneously with consequential interactive effects. Further, most policy instruments have impacts other than those purely on the environment and the magnitude and nature of these are generally not fully known in advance.

NOTES

1. These features have led to one commentator describing transport as 'Industry on Wheels'.
2. For example, the US Air Transport Association recognized the increasing role that environmental concerns will play in air transport policy making in a statement in 1996.
3. Graham and Guyer (1999), for example, while placing some importance on the environmental side of the notion of sustainable air transportation, focus more on the ability of the air transport sector to expand in the face of a variety of potential economic and physical constraints.
4. Safety is often not considered an environmental issue and this is sensible for many aspects of the topic. However, there is the issue of whether people living close to airports have their quality of life reduced through the fear of a plane crashing on them. In the broad definition favored here, this aspect of safety is seen as an environmental concern as much as something such as noise nuisance.
5. Meta analysis of a range of studies looking at noise effects at airports provides some explanation of why these money valuations vary; see Johnson and Button (1997) and Schipper et al. (1998). The initial house price level is an important factor as is the nature of the econometric model specification used.
6. In terms of a sustainable environment, the concept essentially takes a longer time perspective and moves away from the older Coasian framework to embody notions of explicit property rights for future generations.
7. As, for example, seen in 1999 when the European Union moved to ban all older aircraft that did not meet noise regulations without being fitted with 'hush-kits'. The US, where retrospective fitting of these kits has been the preferred option of many airlines, objected on the grounds that the objective of quietening aircraft was being met and that the means of achieving this was immaterial. From a noise abatement position one must have sympathy with the US stance.

REFERENCES

Banister, D. and K.J. Button (eds) (1993), *Transport, the Environment and Sustainable Development*, London: E & FN Spon.
Boeing (1998), *Current Market Outlook*, Seattle: Boeing Commercial Airplane Group.
Button, K.J. (1993), *Transport, the Environment and Economic Policy*, Cheltenham: Edward Elgar.

Policy aspects

Button, K.J. (1994), 'Overview of internalising the social costs of transport', in *Internalising the Social Costs of Transport*, Paris: ECMT/OECD, pp. 7–30.

Button, K.J. (1998), 'Environmental factors in airport competition', in *Les Aeroports de Demain* (Airports of tomorrow), Lyon: Laboratoire d'Economie des Transport, pp. 341–56.

Button, K.J., W. Michalski, B. Stevens and P. Weiss (1997), *The Future of International Air Transport Policy: Responding to Global Change*, Paris: OECD.

Button, K.J. and P. Nijkamp (1997), 'Social change and sustainable transport', *Journal of Transport Geography*, **5**, 215–18.

Feitelson, E., R. Hurd and R. Mudge (1996), 'The impact of airport noise on willingness to pay for residences', *Transportation Research D*, **1**, 1–14.

GRA Incorporated (1998), *Findings Report: Environmental Research Beyond 2000*, Jenkinstown: GRA.

Graham, B. and C. Guyer (1999), 'Environmental sustainability, airport capacity and European air transport liberalization: irreconcilable goals?', *Journal of Transport Geography*, **7**, 165–80.

Hansson, L. (1991), 'Air pollution fees and taxes in Sweden', Annual Meeting of the Transportation Research Board, Washington, DC.

IWW/INFRA (1995), *External Effects of Transport*, Paris: International Railway Union.

Johnson, K. and K.J. Button (1997), 'Benefit transfers: are they a satisfactory input to benefit cost analysis? An airport noise nuisance case study', *Transportation Research D*, **2**, 223–31.

Kageson, P. (1992), *External Costs of Air Pollution*, Brussels: Federation of Transport and Environment.

Levinson, D.M., D. Gillen and A. Kanafani (1998), 'The social costs of intercity transport: a review and comparison of air and highway', *Transport Reviews*, **18**, 215–40.

McMichael, A.J. and A.C. Fletcher (eds) (1997), *Health at the Crossroads – Transport Policy and Urban Health*, London: John Wiley & Sons.

Morrissette, S.E. (1996), 'A survey of environmental issues in the civilian aviation industry', *Journal of Air Transportation World Wide*, **1**, 22–35.

Schipper, Y., P. Nijkamp and P. Rietveld (1998), 'Why do aircraft noise value estimates differ? A meta-analysis', *Journal of Air Transport Management*, **4**, 117–24.

Stanners, D. and P. Bourdeau (1995), *Europe's Environment: The Dobris Assessment*, Luxembourg: Office for Official Publications of the European Communities/ Copenhagen: European Environment Agency.

Turner, K., K.J. Button and P. Nijkamp (eds) (1999), *Ecosystems and Nature*, Cheltenham: Edward Elgar.

World Commission on Environment and Development (1987), *Our Common Future*, Oxford: Oxford University Press.

PART II

Technological Aspects

5. Traffic and transport in the twenty-first century: market chances of new drive concepts for land-based transport

Wim Korver

INTRODUCTION

Incentive and Background for Study

Electricity is an important source of energy for collective passenger transport (train, underground, tram and trolley bus). In individual passenger and freight transport, electricity does not play a significant role. Nevertheless, thanks partly to the increase in environmental awareness, the interest in electricity as a source of energy in traffic and transport has increased in recent years. Intensified use of (new) collective passenger transport, but also large-scale introduction of electrically powered road vehicles can achieve this. The implementation of such ideas has major implications for the supply of energy in the Netherlands. This is also the reason behind doing a large-scale study of the possible image of the traffic and transport system around the middle of the next century. In order to gain greater insight into this issue, NV Sep (N.V. Samenwerkende Elektriciteits-Produktiebedrijven) commissioned a systems study.

The aspect with the most uncertainty is the development of new propulsion systems within individual transport. This could be an all-electric vehicle, but also hybrid-electric or fuel cell vehicles could come into the marketplace. Total electricity demand from the transport sector will to a large extent be dependent on the market opportunities for new propulsion systems. This chapter therefore deals mainly with the market shares of the different propulsion systems. However, the leading principle in this chapter is that such questions can be answered only if uncertainty about future developments is taken into account. Second, assessing the market potential of different propulsion systems can only be done if this is related to overall transport demand. To incorporate these two aspects, a scenario approach is ideal. The objective of a long-term forecasting is not to estimate the correct developments, but to support decision makers. Consistency of the future images and identifying the most important uncertainties are the two main objectives of a scenario study.

Scope of Research

The study was divided into a number of sub-projects, each of which was carried out by a different organization.[1] Figure 5.1 contains a diagram of the research approach.[2] The level of interaction that was required for this study is clearly apparent. One example of this is the reassessment of the vehicle features and energy costs model on the basis of the initial findings of the vehicle selection model. Similar instances of feedback took place on various occasions during the study. Furthermore, the study was divided into two phases, the first of which concentrated on a more or less qualitative description of the matter, while the content of the second phase was of a more quantitative nature. Moreover, the first phase was confined to the period up to the year 2020. The subject for the period from 2020–50 followed in the second phase.

The objective of the chapter is to outline the transport demand (passengers and goods) and to draw up an inventory of the transport systems against a background of the potential developments in the areas of spatial planning, economic activity, the employment situation, recreational activities and sustainability. On this basis, the research findings should give an insight into the future transport power supply and the influence the actors (suppliers, government, car manufacturers and so on) might bring to bear on the development of a future transport system. Therefore, the project has a long-term perspective. In point of fact, the time horizon is the year 2050. To provide more insight into the route to 2050, future visions have also been compiled for 2005 and 2020.

Terminology

This study differentiates between a number of different levels (see Figure 5.2). The explanation of each level follows later in this chapter. Broadly speaking, the approach has been to differentiate between the transport demand (transport system and transport concepts) on the one hand, and the technological content (vehicle concept and propulsion concept) on the other. Nevertheless, the fact remains that these levels have a great effect on one another. If electrical propulsion in a new vehicle concept were to become significantly less expensive, this would have certain repercussions on a transport concept, for example, that of a small vehicle for using in and around urban areas. In short, there is a great degree of interdependence between the levels. Therefore, the study

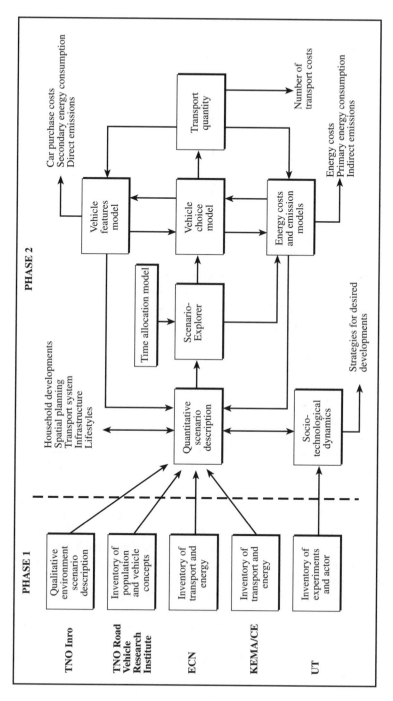

Figure 5.1 Diagram of the entire system study

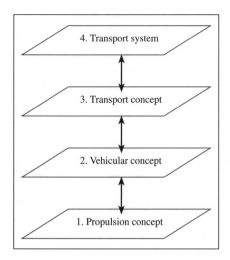

Figure 5.2   Overview of the terminology applied

was carried out in an iterative manner. The process was repeated several times, from top to bottom (see Figure 5.1).

Research Approach

The first step in the study was the scenario construction. In total, four scenarios are developed. It is important to notice that not only the researchers themselves were involved, but also representatives of other organizations (government, private sector and so on). Based on this input, first a qualitative description of the environmental scenarios was made, followed by a quantitative description. The end result is described in the next section.

An important aspect is the consistency of the scenarios. To support the research team a computer model, the ScenarioExplorer 1.0, is used. This enables the user to form a consistent scenario and to calculate the impact on transport demand. The third section presents some results of the outputs and in the fourth section more specific information is given of the different transport concepts to be used.

At the same time, some specific models were developed, namely:

- a vehicle selection model[3] (to determine the share of various propulsion concepts) and
- a model for determining the market shares of the different propulsion systems.

The first model is a system dynamic stock model. It is directly linked to total transport demand, resulting from the calculations with the ScenarioExplorer. The purpose of this model is to take into account fluctuations in overall demand for new cars and also to ensure that the sum of the estimated market shares of the different propulsion systems does not exceed 100 per cent. The fifth and sixth sections go into more detail and present the results for the market shares of the different propulsion systems. The final section offers some concluding remarks.

ENVIRONMENTAL SCENARIOS

Scenario Construction: The Design Dimensions

The scenarios can be split into two dimensions:

- *economic dynamics* this involves two alternatives. A society characterized by extremely high economic dynamics and the accompanying strong economic growth, and one on the verge of stagnation and therefore experiencing relatively little economic growth; and
- *importance of sustainability* this also involves two alternatives. A society in which the pursuit of a sustainable civilization, and therefore a sustainable traffic and transport system, is a generally accepted principle, and one in which it is not.

Four Environmental Scenarios

Four environmental scenarios can be derived from the two design dimensions. These are portrayed in Figure 5.3.

- *Unlimited Growth (UG)* society is characterized by high economic dynamics. This is accompanied by rapid technological progress. However, there is little public support for excessive promotion of a sustainable society. Everyone is in favour of the open market philosophy: the individual holds centre stage. The maximization of income is the guiding principle for the whole of society.
- *Sustainable Growth (SG)* society is characterized by high economic dynamics. This is accompanied by rapid technological progress. However, there is a great deal of public support for the strong promotion of a sustainable society. Everyone is in favour of the open market philosophy: the individual holds centre stage. Yet, this does not lead to the unrestrained maximization of income. Thanks to the introduction of

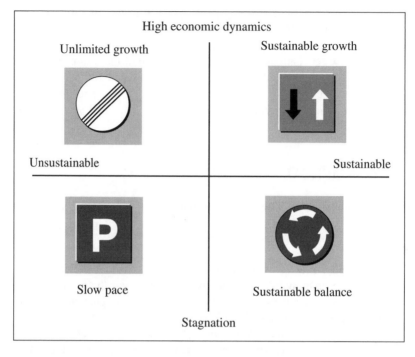

Figure 5.3   Dimensions and position of the various scenarios

a series of market-based policy measures, and the general acceptance of these, the traffic and transport system's environmental and energy impact can be reduced significantly.

- *Slow Pace (SP)*   society is characterized by low economic dynamics. This is accompanied by slow technological progress. However, there is little public support for excessive promotion of a sustainable society.
- *Sustainable Balance (SB)*   society is characterized by low economic dynamics. This is accompanied by slow technological progress. However, there is a great deal of public support for the promotion of a sustainable society.

Socioeconomic Features

Table 5.1 displays a few of the major socioeconomic features of the scenarios. It is clearly apparent that scenarios unlimited growth and sustainable growth are genuine growth scenarios: the economy and the population experience the strongest growth. However, it should not be overlooked that the more 'passive' scenarios (slow pace and sustainable balance) still display

Table 5.1   Several features of the various scenarios

Variables	UG	SG	SP	SB
Population (> 12 years; * 1,000):				
2005	13,721	13,720	13,957	13,525
2020	14,626	14,629	14,077	14,053
2050	14,629	14,343	13,121	13,682
Growth GDP (%)				
1990–2005	3.10	2.60	2.0	1.7
2005–2020	2.80	2.10	1.3	1.0
2020–2050	2.75	2.25	1.5	1.0
Household income (1990 = 100):				
2005	158	150	156	151
2020	217	206	198	192
2050	351	323	258	234
Employment (*1,000):				
2005	6,669	6,601	6,672	6,596
2020	6,958	7,023	6,888	6,880
2050	6,161	6,142	5,842	6,160
Households (* 1,000)				
2005	7,243	7,234	6,924	6,939
2020	8,201	8,058	7,422	7,421
2050	8,665	8,183	7,607	7,548

Note: *1000 – in thousands; # number of households.

considerable dynamism, and that the employment and population figures continue to increase until the year 2020. Economic growth is also substantial, when measured throughout the whole period.

It is distinctive that all the scenarios show considerable growth in both population and employment until 2020. These later stabilize, and in many cases even decline. The effect of the ageing population is apparent in each of the scenarios. In conjunction with this, it becomes evident that the number of households will continue to grow. Even slow pace and sustainable balance scenarios display this development. Underlying socio-cultural factors (continuing individualization) and age factors (the aged often live alone) are the cause of this.

Spatial Features

The relative spread of available housing over the various spatial areas is displayed for each scenario in Figure 5.4. Although this indicates a shift, it also shows that the spread of housing over the various spatial areas will remain

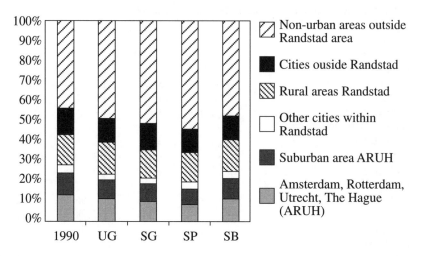

Notes: UG Unlimited growth; SG Sustainable growth; SP Slow pace; SB Sustainable balance.
Randstad is the urbanized western part of the Netherlands

*Figure 5.4   Relative spatial spread of housing in 1990 and in each of the
scenarios (2050)*

reasonably stable in relation to that of 1990. Given that a great deal of new
housing will be built while at the same time at least 60 per cent of the housing
currently available will still be in use in 2050, means that substantial changes
simply cannot be expected. The environmental structure has largely been
determined already, and will experience little change in the years to come.

Although the environmental spread is reasonably stable, there will of
course be growth. A considerable number of houses will be added in each of
the scenarios: this varies from 1.5 to 2.5 million houses in 2050. The strongest
growth occurs in the category 'Other, the rest of the Netherlands' (see Figure
5.5). In terms of housing figures, this is the largest category in the Netherlands,
44 per cent, and this will only continue to increase. The strongest growth is
forecast in scenarios unlimited growth and sustainable growth. However,
scenario slow pace also experiences relatively strong growth: +50 per cent.
Despite specific government policy, growth will continue beyond the urban
areas in particular.

Transport Costs: Passenger Transport

Figure 5.6. indicates the energy costs and the total variable costs per veh-
icle-kilometre. The energy costs are expressed as the weighted price per

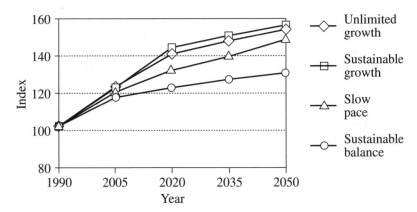

Figure 5.5   Change in number of houses per scenario beyond the 'Randstad' in the non-urban areas (1990 = 100)

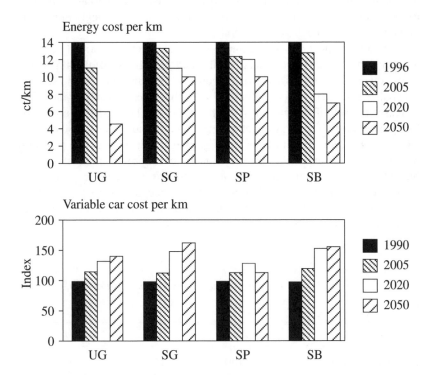

Notes: UG unlimited growth; SG sustainable growth; SP slow pace; SB sustainable balance.

Figure 5.6   Energy costs and total variable car costs per kilometre

kilometre. That is to say, changes within the vehicle fleet have been taken into account (see below). One general conclusion can be drawn, and that is that energy costs will fall drastically in each of the scenarios. This drop will take place mainly in the 1996–2020 period. The reason is three-fold:

- improved fuel efficiency (per vehicle, and as a result of the altered vehicle mix within the fleet);
- reduction or abolishment of fuel tax (particularly in scenario unlimited growth); and
- reduced energy charges.

Nevertheless, the variable car costs will increase in each of the scenarios. Due to the introduction of a range of cost-increasing measures (road pricing, parking charges and so on) it will become more expensive to drive a car. In the long run, this means that energy consumption will play an increasingly minor role in the prospective purchase of a private car.

The fares for public transport increase in each of the scenarios (see Table 5.2). The sharpest increase occurs in unlimited growth scenario: 140 per cent in relation to those of 1990! The rise is considerably lower in scenario sustainable balance: 42 per cent in relation to 1990. There is a tendency towards fare increases in each of the scenarios. As a result of the large portion accounted for by wage costs (varying from 50 per cent on trains to more than 80 per cent on buses), the direct result of economic growth is higher fares. The possibilities of counteracting these costs by means of improved productivity are limited. Furthermore, the government's continuing readiness to provide the running costs remains a crucial point. With the exception of scenario sustainable balance, it is assumed that this contribution will decrease; this automatically leads to higher fares.

Table 5.2   Fares for collective passenger transport per scenario (1990 = 100)

Scenario	2005	2020	2050
Unlimited growth	149	180	240
Sustainable growth	139	150	188
Slow pace	130	139	162
Sustainable balance	113	122	142

TRAFFIC AND TRANSPORT SYSTEM

Typology

The total traffic and transport system can be divided in several ways. Throughout this study we shall differentiate between three components:

- *individual passenger transport*   this entails transport by means of one's own, generally motorized, vehicle;
- *collective passenger transport*   this entails transport that is largely organized and provided by some form of organization, and is available to everyone (public transport); and
- *goods transport*   this entails the transport of goods by professional organizations.

This study is limited to the purely domestic aspect of transport. This means that the domestic leg of international transport is taken into account, but not the foreign leg. Air transport is not taken into consideration at all.

Scenario Characteristics

Table 5.3 provides a summary of the traffic and transport system components of the various scenarios. The underlying choices and argumentation are the result of several workshops, both with only project members as with external experts. It is important to notice that before this process a literature study was held which resulted in systematic description of a number of possible transport concepts (see also the next section). Looking at the transport system of the future one thing that emerges is the automation of traffic flows in one way or another. Furthermore, three of the four scenarios involve substantial changes in the composition of the traffic and transport system. Only in the scenario slow pace does the structure of the traffic and transport system remain the same.

Transport Performance: Passenger Transport

Total mobility continues to increase in each of the scenarios, however, the variations in growth rates are considerable (see Figure 5.7). As expected, scenario unlimited growth displays the greatest increase (index 167). The other scenarios experience more moderate growth. Scenario sustainable balance displays the least growth: only 15 per cent growth in relation to 1990. Scenarios sustainable growth and slow pace are pretty much the same, although the volume of mobility in scenario 'sustainable growth' is consistently slightly higher than that of scenario slow pace.

Table 5.3   Overview of traffic and transport system components per scenario

Unlimited growth	Sustainable growth
Individual transport	Individual transport
AVG, emphasis on smart cars	Dedicated cars (urban and neighbourhood
Special high speed automobile network	car) first car
(HSA)	AVG, emphasis on smart and clean car
Average car is larger and more luxurious	Limited AVG network (partially reserved
Special vehicle for long-distance transport	for environmentally friendly vehicles)
Road pricing on a substantial part of the	Road pricing closely linked to
road network, this will replace taxes, such	environment tax, with particular regard
as road tax	to CO_2 emissions
Dedicated cars: second and third cars	Collective transport
for leisure transport	Integration of existing systems to form
Collective transport	one system
New systems by linking existing systems	Automation of existing systems
Automation of existing systems	New automatic systems
Sharp reduction in volume	Environmentally friendly urban transport
No government contribution towards	Integrated car/collective transport system
public transport	Limited subsidy for public transport
Goods transport	Goods transport
Switch to diesel rail transport	Urban distribution centres
Double stack rail transport	Modular inland navigation
AVG and road trains	

Slow pace	Sustainable balance
Individual transport	Individual transport
AVG, emphasis on smart infrastructure	External speed control
Separate AVG network	Covered bicycle (Twike)
Taxes and charges at current levels	High variable costs for cars
Collective transport	Collective transport
New systems by linking existing systems	Environmentally friendly urban transport
Sharp reduction in volume	Integrated car/collective transport system
No government contribution towards	Extensive demand-controlled transport
public transport	system
Goods transport	Similar public transport subsidies to
HSG (fast train)	current ones
Partial switch to diesel rail transport	Goods transport
Separate AVG	Electric rail transport
	Combined transport
	Large-scale inland navigation
	Urban distribution centres
	City centres largely inaccessible

It is distinctive that the differences between unlimited growth scenario and the other scenarios continue to increase with the course of time. While the growth rate in unlimited growth scenario remains almost constant, the other scenarios display a distinct drop in growth after the year 2000. Given the straight line it displays, unlimited growth scenario can be considered the linear extension of the growth in mobility experienced in the Netherlands in recent

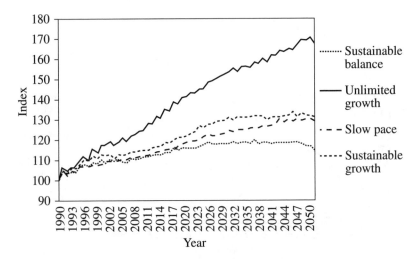

Figure 5.7   Total mobility growth (passenger-km) between 1990 and 2050, for the four scenarios (1990 = 100)

decades. For various reasons, the other scenarios experience much less growth. It is interesting to discover that economic growth and mobility growth appear to be separable. The sustainable growth scenario proves this.

How do these forecasts compare with other long-term studies? A good benchmark are the recently published long-term scenarios of the Dutch Planning Agency (CPB, 1997). These scenarios forecast a mobility growth of less than 20 per cent between 1995 and 2020. This is quite similar with three of the four scenarios, only the unlimited growth scenario deviates from this. More European-based scenarios show for the period to 2020 more or less the same growth rate: almost 1 per cent per year. More uncertainty exists for developments after 2020; no good benchmark could be found.

Car-kilometres

Figure 5.8 indicates the growth in the number of car-kilometres. It presents an almost identical picture to that of total mobility growth. Scenario unlimited growth is the most rapid grower: more than double the number of car-kilometres compared to the current situation.[4] However, slow pace and sustainable growth scenarios also display a considerable increase in the number of car-kilometres: more than 70 per cent in relation to 1990. Scenario sustainable balance experiences only limited growth in the number of car-kilometres: some 37 per cent in relation to 1990. When compared to the current situation, this practically amounts to stabilization.

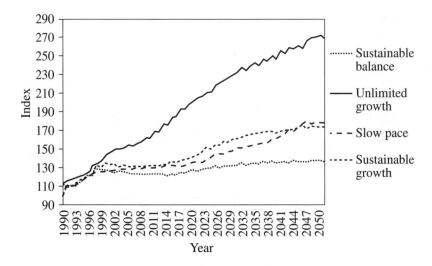

Figure 5.8   Change in the number of car-kilometres between 1990 and 2050, for the four scenarios (1990 = 100)

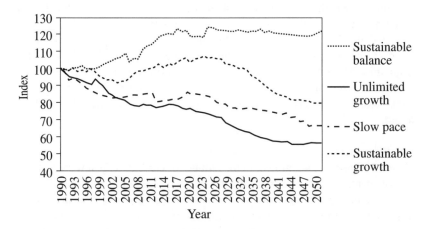

Figure 5.9   Change in the number of public transport passenger-kilometres between 1990 and 2050, for the four scenarios (1990 = 100)

Collective transport (public transport)

The number of person-kilometres travelled on public transport fluctuates greatly. As Figure 5.9 indicates, sustainable balance scenario experiences the strongest growth: + 21 per cent in relation to 1990. However, almost all of this growth occurs in the period 1990–2020. After this, the number of public transport-kilometres stabilizes. All the other scenarios display a reduction in the use of public transport. The sharpest reduction takes place in scenario unlimited growth; where the use of public transport is almost halved.

Transport Performance: Goods Transport

Table 5.4 indicates the change in transport performance for goods transport. This presents a similar picture to that of passenger transport. The sharpest growth is in unlimited growth scenario and the least is in scenario sustainable balance. It is also conspicuous that growth, expressed in ton-kilometres, surpasses that of passenger transport. The growth scenarios in particular display explosive growth figures.

The market share of goods transport by road remains substantial in each of the scenarios (see Figure 5.10). However, in the sustainable scenarios this share will eventually decline to less than 50 per cent.

Table 5.4   Transport performance goods transport (ton-km), per mode of transport (1990 = 100)

Scenario	Year	Road	Rail	Inland navigation	Total
Unlimited	2005	133	111	95	115
growth	2020	220	93	174	192
	2050	465	49	461	437
Sustainable growth	2005	90	145	116	105
	2020	142	188	204	172
	2050	269	254	504	371
Slow pace	2005	94	154	65	85
	2020	144	187	106	130
	2050	214	181	188	201
Sustainable	2005	73	138	102	90
balance	2020	114	179	168	142
	2050	147	225	249	197

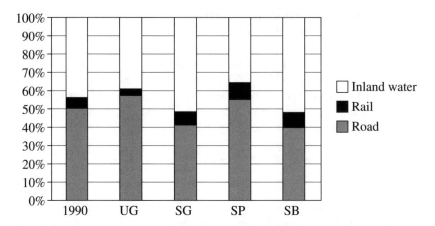

Notes: UG unlimited growth; SG sustainable growth; SP slow pace; SB sustainable balance.

Figure 5.10   Modal split in goods transport in 2020

TRANSPORT CONCEPTS: INDIVIDUAL AND COLLECTIVE TRANSPORT

Typology

If we look to 2020 and beyond, the current division of transport modalities will no longer be sufficient. The assumption that nothing will change is an unlikely prospect. On the other hand, new transport concepts are bound to be based on existing models. Technological development is an evolutionary process. Sudden breaks with tradition rarely occur, and if they do, one of the major preconditions is that this technology can succeed in creating a new market. This is no small task in the traffic and transport market. However, that does not mean that an evolutionary process will eventually lead to a completely new traffic and transport system (see below).

On the grounds of feedback within the project group, only a limited number of transport concepts remain. These are:

1. the *individual, conventional vehicle*   all journeys are carried out with a single vehicle (purpose and distance);
2. the *dedicated car*   use of an individual vehicle for a limited number of types of journey. This may be based on purpose (fun car) or distance (urban car/neighbourhood car);
3. *automatic vehicle guidance (AVG)*   the driver is (partially or completely) relieved of the task of driving. This alters the value of the

driver's time, and therefore the decision to use the car or some other form of transport;

4. *car sharing* instead of personal possession of a car, ownership is shared with others. The factors influencing the decision to use the car are then totally different;

5. *organized collective passenger transport by road* scheduled bus transport in urban and rural areas;

6. *collective road transport according to demand* vehicles are deployed according to the actual demand (mainly in rural areas, but also in urban areas). The vehicles used may be taxis, minibuses or 'ordinary' buses;

7. *individual public transport* these are systems that give the user the option of renting/using a vehicle for a particular journey. The Praxitelle and Tulip systems are examples of this;

8. *urban rail transport* further expansion of the existing tram, express tram and underground concepts;

9. *regional rail transport* the type of rail transport currently provided by the NS (Dutch Rail), up to a distance of about 50 km and

10. *long-distance rail transport* train journeys in excess of 50 kilometres. The competitive position of this transport concept is increasing, largely due to the anticipated arrival of the high-speed train.

Change in Transport Performance, Individual Passenger Transport

Table 5.5 contains an overview of the vehicle-kilometres per transport concept, with the note that dedicated car in the sustainable growth scenario has a different meaning to that in the unlimited growth scenario. The mix of transport concepts changes radically in all but the slow pace scenario.

Use of the all-purpose car declines in the sustainable growth scenario only. In sustainable balance and unlimited growth scenarios use of the all-purpose car stabilizes after 2020, while in the slow pace scenario it continues to increase. In unlimited growth and sustainable growth scenarios, all growth after 2020 takes place in new transport concepts. It is notable that the role of AVG in the sustainable growth scenario is even more substantial than in the unlimited growth scenario. The strong link between an environmentally friendly propulsion concept and the use of AVG apparently provides an extra incentive.

It is also distinctive that sustainability does not automatically imply a completely different traffic and transport system. Although scenario sustainable balance does involve new transport concepts, on balance the emphasis remains on the all-purpose car. Due to the great emphasis on volume policy and the promotion of the use of smaller vehicles, the consumer is likely to select a small clean vehicle. This causes the competitive position of

Table 5.5   Change in vehicle-kilometres (in billions) in individual passenger transport, 2020 and 2050

Scenario	Transport concept	1990	2020	2050
Unlimited growth	All purpose	735	111.1	111.4
	AVG	0	28.1	64.9
	Dedicated	0	9.3	21.4
Slow pace	All purpose	73.5	101.9	133.6
	AVG	0	0	0
	Dedicated	0	0	0
Sustainable growth	All purpose	73.5	37.8	6.8
	AVG	0	37.1	72.0
	Dedicated	0	30.3	50.6
Sustainable balance	All purpose	73.5	80.4	83.1
	AVG	0	0	0
	Dedicated	0	6.8	13.3

completely new transport concepts to deteriorate. After all, smaller vehicles are already much cheaper than conventional ones; so the price incentive to switch to a different transport concept is lost.

A special calculation method was used for the transport concept car sharing. Given its totally different nature, it was impossible to specify the number of vehicle-kilometres for this transport concept. However, the number of shared cars has been estimated in Table 5.6. This pertains solely to the sustainable scenarios. It is assumed that the share of the shared car transport concept in the other scenarios will be negligible. The role of the shared car varies greatly from one scenario to the other:

Table 5.6   Number of shared cars in the sustainable scenarios

Scenario	Description	2005	2020	2050
Sustainable growth	Number (*1,000)	24	222	504
	% of fleet	0.3	2.7	5.2
Sustainable balance	Number	159	327	676
	% of fleet	2.0	4.0	8.0

Note: 1000 – in thousands

- in scenario sustainable growth, it mainly involves long journeys. Therefore, we are talking about long-distance cars in most cases, and
- in scenario sustainable balance, it involves mainly short journeys. The shared car takes the place of the private car in many households. Therefore, to a great extent we are talking about all-purpose cars. The significance of car sharing is consequently the greatest in this scenario (8 per cent of all cars).

Change in Transport Performance, Collective Passenger Transport

During the 1990–2020 period, the transport performance of collective passenger transport increases in the sustainable scenarios, and declines in the other two scenarios (see Table 5.7). After 2020 use stabilizes or declines. The situation varies considerably from one transport concept to the other. For example, in scenario unlimited growth the use of urban rail transport increases, despite a substantial drop in the use of collective passenger transport in general. One transport concept experiences a decline in all the scenarios; scheduled road (bus) transport. If growth is to be achieved in collective passenger transport, it will have to be sought in new transport concepts, such as transport by demand and individual public transport.

VEHICLE CONCEPTS: INDIVIDUAL TRANSPORT

Typology

This study differentiates between three vehicle concepts:

1. *All-purpose car* this is basically the current private car. The vehicle is suitable for any distance and all purposes (hence the name).
2. *Long-distance car* this is a vehicle specially designed for long distances. This is also closely linked to the introduction of AVG, which will be used mainly for longer journeys. As the driver is (partially or completely) relieved of the task of driving, there is time to perform other activities during the journey. In the long run, this will lead to the development of vehicles specifically for this type of journey.
3. *Dedicated car* this is a vehicle specially designed for a certain type of journey. The design may be distance or purpose orientated.

Car Park

The car park continues to grow in each of the scenarios. Scenario unlimited growth displays the sharpest growth: doubling the volume in 1990 to some 11

Table 5.7 Change in passenger-kilometres (in billions) in collective passenger transport, 2020 and 2050, per transport concept

Transport concepts	1990	2020				2050			
		UG	SG	SP	SB	UG	SG	SP	SB
Scheduled road transport	6.5	3.0	4.6	3.7	5.5	1.5	2.3	2.2	4.4
Transport according to demand	0	0.5	1.0	0.7	1.1	0.5	1.3	0.9	2.1
Individual public transport	0	0	0.4	0	0.1	0	0.8	0	0.1
Urban transport (rail)	1.3	1.5	1.6	1.4	1.8	1.6	1.6	1.4	2.0
Regional rail transport	7.0	5.5	7.1	6.2	8.6	3.2	5.0	5.0	8.4
Long-distance rail transport	5.9	5.4	6.8	5.8	7.7	4.7	5.8	5.4	7.8
Total	20.7	15.9	21.4	17.8	24.6	11.6	16.8	14.9	24.8

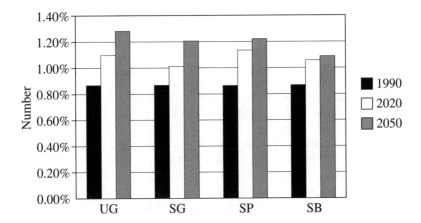

Notes: UG unlimited growth; SG sustainable growth; SP slow pace; SB sustainable balance.

Figure 5.11   Number of cars per household

million cars in 2050. However, even in the relatively car-free sustainable balance scenario, the volume increases to about 8 million private cars. The figures for scenarios sustainable growth (9.8 million) and slow pace (9.3 million) lie somewhere between the two.

To gain better insight, it is useful to relate car ownership to the number of households. This is displayed in Figure 5.11. It is evident that the differences then actually become much smaller. The individualization trend experienced in the growth scenarios in particular, leads to a marked increase in the number of one-person households. Private cars become more expensive. The largest increase occurs in the unlimited growth scenario: practically treble the 1990 price in 2020, and this continues to rise even more. The unusually vigorous economic growth allows for such astronomic price rises. This also means that there is space in this scenario for new features in the car. The most important of these is AVG. This is highly expensive, but affordable given the circumstances. In the sustainable growth scenario, the average purchase price also increases. This increase is less substantial than in the unlimited growth scenario, as the cars will be considerably smaller. The price rise in the sustainable balance scenario is the lowest. As a result of the downsizing of the all-purpose car and few technological innovations, the average purchase price hardly increases at all. The overall result is that the propulsion unit's portion of the total cost price of a car declines sharply. In all but the sustainable balance scenario, the costs of the propulsion unit will become less important.

PROPULSION CONCEPTS: INDIVIDUAL TRANSPORT

Typology

This study differentiates between four propulsion concepts:

1. *ICE* — the conventional internal combustion engine. Despite having been around for decades, this concept can still be improved upon and is quite capable of dismissing competing propulsion concepts.
2. *BEV* — the completely electrically powered vehicle. At the moment, this propulsion concept cannot compete with conventional systems. However, on the assumption of an extra incentive (to achieve sufficient scale size) and marked progress in battery technology (particularly the operating radius), this propulsion concept could play a major role.
3. *Hybrid (HEV)* — a combination of an electric motor and a (small) conventional internal combustion engine. The beauty of this concept is that the problem of the BEV's limited operating radius is overcome, while retaining the appealing environmental aspects.
4. *Fuel Cell (FCEV)* — a unit that directly converts fuel (generally hydrogen) into power, electrochemically.

Methodology for Determining Market Share of (New) Propulsion Systems

For determining the market share of (new) propulsion systems the basis was the expected development cost. Per combination of propulsion system, fuel used, vehicle concept and scenario (after filtering for the very unlikely combinations 31 combinations remained) an assessment is made of expected development of the purchase price (excluding purchase taxes and VAT) and operational costs (based on energy cost, fuel taxes and fuel efficiency per combination). These cost are assessed by three organizations:

- Road Vehicles Institute of TNO (TNO-WT) assessed the car purchase price (excluding taxes). The assessment is based on expected cost price developments of all engine components;
- Centre for Energy Saving and Clean Technology (CE) assessed the developments of the energy prices. This includes the production and distribution cost of fuel. In this way electricity and conventional fuels are comparable; and
- TNO Inro assessed the fuel taxes, which differed per scenario.

Based on these assessments it was possible to construct time series for all combinations. The propulsion system choice model is based on the relative changes in the purchase prices and operational costs. The combination with the largest cost decrease is most likely to gain market share. The general form of the model is:

$$A_i^t = A_i^{t-1} * (1 + \varepsilon_1 \Delta P + \varepsilon_2 \Delta K),$$

Where:

A_i^t = share of propulsion system i in year t
ε_1 = elasticity
ΔP = relative change of the purchase price
ΔK = relative change of the operational costs.

It is important to notice that this model is used only to determine the market shares of the different propulsion systems in the new car sales. Total car ownership is assessed (within the ScenarioExplorer) simultaneously with the transport demand forecast. In addition, an inventory model is used to calculate the number of cars coming into the market. This means that all kinds of policy measures to stimulate environmental vehicles are incorporated in the transport model. It also assumes that no specific policies exist to stimulate one specific propulsion system (for instance, the Californian demand to sell at least 10 per cent zero emission vehicles). In other words it is assumed that in the long run, transport demand and costs (including environmental taxes) are the driving forces for consumer choice behaviour.

Transport Performance

Figure 5.12 shows the transport performance of each propulsion concept. One important conclusion that can be drawn is that ICE experiences very little growth in any of the scenarios. The second conclusion is that its most promising successor is the hybrid propulsion unit. The hybrid plays a major role, even in the slow pace scenario. The third conclusion is that the fuel cell could play a major role, but that this, apparently, depends on economic growth. Only in the growth scenarios does the fuel cell propulsion concept achieve substantial figures. Only in a sustainable environment does completely electrical propulsion (the BEV) have any chance of gaining a market share. To which it must be added that BEV propulsion will never capture the majority of the market, and active encouragement is vital. Without incentives (price incentives and preferential treatment within built-up areas) it will never achieve more than a modest share of the market.

Propulsion Concepts in Collective Passenger Transport

While ICE will be able to hold its ground in individual transport, this is much less the case in collective passenger transport. Due to the combination of

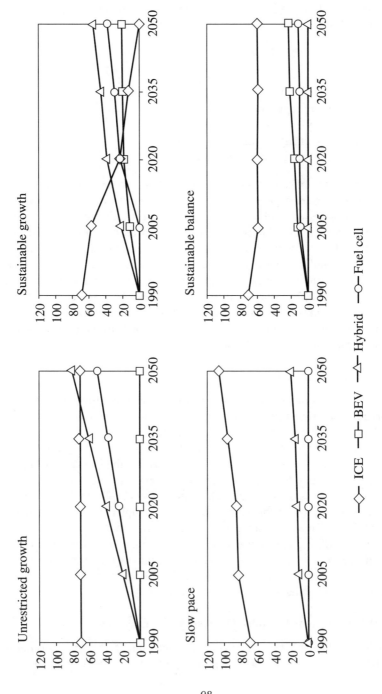

Figure 5.12   Change in vehicle-kilometres per propulsion concept in indivdual passenger trasnport (bn per year)

declining volumes and the (government) desire to promote environmentally friendly propulsion concepts in each of the scenarios, the use of conventional propulsion concepts in collective passenger transport will decline. The volume of electrically powered transport will also decline. The exception is the sustainable balance scenario, which experiences substantial growth. However, even in this scenario, the use of electricity declines. (See Figure 5.13.)

Propulsion Concepts in Goods Transport

Goods transport has been divided into road and other modes of transport. In the case of the road sector, new propulsion concepts will play only a minor role. In the case of trucks, only in the sustainable growth scenario will the fuel cell gain a substantial market share (about 33 per cent in 2050). For vans, the hybrid propulsion concept will become commonplace. However, the percentage of the total transport volume accounted for by vans is rather small (about 2 per cent).

In the other sectors, rail and inland navigation, the former is expected to be the more dynamic. The determining factor is whether or not society focuses on sustainability. If this is not the case, the transport of goods by rail will stabilize and the use of diesel traction will increase further. If the focus is set on sustainability, the volume of rail transport will increase sharply (260 to 280 per cent). Furthermore, electrical propulsion will play an even greater role in this sector.

CONCLUDING REMARKS

In this study four scenarios were developed. These scenarios provide a clear picture of the developments that may occur: unlimited expansion of (car) mobility, stabilization of mobility and a moderate increase in mobility. This is expounded on in terms of various developments within the traffic and transport system. These range from completely new transport concepts to limited upgrading of existing transport concepts. A whole range of techniques may be introduced within this framework. In short, the number of possible developments is vast. This causes a great deal of uncertainty among actors involved in long-term planning (government bodies, transport companies, vehicle manufacturers, power companies and so on). There are so many options, and which 'solution' will be the ultimate winner? Scenario studies such as 'Traffic and transport in the twenty-first century' attempt to answer this question.

This study revolves around propulsion concepts. From the point of view of the electric utilities, the prospects for electrical propulsion are particularly relevant. The ultimate prognosis is that it is highly likely that electrical propulsion

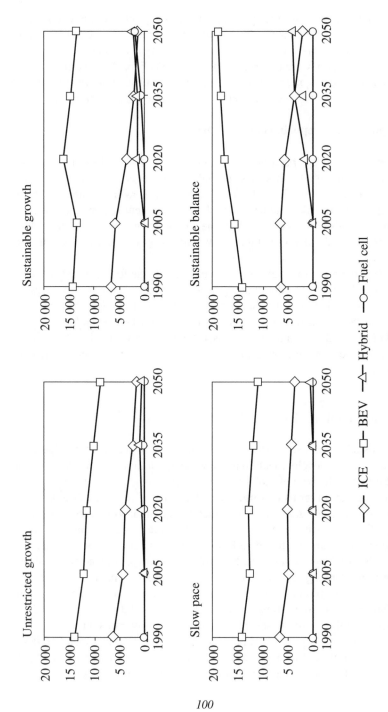

Figure 5.13   Change in passenger-kilometres per propulsion concept in collective passenger transport (m per year)

will play a major role, but that 100 per cent electrical propulsion (BEV) seems unlikely to achieve more than a 25 per cent share of the market. The future appears to lie in the combination of electrical propulsion and a small conventional engine (hybrid propulsion), and ultimately in the form of a fuel cell. However, the conventional internal combustion engine (ICE) is a strong competitor. The scenarios show that unless explicit incentives are given, ICE will retain the lion's share of the market. There is still plenty of scope for improvement of ICE (both in terms of emissions and energy consumption). This is a factor that actors involved in long-term strategy development must bear in mind. Any attempt to promote a new propulsion concept will trigger a reaction from the current basic technological design, in this case ICE technology.

From a methodology point of view it is difficult to interpret the results. Scenarios are, first of all, not a prediction of the future but an aid to structuring our thinking about the future. Therefore it is essential that within a scenario study interaction exists between the researchers and the outside world. But even then, many of the results are determined by the inputs. In this study the use of the ScenarioExplorer prevents illogical combinations from being made (for example, an increase in households is not related to employment and housing developments). Nevertheless, the views laid down in the scenarios are the views of a limited number of people, mainly experts. This should always be taken into account when looking at the results of a scenario study.

NOTES

1. Involved were: TNO Inro, TNO Road Vehicle Research Institute, University of Twente (UT), Energy Centre Netherlands (ECN), the Centre for Energy Saving (CE) and the KEMA.
2. The approach outlined here applies mainly to passenger transport. The same basic approach was taken to outline goods transport, on the understanding that neither the lifestyle aspects nor the corresponding time allocation model (the sub-project carried out by ECN) were taken into account. And second, that the ScenarioExplorer was not used for goods transport, but a combination of two specialized goods transport models, ATTACK and FORWARD.
3. It must be borne in mind that this involves three versions: individual passenger transport, collective passenger transport and goods transport.
4. This strong growth is supported by a change in lifestyles. The egocentric citizen is a good typecasting of this lifestyle.

BIBLIOGRAPHY

(all publications are in Dutch, unless the title is given in English)

Centraal PlanBureau (CPB) (1992), *Scanning the Future: A Long-term Scenario Study of the World Economy 1990–2015*, 's Gravenhage: SDU-uitgeverij.

Centraal PlanBureau (CPB) (1997), *Economie en fysieke omgeving: Beleidsopgaven en oplossingsrichtingen 1995–2020* (Economy and Physical Environment: Policy Demands and Possible Solutions 1995–2020), 's Gravenhage: SDU-uitgeverij.

Elzen, B., F. Geels, R. Hoogma, J. Schot and R. te Velde (1997), *Verkeer en Vervoer in de 21e eeuw; Deelproject 3: strategieën voor innovatie* (Traffic and Transport in the 21st Century; Part 3: Strategies for Innovation), Enschede: Universiteit Twente, Rapportnr. SEP-97.doc.

Elzen, B., R. Hoogma and J. Schot (1996), *Strategieën voor innovatie: experimenten met elektrische voertuigen als opstap naar marktontwikkeling* (Strategies for Innovation: Experiments with Electric Vehicles as a Start-up for Market Development), Enschede: Universiteit Twente.

Gerwen. R.J.F. and P. Toussaint (1997), *Wegwijzers naar 2050; Verkeer en Vervoer in de 21e eeuw* (Mapping the Road Towards 2050; Traffic and Transport in the 21st Century), Arnhem: NV Sep, Rapportnr. 42020-KST-97-3250.

Korver, W., C.A. Smits and M.J.M. van der Vlist (1997), *Verkeer en Vervoer in de 21e eeuw; Deelproject 1: vervoerbehoefte en vervoersystemen* (Traffic and Transport in the 21st Century; Part 1: Transport Demand and Transport Sysems), Delft: TNO Inro, INRO-VVG 1997–15.

Roos, J.H.J., F.J. Rooijers and J. van Swighem (1997), *Vervoer en Energie in de 21e eeuw; Deelproject 5: energie in de 21e eeuw* (Traffic and Transport in the 21st Century; Part 5: Energy in the 21st Century), Delft: Centrum voor Energiebesparing en Schone Technologie, Rapportnr. 3.3831.1.

Schol E. and K.F.B. de Paauw (1997), *Verkeer en Vervoer in de 21e eeuw; Deelproject 4: Personenvervoer en leefstijl* (Traffic and Transport in the 21st Century; Part 4: Passenger Transport and Lifestyle), Petten: ECN-Beleidsstdudies, ECN-BS/ES/7.7019/98.

Schuld, J.H. (1997), *Verkeer en Vervoer in de 21e eeuw; Deelproject 5: Elektrische Infrastructuur* (Traffic and Transport in the 21st Century; Part 5: Electrical Infrastructure), Arnhem: KEMA Transport en Distributie, Rapportnr. 59718-TDP-107236.

Smokers, R., J. van de Venne, P. Hendriksen, J. Prikken, D. Schmal and R. van der Graaf (1997), *Verkeer en Vervoer in de 21e eeuw; Deelproject 2: nieuwe aandrijfconcepten* (Traffic and Transport in the 21st Century; Part 2: New Propulsion Concepts), Delft: TNO-WT, Rapportnr. 97.OR.VM.089.1/RSM.

Verroen, E.J., C.A. Smits and T. van Maanen (1994), *De ScenarioVerkenner, versie 1.0. Deel 3: Technische documentatie Scenariobouwmodule* (The ScenarioExplorer Version 1.0. Technical Documentation), Delft: TNO Inro, 94/NV/058.

Wilkinson, L. (1995), 'How to build scenarios: planning for "long fuse, big bang" problems in an era of uncertainty', Wired special edition.

6. Electric vehicles: a socio-technical scenario study

René Kemp and Benoît Simon[*]

INTRODUCTION

Many car manufacturers today are doing research on electric vehicles. Some car industry commentators, like Sperling (1995), believe that the shift towards electric vehicles (EVs) is inevitable – because of the insufficient environmental stretch of other types of vehicles and ultimate depletion of the gasoline feedstock. Other people believe that EVs will have no future, arguing that EVs are a 'turn off' (*Financial Times*, 12 June 1997) – because of intrinsic disadvantages (notably the short range and high purchase price) relative to internal combustion vehicles. This chapter will examine the future for EVs in a more structured way, using a method which combines insights from technology dynamics studies (especially evolutionary theories of socio-technical change) with scenario analysis. The method – called the co-evolutionary socio-technical (CEST) scenario method – differs from other prospective methods such as trend extrapolation (curve fitting exercises), Delphi studies and traditional scenario studies, by focusing on the interplay (co-evolution) of technological possibilities, supply-side policies, government policies and market demand – how such an interplay gives rise to particular passenger transport development patterns.

A key element of the co-evolutionary socio-technical scenarios is the focus on the interaction between technologies and society. In the scenarios we describe how transport technologies, manufacturing strategies, government policies and travel practices co-evolve and change through a process of interaction in multiple marketplaces, social communities and policy arenas. Actor strategies, including government policies, are not exogenous but endogenous to the process by building on previous experiences with transport technologies, policies and investments. Likewise, user needs and requirements, travel

* This chapter was written as part of the Strategic Niche Management project for the Environment and Climate programme of DGXII of the European Commission. A first version was presented at the 6th Greening of Industry Conference, Santa Barbara, CA, 16–19 November 1997. The authors would like to thank Kanehira Maruo, Boelie Elzen, Sytze Rienstra and two referees for comments on an earlier version.

behaviour and car ownership patterns co-evolve with new technologies and user experience.

In the chapter we describe two scenarios for EVs: one in which EVs are used in small niche markets of the car-based travel regime, and one in which they are used as part of a regime of intermodal travel.

THE CEST SCENARIO METHOD

Companies and governments alike feel a great need to orientate themselves to the future. Whereas companies want to be better prepared for future events and developments, to take stock of emerging threats and opportunities, governments have a greater ambition to create the future or shape it in a beneficial way.

To gain insight into the future, different methods and techniques have been developed and used. The methods may be grouped in two categories: (i) forecasting methods that aim to predict the future, and (ii) foreseeing methods aimed at outlining future possibilities rather than future states. Foreseeing exercises are more explorative and narrative. The goal is not to give accurate predictions but to outline possibilities, so as to elicit discussion and to challenge existing views of reality. Scenarios and cross-impact studies are examples of foreseeing exercises.

In the field of technology, the diffusion of a new technology is a popular topic for prospective study. The method most widely used is that of curve fitting. Usually, an S-shaped curve is fitted to historical data. This work has been pioneered by Bass (1969). Curve-fitting exercises are predicated on the idea that the diffusion process will follow a commonly observed sigmoid pattern. In our view, curve-fitting exercises are *not* a good method for prospective analysis, at least not if you are dealing with competing (systemic) technologies of which it is uncertain which one will gain dominance, as in the case of transport. It is also not well suited for emerging or embryonic technologies that have only a short diffusion history, but even for well-developed technologies the predicted diffusion pattern may be well off the mark: the diffusion process may peter out because of shifts in the adopter environment (such as price changes, regulations, taxes, user preferences), or the emergence of new technologies. Also, the diffusion ceiling may elevate due to important improvement in the techno-economic characteristics of the diffusing technology, changes in the price structure, or, in the case of systemic technologies, the availability of complementary technologies (like fast-recharging stations in the case of electric vehicles and real time travel information systems) which make the new technology more attractive for prospective users.

If there are many, undetermined variables affecting the diffusion of a new technology, as in the case of electric vehicles, it is better to use a different method, one which takes stock of possible changes in technologies and the *system* aspects of technologies. In this chapter we develop such a method that may be used for examining the prospects of systemic technologies: the co-evolutionary socio-technical (CEST) scenario method. This is a foreseeing method that combines elements of different futures studies, especially scenario analysis and cross-impact studies, and social studies of technology – in particular economic evolutionary theories and sociological studies of technical change.

The characteristic elements of the CEST method are that it:

- looks at actor strategies and goals;
- builds upon real existing technological possibilities;
- takes a system view;
- focuses on trends; and
- looks at interactions and cross-impacts.

Trends and actor strategies and goals are used as an important source of information for the scenarios. Of course, the focus on trends is common in scenario analysis. The focus on actor strategies and goals is something new. In our view it is important to take them into account because history is not an autonomous process but the long-term outcome of the strategies, actions and policies of actors. Which transport technology will be used in 5 or 25 years' time depends on the investments in alternative transport technology today – it depends on the research and development (R&D) efforts of automobile companies and suppliers of alternative power sources, and on government programmes for alternative vehicles and emission control policies. Thus, the expectations, plans, competencies and strategies of key actors tell us something about the technologies that will be available in the (near) future and the likely techno-economic characteristics of the technologies. It is important therefore to look at investment plans, R&D efforts, the technological expectations of suppliers, and at the support and control policies that are being implemented and currently considered by public authorities. It is also important to look at the first experiences with EVs: how EVs are doing in the driver tests and the marketplace, what barriers they meet and what the prospects are for overcoming them.

A third feature of the CEST method is that it looks at real technological possibilities, both existing ones and those that are 'in the pipeline'.

A fourth feature is that it adopts a systems view, to account for the fact that most technologies are part of socio-technical systems or regimes, involving a set of interrelationships and institutions, a capital and knowledge base, and, especially in the case of transport, a physical infrastructure. For example, the travel choices of individuals are made in the context of the existing regimes of individual car-based and public (collective) transport, in which the use of individually owned cars is supported by the present ownership structure in which almost every household has a car (waiting to be used). Furthermore, the use of cars is supported by the existing road infrastructure, the marketing activities of car manufacturers, a well-developed system of car maintenance and fuelling, and by a set of cultural values of freedom and status. Thus, the economics of car use depend not only on car and fuel prices but also on ownership structures, infrastructures, tax policies and so on. But it is not the economics of vehicle use that determine vehicle choices and travel behaviour. Apart from the economics of costs, there are also important considerations of speed, convenience, safety, privacy, status and freedom that exercise an influence on travel choices. In the scenarios, we look at the systems aspects of travel choices and at other aspects such as established travel habits and the emergence of new concepts of what a car is and should do.

A fifth aspect of the CEST method is the focus on the interactions between actors and the co-evolution of technology and social change. Actor positions are *evolving* as a result of individual experiences, social interactions, government interventions, certain events and so on. One important aim of the method is to examine possible and probable outcomes (cross-impacts) of such interactions.

A final element of CEST scenarios is the focus on the interaction between technologies and society. This means that technological change (broadly defined) is *endogenized* instead of being exogenous as in traditional scenario analysis and technology assessment studies. In the scenarios, we describe how technologies and society interact and change through a process of co-evolution. In the development process there are endogenous change mechanisms. For example, the use of electric vehicles in niche markets (such as fleets and second household cars for urban use) opens up new possibilities for hybrid electric drive systems: electric hybrids with combustion engines, gas turbines or fuel cells; the introduction of a system of self-serviced electric vehicles, such as in St-Quentin-en-Yvelines (France), will provide car drivers with a new driving experience that may persuade them to buy and/or use an electric or hybrid vehicle; and once EVs are proved to be a 'real' vehicle, municipalities with strong preferences for non-polluting, silent cars may be induced into giving EVs a favourable treatment in their zone access and parking policies, giving further momentum to EVs. These are all examples of virtuous circles or 'snowballing' effects. But it also possible that the new development will not take off because of competition from environmentally improved internal combustion engine vehicles (ICEVs), or that the kind of momentum for EVs is simply too limited, where the small base keeps EVs an expensive vehicle, having a negative effect on public and private EV support policies.

The CEST method combines elements of different futures studies, especially trend analyses and cross-impact studies. It does not rely on a fully specified causal model, which can be used to arrive at quantitative outcomes. The method is more a qualitative than a quantitative approach, which is suited for analysing emergent processes that lead to structural change.

POSSIBLE SOLUTIONS TO THE PROBLEMS OF TRANSPORT-RELATED POLLUTION AND CONGESTION

The present regime for passenger transport, with its two subsystems of individual car-based and collective transport, is not sustainable. The total costs of road-based transport are estimated at more than 4 per cent of GDP (excluding global warming).[1] Each year about 250,000 people are killed in road accidents while 10 million people are injured. Congestion is a major problem in urban areas all over the world. Automobile exhaust emissions give rise to problems of local air pollution and are a major contributor to the build-up of greenhouse gases, which may lead to climate change. In the European Union (EU) almost 80 million people (20 per cent of the population) are subjected to noise levels above what is considered to be acceptable by the World Health Organization. Other problems associated with road transport are land use (especially in urban areas), energy dependence, and the undermining of communities (Hodge, 1995).[2]

Most of the problems are not new; they have existed for years but gradually have grown worse. Surprisingly there is no shortage of possible solutions. Exhaust emissions may be controlled by pollution control devices, more fuel-efficient cars, and the shift to alternative fuel vehicles. Road congestion may be reduced through road pricing and traffic information services. Safety may be enhanced through air bags, collision warning systems, roadside information panels and safer driving behaviour. A wide range of solutions has been tried and tested; some have been implemented (such as the three-way catalyst and airbags), while others, especially advanced transport telematics (ATT), are under development.

This section will describe a number of key technologies and social and organizational innovations that may help to alleviate the problems of transport-related pollution and congestion. The innovations constitute in our view the most auspicious solutions. There is a broad consensus among private and public transport experts that these are the most promising solutions; important differences of opinion exist, however, as to what are the best solutions and the likely prospects for diffusion.

The innovations are mapped in terms of the two regimes of individual car ownership and collective transport. The reason for mapping the innovations is that the innovations should be seen in the context of ownership structures, established practices, technologies and transport (maintenance) infrastructures as the setting (context) in which travel choices and vehicle manufacturing and purchasing decisions are made. In passenger transport there are two regimes: that of individual car-based transport and that of collective transport, each with its own unique features and problems. A description of the two regimes is given in Table 6.1.

The first regime is that of individual car-based transport, with car manufacturers as the dominant actor, in which individually driven and privately owned cars are used to satisfy almost all travel purposes, even though they are highly overmotorized for some purposes, which suggests that they are suboptimal. A second source of suboptimality is their high energy consumption per passenger-km, which has to do with the low efficiency of the combustion process – between 30 and 35 per cent of the energy is converted into motive power. The reason why they are still the dominant choice is that they have benefited from an array of improvements in performance and manufacturing. Cars are sustained by a system of interorganizational relationships (between oil and automobile companies, dealers, garages, insurance and leasing companies, transport departments) and infrastructures and a set of institutions that give the system coherence and stability. Car use is deeply embedded in social and cultural systems, which means that a car is more than a convenient means of transport to get from A to B: it is a symbol of freedom, it signals social status and is an expression of one's identity ('you are what you drive').

The system of private transport is complemented by a public transport system of trains, buses, trams and metro organized, controlled and operated by public transport companies. Public transport does not provide door-to-door transport services but uses a fixed routing system which is traversed according to a schedule. In order to get to your destination you may need to change transport modes at fixed transport nodes. Historically, car owners used to make use of public transport services, especially in cities. Nowadays, car owners use less and less public transport in relative terms. In Île-de-France (the Paris region) just 15 per cent of daily trips for people travelling within the suburbs are made by collective transport. This percentage rises to 30 per cent for trips between Paris and the suburbs and to 60 per cent for trips made within the city of Paris.

At present, we have two separate systems with little integration, each prone to specific problems for the individual user and society. In the case of the car, the main problems are safety, road congestion, and transport-related noise, pollution and land use. In the case of public transport for public transport users, the main problems are long travelling times, lack of flexibility and (for men) the lack of privacy.[3]

In the regimes there are different actors with differing interests, capabilities,

Table 6.1 *The present situation: two (highly disjunct) regimes of passenger transport*

	Regime of individual car-based transport	Regime of collective transport
Key actors at supply side	Individual use of multipurpose vehicles produced by (oligopolistic) car manufacturers and sold through dealerships; supported by marketing efforts by powerful car producers	Collective transport by (local, regional and national) public and private transport companies
Production system	High investment costs and technical and organizational complexities in car manufacturing create an entry barrier for newcomers and for alternative vehicles	
Maintenance	External maintenance in garages by mechanics trained in the repair of ICEVs	Internal maintenance by transport companies
Supportive infrastructures and policies	Car use is supported by extended road network and filing system and by land-use planning, fiscal policies, car insurance, leasing facilities and the only partial internalization of external costs	Less-developed network in rural areas, well-developed system of mass transport in big European cities but little optimization across transport modalities
Ownership	Individual ownership and use	Public and private ownership
Costs	Expensive plus underestimation of the total cost of car ownership and use	User costs per ride are visible
Vehicle performance	Flexible (possibility of combining different tasks: going to work, taking children to school, doing shopping)	Fixed routing system + time schedule (no door-to-door service)
	Instant availability	Non-instant availability
Cultural meaning	Part of high-mobility lifestyle	Lack of privacy
	Symbol of freedom and independence	Seen as a functional means of transport with a bad public image
	Type of car expresses personal identity	
Problems	Gives rise to problems of road congestion, pollution, noise and accidents	Same as cars but to a lesser degree

views and goals and respective policies and strategies to achieve these goals. At one level, these actors are part of socio-technical constituencies (Molina, 1993) who compete with one another, and, through their interactions (in markets, networks and policy arenas), generate techno-economic trends. The actors are not freewheeling individuals but are configured: they are equipped with certain skills, an outlook and set of beliefs, and bonded institutionally, for example through the rules of the organization that employ them and the rules of the markets they are in. Apart from the institutional matrix there is also the material world of artefacts (brakes, steering wheels, traffic lights, buildings) and infrastructures and the spatial dimension of settlements which prestructures change. A set of relations and rules has been established through past interactions. The rules consist of formal rules, such as technical standards and less formal rules such as standard operating procedures, ways of doing things, routines. This rule system is partly technology specific; different technologies incorporate different rule systems and grammars. A key rule of the present car regime is that cars are used for a range of activities: commuting, shopping, vacations. Cars are designed towards this end (and other ends such as safety), and evaluated by consumers with regard to the extent to which they satisfy multiple requirements. Collectively the rules of established product requirements and ways to satisfy them – through product designs and certain standardized ways of manufacturing – form a *technological regime*, which is the interface between the micro level of local practices and the macro level of the overall socio-technical landscape.[4] Instead of rules one can talk about institutions. In our view it is important to see the technological innovations as part of evolving socio-technical regimes and not to portray them as sole technical configurations. A change in the cost and demand conditions will not cause actors to change their assumptions and practices. It is a big step for a car manufacturer to become a mobility provider or to start producing vehicles that constitute a big departure from what they have produced in the past.

Within each regime, various technical solutions are developed to solve the above-mentioned problems. These innovations can play two distinct roles in the future of the regime: they can either help the existing regime become more sustainable by helping it to overcome internal problems to sustained growth and accommodate external pressures, or, alternatively, contribute to a transformation of the existing regime. The remainder of this section describes the innovations, first those within the car-based regime of individual transport.

In the car-based regime of individual transport the following four types of technological innovations are pursued by industry in accordance with their own interests, capabilities and expectations.

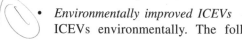

- *Environmentally improved ICEVs* There are many ways to upgrade ICEVs environmentally. The following three types of technical improvements receive most attention: fuel-efficient engines (direct injection engines for instance), end-of-pipe devices (catalysts such as NO_x catalysts) and new car design (less drag and weight).

- *Alternative fuel vehicles (AFVs)*   These are the second option, of which liquefied petroleum gas (LPG) and compressed natural gas (CNG) are considered as the most promising alternative fuels with CO emissions cut by 80 to 90 per cent, HC emissions by 70 to 80 per cent and CO_2 emissions by 14 per cent for LPG vehicles. They are used preferentially in high-mileage commercial fleet vehicles, where low fuel costs compensate for high engine and fuel storage costs which are today the largest obstacle to their wide adoption.

- *Electric drive technologies*   These comprise battery-powered electric vehicles (BEVs), hybrid electric vehicles (HEVs) and fuel cell vehicles (FCVs). The hybrid vehicle is viewed as the most attractive option from a user point of view. It provides a solution for the limited range problem of BEVs by combining an electric motor with an ICE (petrol or diesel engine, gas turbine). There are two different design configurations: parallel hybrids and serial hybrids. In the case of the former, the electric motor is used for urban drive and the ICE ensures a sufficient range (in the order of 500 km) and speed to drive on motorways. In serial hybrids the ICE functions as an electric generator to drive the electric motor, which in turn drives the wheels; electric energy is also received from a battery, which is recharged by the generator. Hybrid systems can easily be optimized, resulting in very low fuel consumption (3l/100 km). Different projects are under way to design and test prototypes, and Toyota commenced commercialization of its Prius in Japan in December 1997. An FCV is powered with electricity resulting from the electrochemical reaction between oxygen and hydrogen. The vehicle has many advantages: silent driving, little or no emission (depending on the way in which hydrogen is generated), good behaviour when it charges partially, short production time, easy maintenance and no range restriction. When fully developed, FCVs could probably quickly replace ICEVs. Several experimental FCVs have been built by large car manufacturers but sales are not expected before 2005.

- *Advanced Transport Telematics (ATT) systems*[5]   These are telematics applications in transport aimed at providing travel information to drivers, transport companies, users and to traffic management authorities. ATT systems may help to improve road safety and traffic flows, while at the same time reducing energy consumption associated with congestion. Applications of ATT can be divided into three categories: traffic management systems, static and dynamic route-guidance systems and advanced driver support.

Most of these technologies offer incremental improvements of the car-based transport regime. They add some new features to current cars in order to avoid the main drawbacks associated with the use of ICEVs: pollution and congestion. Electric drive and ATT can do more: they can help to achieve a change in travel-use patterns and thus be an element in regime change. Whether BEVs will be part of a new regime depends on the way they are used, which depends on the characteristics of the vehicle, the ownership of the vehicle and the cultural meaning of EV driving. There is an important link between EV characteristics and the latter aspects. For example, the limited range and speed of BEVs, combined with increased comfort and susceptibility to the surroundings, could lead to a different conception and use of cars. The reduced range of BEVs may stimulate better trip planning among car drivers, who would then perhaps change to public transport for longer trips. BEVs may also be used in public transport such as self-service rented vehicles for urban use (as in the Praxitèle project). In such an application, the limited range does not count as a disadvantage: the multiple use benefits from the BEV's advantage of low fuel costs. BEVs could aid in making a shift to collective use and ownership of cars, which would constitute a radical departure from the existing regime of individual car-based transport. Vehicle characteristics and usage interact. What we have is a process of *co-evolution*.

We now come to talk about innovations in the collective use of transport means. They consist of innovations in public travel services and systems and the collective use of cars, taxis and bicycles. Innovations to make public travel systems more environmentally sustainable and at the same time more attractive to users are: the provision of travel information, the integration of public travel schemes, the use of more clean, silent, comfortable and fuel-efficient transport means (natural gas buses and so on), and the customization of public travel services to individual transport needs. This last group of innovations tends to individualize public transport systems in order to increase their efficiency and to offer a convenient transport service to people who are not well connected to public transport means (people living in suburbs or near-city countryside who may have different transportation needs).

Individualized public transport innovations are a way for public transport companies to regain the lost share in passenger transport, helping society to move away from the current transport system based on the predominant use of individual cars that today satisfies more than 80 per cent of people's mobility needs. Examples of individualized collective transport are:

- *Self-service rented public vehicles systems*, where public vehicles are offered for rent by public transport companies on a short-term basis. After use, the car is collected by the system operator and made available to the next user. Hence, use-per-car is optimized for cost-effectiveness and environmental effects. In the case of Praxitèle and Liselec (another French system which has been tested in La Rochelle since September 1999), the cars are small BEVs that are under the constant control of a central computer. Users rent cars at special stations located in different parts of the city, where maintenance and recharging also take place. Computer and communication technologies enable the location of cars to be known and distribution to be made according to demand (Simon, 1998).

- *Dial-a-ride services* provided by bus companies are another intermediary step between individual and collective transport. People are picked up from home or some meeting point by minibuses and driven to their point of destination or to a transport node. Dial-a-ride services give further flexibility and efficiency to bus operations and are achievable thanks to advances in information and telecommunication technology. Such services exist in several cities in England, Germany and the Netherlands. The ASTI experiment in London (Potter, 1997) is a good example of combining dial-a-ride service and cleaner drive technologies (electric and CNG buses).

Examples of the new developments in the collective use of traditionally private transport modes are:

- *Organized car-sharing* through special car-sharing organizations or household cooperatives. Instead of privately owning a car, users join a cooperative or a commercial car-sharing organization that provides a vehicle when needed. Innovations are at different levels: the system as a whole (reservation system, fleet management), users' behaviour (new mobility forms requiring trip planning, new costs structures and so on) and technology (for car reservation: audiotex system and attended telephone line; and for access control: satellite communication). In a broader sense, car-sharing may be seen as an important element of integrated mobility services, where several means of transport are used to deliver reliable transportation services to users. They are a substitute for private ownership of individual cars and at the same time a complement to traditional public transport as car-sharing users tend to use public transport more while the number of kilometres driven is decreased. Large car-sharing organizations exist in the Netherlands (Call-a-car), Germany (StattAuto and Mobil Konzept), Austria and Switzerland (ATG and ShareCom, now merged into Mobility). This system could have a positive impact on traffic congestion, energy consumption and air emissions if widely adopted (Harms and Truffer, 1998a and b).

- *Ride-sharing* where people share the use of their individual car for commuting in order to reduce the number of single drivers in four-seated cars in urban trips – the average is 1.5 person per car in most cities – which is highly inefficient from both the economic and the environmental point of view. Many experiments have been undertaken in the last years, but without much success. Special lanes for high-occupancy vehicles may change this, as may company transport management systems offering informational services and incentives for people to engage in ride-sharing. In general, the desire for privacy and the need to pick up fellow passengers and drop them off at some place, plus the necessity to respect a given time schedule, have been a major drawback for a widening of this scheme.
- *Train taxis* are taxis that move people from the train station to the place of their destination, or bring them to the train station. Train taxis are a big success in the Netherlands, despite the initial opposition from taxi companies that were not part of the scheme. The small delay in time compared to a normal taxi drive is compensated by a much lower price (a fixed fare of Dfl 7, about 25–35 per cent of the normal taxi fare).
- *Station cars* are public or neighbourhood cars that drive to and from public transport nodes such as train stations.
- *Bicycle pools using advanced access systems*   Bicycle pools can be another complement to traditional public transport, especially for short distances within compact cities, on campuses, business parks and so on. Such schemes have been tried out in a number of European cities over the last few decades, but these schemes have usually failed due to bikes getting lost or stolen. Automatic access systems (like the Bikeabout systems in Portsmouth, UK) can make such systems more attractive and economic (Black, 1998).

All these innovations serve to make public and collective transport more attractive for users. They combine advantages of individual and collective transport. They are neither widely introduced, nor an immediate success although some schemes experience quite high growth rates but from a low base,[6] which may suggest that they have little potential. However, one should assess their prospects differently: not in the context of the existing transport system but in the context of the *future* transport system of which they will be part, a context which will consist of the following innovations:

- cheap, widely accessible *travel information systems* providing (real time) information about public transport services (train, bus) before and during a trip;
- *mobility cards*: chip cards, which can be used to pay for different means of transport and road tolls;

- *transferia*: park and ride stations near public transport nodes (train and metro stations) where people can park their car; and
- *advanced means of public transport*: high-speed trains for trips between 200–700 km and the introduction of light rail in urban areas providing fast and convenient transport services.

Apart from these innovations there will be travel demand management systems aimed at promoting collective forms of transport, such as:

- *road pricing* and other types of traffic management systems such as *restricted zone access systems* (see the experiment in Bologna, Hoogma, 1998);
- the *integration of public transport in urban planning*; and
- *company transport management schemes* that give a preferential treatment to public transport, for example by charging employees for parking places, arrangements to provide collective transport of employees, encouragement of ride-sharing through informational schemes and financial incentives and so on.

An overview of the different innovations is provided in Figure 6.1. The innovations are mapped in terms of the two regimes of collective and car-based transport. The innovations that are part of the individual car-based regime help to deal with the problems connected with the individual use of cars (congestion and pollution), whereas the innovations in the collective transport regime help to achieve environmental and social benefits through a modal shift to collective transport. The innovations in the middle help to better integrate the two regimes, allowing for a new type of transport practice which is intermodal travel to satisfy specific mobility needs (commuting, shopping and so on) and at the same time achieve environmental and social benefits.

In this section we described the most important innovations for making the existing transport system more sustainable. The innovations are mapped in terms of the two presently disjunct regimes of individual car-based and collective transport. The regimes provide the context in which the innovations are produced and used by differing actors. Regimes consist of a set of interconnected rules, practices, technologies and infrastructures that sustain a particular technology (here mode of transport). In the different transport regimes, different actors are interacting: car manufacturers, public transport companies, local and state authorities, and users. The interaction produces outcomes and patterns: the availability of new types of vehicles widens the choice of automobile users, it forces other manufacturers to rethink their car design and manufacturing policies; prototypes of alternative vehicles and expectations about new technologies may pave the way for the promulgation of emission

Collective transport   Individual car-based transport

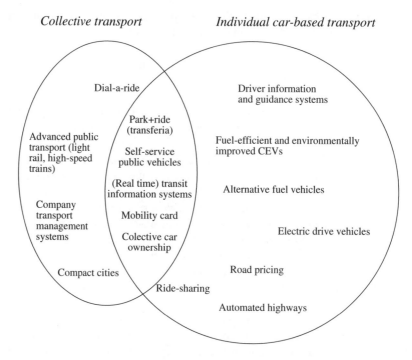

Figure 6.1   Innovations in the transport system that may help to solve problems of environmental pollution and road congestion

limit values standards for new automobiles and the implementation of other policies aimed at promoting the development and use of low-emission, fuel-efficient vehicles (such as fuel taxes, fuel economy standards). Likewise, the problem of congestion may prompt transport authorities to introduce and extend road pricing and will stimulate the diffusion of real time driver information systems, both of which will change the behaviour of car users. The coupling of travel information and monitoring systems will help to enhance the capacity of the existing road infrastructure, to control traffic flows better and aid the integration of different modes of transport.

A key characteristic of transport is that there is no actor in command and control of what goes on, 'in the driver seat' so to speak to use a phrase from transport. Each actor acts and reacts, and it is through these interactions of multiple, interdependent actors that the system of transport changes. In the scenarios section, we shall describe how particular interactions produce particular outcomes and development paths. In the process, there are also exogenous changes such as external events and socio-technical, demographic and cultural trends impacting 'from the outside' on the transport system. Examples are advances in materials and information technology that may be used in transport, the rise in economic wealth, the growing number of households and the trend towards suburbanization.

For the short to medium period we identified the following four transport-relevant trends:[7] (i) increased demand for mobility because of suburbanization and increases in economic wealth; (ii) declining tolerance of congestion and pollution (this means that even when congestion and pollution are not increasing, there will be anti-congestion and anti-pollution policies); (iii) a need for fast, safe and convenient means of transport; and (iv) advances in electronics, telematics and drive systems, especially electric drive systems.

Given these trends and the innovations described above, different futures are possible. In the next section we describe two scenarios for more sustainable modes of passenger transport. They are based on the innovations and trends identified here, and the co-evolutionary model of socio-technical change.

TWO SCENARIOS FOR PASSENGER TRANSPORT

In the previous section we described a wide range of technological and social innovations that could help to alleviate transport-related problems of road congestion, safety, pollution and land use. The multiplicity of transport solutions and uncertainty about travel needs means that the future transport system may take different forms. In this section we shall describe two distinct futures for passenger transport. They are:

- a radical upgrading of the car-based system in terms of vehicle energy efficiency and exhaust emissions and accommodation of the increase in automobile mobility through enhancement of the road capacity;
- the integration and convergence of the two regimes of individual car-based and collective transport.

The first scenario entails a modification of the car-based regime, the second the development of a new regime, that of intermodal travel. The first scenario may be termed 'system optimization'; the second scenario 'system renewal'. The use of a scenario of system renewal is deliberate. We wanted to explore the possibility of structural change in which there is a fundamental change in the rule set. System optimization and renewal thus constitute two ideal types of changes, which do not need to be mutually exclusive. Within these broad categories there is a range of possibilities. We are limiting our attention to two scenarios, both of which are feasible and plausible as they are based on available and emerging technologies, are consistent with social-economic trends (such as income growth, increasing mobility, higher demand for convenience, personal comfort, safety and environmental qualities), and supported by important actors and interests.[8]

Scenario 1 A Modification of the Existing Regime of Car-based Transport – More, But Different, Individually Used Cars

The automobile-based transport regime meets with growing pressure because of environmental problems associated with car use and problems of congestion. In most industrialized countries, stringent car emissions standards are promulgated for coping with air pollution. In addition to these regulations, many R&D programmes have been instituted for developing alternative fuel vehicles and ATT systems to deal with problems of pollution and congestion. Most efforts from both industrialists and policy makers are directed towards the improvement of the existing regime; they do not aim to make a shift away from the car-based regime, as this is perceived to be infeasible given user requirements.

In this section we shall describe the scenario of an optimization of the current regime of car-based transport. This scenario has a high likelihood of coming true because it is in line with current policies and strategies of industry and government, as the discussion below will show. We describe the main regulations and R&D programmes under way in Europe, Japan and the US, which will shape transport futures. This is followed by a description of car manufacturers' strategies to cope with air pollution and congestion, and the time scales for developing alternative technologies as the outcome of the strategic decisions and policies.

Regulations
In the short term, the likely evolution of regulations is a tightening of car emissions standards that has already started in OECD countries. For instance, in the European Union, current emissions standards are on the way to be further tightened by 2000 and 2005 (see Appendix 6A, on regulations). The European Commission also adopted in December 1995 a communication describing a strategy for reducing CO_2 emissions of individual cars and for improving fuel efficiency by 2005. This strategy defines the following objectives: 5 litres for 100 km for gasoline cars and 4.5 litres for 100 km for diesel ones, that is equivalent to respective CO_2 emissions of 120 g/km. This process of tightening also holds for the United States and Japan.

In the United States, the 1990 Clean Air Act introduces the following emissions standards: 0.25 gpm non-methane HC and 0.4 gpm NO_x, as compared to existing standards of 0.41 gram for HC and 1.0 for NO_x. The Environmental Protection Agency (EPA) is required to study whether even tighter standards are needed, technologically feasible and economical. If the EPA determines by 1999 that lower standards are warranted, the standards will be cut by half, beginning with 2004 model year vehicles.

In California (and other states now), these standards have been further strengthened by the definition of four categories of vehicles (transitional low-emission vehicles, low-emission vehicles, ultra-low-emission vehicles and zero-emission vehicles) whose sales have to increase from 10 to 75 per cent by 2003, according to the category (see Appendix 6A, on regulations). However, as most people know, intermediary steps toward ZEVs have been cancelled under the pressure of the big three, and only the final objective of 10 per cent new car sales for ZEVs has been kept.

Another influential regulation in the US is the National Energy Policy Act of 1992, which created both incentives and a regulatory programme for fleet operators to use alternative fuel vehicles within their fleet. The AFV requirements for 1999 amount to approximately 200,000 AFVs, increasing to 1 million vehicles in 2006.

In Japan, the main regulations to cope with air pollution are the 1994 Plan for the Environment and the 1993 emissions standards. Under the plan, individual car fuel efficiency has to be improved by 8.5 per cent between 1993 and 2003; for company cars the aim is a 5 per cent improvement; for NO_x emissions, long-term objectives forecast reductions from 16 to 65 per cent according to the type and size of the vehicle, based on standards implemented by the end of the 1980s; finally, particles should be cut by 60 to 64 per cent. In the urban areas of Tokyo and Osaka, the 'Law on NO_x emissions by cars' set up a reduction objective of 30 per cent by 2000 when compared to the 1990 level.

However, we should like to point out that we do not foresee in the short term any change in other fields of public policy that impact the evolution of transport systems. For instance, there is no evidence of change in fiscal regimes (taxes on car ownership, tolls, fuels, but also housing policy) or in energy policies that could offer long-term incentives to shift away from individual car ownership and use. For instance, it is well known that housing policies tend to reinforce the trend of suburbanization which increases the need for an individual car to commute. There is a growing awareness of the disadvantages of suburbanization, but few policies to reduce the need for travel through urban planning.

Public R&D programmes
The European Commission (EC) is strongly promoting R&D programmes that aim to improve car emissions and traffic congestion. In the fourth framework programme, 256 million ecus were spent on transport R&D. A Task Force 'Car of Tomorrow' was set up, but stopped for budget reasons. There is also the

Auto Oil Programme, a three-year technical programme involving the European oil and manufacturing industries, in which many studies have been undertaken to help the EC to formulate a strategy for the control of emissions from road transport. ATT have been the object of numerous programmes: 65 R&D projects were funded for an amount of 141 million ecus under the third framework programme (1992–94); many others were supported within the fourth framework programme (1994–98), Prometheus and Drive, for instance. Furthermore, the development of ATT systems is supported by the EC, which is elaborating a community strategy and a development framework for the use of road telematics (20 May 1997).

In the United States, the FAST-TRAC (faster and safer travel through traffic routing and advanced controls) is one of the largest IVHS (intelligent vehicle technology and highway system) R&D programmes. It displays impressive goals with regard to the number of injuries (–27 per cent) and serious injuries (–100 per cent) while increasing average speed on major arterial roads by 19 per cent.

In Japan, the main focus is on the deployment of advanced traffic management systems and the development and marketing of automobile navigation systems as a platform for in-vehicle information. R&D has largely been supported under the advanced travel information system (ATIS).

Carmakers' strategies

In order to cope with these challenging limit values and also with congestion problems, car manufacturers have committed themselves to important R&D programmes. This is done both at the company level and within cooperation organizations like EUCAR in Europe and USCAR and PNGV (Partnership for a New Generation of Vehicle) in the United States. The reason for this is not just the threat of emissions standards. Automobile manufacturers increasingly realize that the image of the car is in danger. Thus they have to provide cleaner cars quickly, or a more radical change in transport users' behaviour could emerge that would simply reject the car, damaging the future of the car industry. Their long-term strategy is to be able to sell clean(er) cars to replace currently polluting vehicles. In order for this strategy to be successful, large carmakers need to develop a competence in more environmentally benign drive systems and technologies.

Current competencies of carmakers are based on the mass manufacturing of vehicles. They are good at marginally improving their products, on the basis of accumulated knowledge, routines and production methods. The dominant technological strategy of major car manufacturers is to improve the internal combustion engine and to introduce ATT technologies within the car in order to cut car emissions and reduce congestion. They are ready to modify internal combustion engine vehicles in order to operate on different fuels (gasoline, LPG or CNG), even to couple the ICE with an electric motor (HEVs), but they are unwilling to do away with the ICE. They are reluctant to make a change to a completely different drive train, such as an electric one based on the use of batteries, not just because the knowledge base is different but also for fear that consumers will not opt to buy vehicles with a range of only about 100 km (Simon, 1997b). They expect that HEVs will be able to solve most problems, without great sacrifices in terms of user benefit: performance characteristics will be equivalent to current gasoline cars while decreasing polluting emissions considerably (thus making them easier to sell) and without the need to achieve a significant reduction in weight (which means no change in the materials used).

Car manufacturers are stepping up their efforts to commercialize HEVs as soon as possible. But apart from Toyota, which is selling the Prius only in Japan but is anticipating selling it in Europe and in the US in 2000, most carmakers will not start commercialization before 1999–2000 and then only on a small scale (for example, Fiat Multipla, Audi bimode, Mitsubishi) or they will still be in the development phase: PSA and Renault with the results of the VERT project (both have a prototype – 405 and Espace), GM with the HX3, Chrysler with the Dodge Intrepid ESX, and Mitsubishi with the SpaceWagon and Chariot. The objective is to convince potential users and public authorities that this is *the* individual transport technology of the future. This may have the effect that policy makers will redefine their support and control policies, for example in California, the 10 per cent ZEV requirement may be annulled or revised so that HEVs qualify (due to the pressures of car manufacturers and political support from automobile users). The expectation that HEV will be the vehicle of the future may act as a self-fulfilling prophecy by slowing down research activities and support for other types of vehicles, for example, AFVs.

Fuel cell electric vehicles are often seen as the long-term 'sustainable' solution. There is a clear acceleration of R&D on this technology (the recent cooperation between Daimler-Benz and Shell is a good example) but only prototypes are on the road today and it seems unrealistic to expect FCEVs to be commercialized before 2005.

With regard to BEVs, carmakers' strategy is mainly:

- to keep control over the development of BEVs through a minimal investment with the aim of deterring potential competitors from entering the market (for instance, PSA and Renault decided to invest in BEVs so as to kill small manufacturers like SEER Volta – which is already selling a few cars);
- to maintain high prices (in order to deter potential customers from buying these cars); and
- to state that performances are too low and that we should wait for other types of vehicles, such as HEVs.

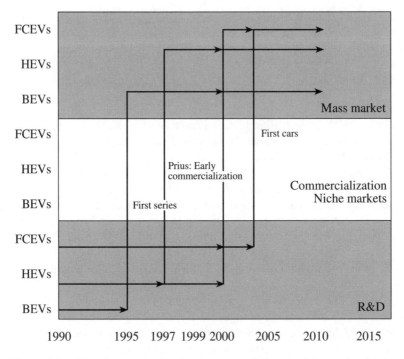

Figure 6.2   Time frames in the development of electric drive technologies

This suggests that the prospects for BEVs are poor. However, we should point out that the development and marketing of HEVs or FCEVs could have a knock-on effect on the development of BEVs, through increasing knowledge about electric drive technologies (Kirsch, 1996). It is still an open issue whether the automobile industry will be willing to take this last step, which will require important changes. Figure 6.2 shows the time frames in the development of electric drive technologies.

There still remains the congestion problem, which will not be solved through a different type of vehicle. To cope with this problem, many solutions are available. Most of them entail a larger use of collective transport means and/or the development of individual public transport systems. Within the car-based regime, the solution that is favoured by both carmakers and public authorities is the extended use of ATT, for which there has been a large R&D effort: (real time) driver information systems (beacons, on-board systems), which will develop from static information to dynamic (interactive) information systems, which will be part of a fully integrated ATT system that allows for the management and control of automobile traffic. The question then is: will ATT technologies that are currently developed by carmakers be able to decrease congestion in the long run? We think not. We expect ATT technologies to be merely a temporary solution to the congestion problem, just like building new roads: as the traffic improves, more people will be attracted to use their individual car, bringing back the congestion at the initial point, if not worse.

Thus, to deal with the problem of congestion, other solutions will be needed such as the implementation of restricted zone access policies for cars (in city centres, for instance) and/or road-pricing policies. It may also be that congestion will remain an accepted part of modern life, and that only the worst forms of congestion will be alleviated through anti-congestion policies.

Car manufacturers do not decide alone what will happen. The respective diffusion of the different competing transportation technologies will also depend on the different regulations (especially emission standards) in different countries and the evolution of user preferences. Apart from environmental aims, national policies will be based on the need to protect national industries (and employment), which could lead to a distinct evolution of the diffusion of alternative innovations. This also holds at the local level where most stringent policies are likely to be implemented (road-pricing, electronic zone access, ban of cars). Users, too, will shape the profile of diffusion for each technology according to their mobility needs, travel behaviour, and attitude (aptitude) towards owning an individual car. If we add today's penchant for cars with tomorrow's vehicle offers and economic wealth (which doubles every 25 years under the present growth trend), we get a household that will own or use different vehicles: a long distance vehicle (LDV), an urban car (for example, a micro compact car or EV) and a sports vehicle. In this scenario, BEVs would be used as a second or third household car, which is used for urban travel. This scenario is seen as the most likely one in the eyes of many people, in part because it is an extension of current developments. It is not the only possibility, however.

Scenario 2   The Integration and Convergence of the Two Regimes of Car-Based and Collective Transport – Towards Intermodal Travel

The second scenario is that of integration and convergence of collective and individual transport. At this moment the two systems are not integrated but highly disjunct. As noted in the previous section, there are many opportunities to integrate the two systems in ways that offer benefits both to individual users and society. Especially *intermodal travel* and *personalized public transport* hold great promise with the following innovations: dial-a-ride services provided by bus companies, collective taxis, self-serviced public vehicles offered for use by public transport companies, car-sharing organizations and so on. Most of these innovations have been made possible because of the progress in the field of information and communication technologies: on-board computer, global positioning system (GPS), global system for mobile communication (GSM) and so on are all incorporated and participate in the likely success of these new public transport schemes. Experiments of individ-ualized public transport schemes that failed in the 1970s (such as in Amsterdam, Brussels or Montpellier) because of the non-existence of adequate tools for managing fleets have restarted, with great hopes in the improvement of public transport services' quality, efficiency and flexibility.

Unlike scenario 1, where the problem of congestion will continue to exist, this scenario would bring sustainable solutions to problems both of congestion and of pollution. As mentioned above, mitigating air pollution does not help to reduce congestion, while fighting congestion also helps to decrease car emis-sions. In addition, we believe that this scenario would also bring sustainable solutions to life in cities (less space dedicated to roads and parking lots, less noise and so on).

Social innovations are an important element in this scenario. They include, apart from the collective ownership and use of cars (car-sharing and riding): (i) the creation of so-called mobility agencies, providing intermodal transport services,[9] (ii) the integration of collective transport schemes by transport companies (particularly railway and bus companies but also car rental compa-nies),[10] and (iii) the introduction of traffic management systems in compa-nies.[11] These innovations mutually support each other. In this respect the scenario differs from the first one, which relies predominantly on technical innovations.

In the scenario there is still a strong reliance on the individual use of cars: gasoline and diesel (few LPG and hybrids) vehicles used by households and the use of battery electric vehicles in public transport. The reason for choos-ing BEVs in public transport is founded on three considerations. First, the fact that they are so far the only cars that do not pollute at the point of use, second, their low operating costs, and third, the idea that for reasons of image an inno-vative system cannot be based on old technologies.

The shift to intermodal travel is supported by many innovations that sustain one another. Transit information systems and transferia (park and ride stations) aid the use of (more flexible) public transport and the use of car-sharing, as do mobility cards provided by newly founded mobility providers. Apart from the synergetic effects between the above innovations there are also positive network externalities at work, especially for car-sharing. The growth of car-sharing networks makes it more attractive for people to join a car-sharing orga-nization. In Switzerland in 1997, the two car-sharing companies joined forces to create one company called Mobility Carsharing Swiss (Mobility for short) and there are also plans to expand their networks internationally, into neigh-bouring countries. The current high growth rates of 50 per cent in car-sharing, helps to mobilize the support of other actors, such as investors and governments. In the Netherlands, the Minister of Traffic and Transport has stated that 2 million people should share cars by the year 2010. It is unclear how they will succeed in doing so, but the ministry is actively involved in the construction of several transferia (park and ride stations) to promote ride-sharing and car-sharing.

The above developments in public transport and ownership are likely to foster the diffusion of battery electric vehicles. BEVs are attractive for multiple use and for making short trips. Experiments with EVs in La Rochelle (France), Rugen (Germany), Mendrisio (Switzerland) and Coventry (UK) studied in the Strategic Niche Management (SNM) project showed that people like electric driving. Hence, market niches for this alternative fuel vehicle could be larger than expected, even if its intrinsic characteristics were to constrain its use to urban areas. Other types of vehicles will be used for long-distance travelling, such as hybrid electric vehicles, fuel cell vehicles or gasoline direct injection vehicles (even if long-distance public transport were also to be upgraded thanks to a well-developed trans-European network of high-speed trains, for instance).

The position of carmakers like Renault and PSA that produce EVs is ambiguous. They are involved in individualized public transport schemes (respectively in the Praxitèle and Liselec projects) but the success of such schemes may not be in their long-term interest when it means that fewer people will own a car. However, as there is still uncertainty about future vehicle design (ICEV or EV), they adopt a wait-and-see strategy via minimal investment in the different alternatives (which does not prevent them from lobbying for maintaining the dominance of individually owned and used ICEVs for satisfying mobility needs). Governments of automobile-producing countries also adopt a wait-and-see approach; they are reluctant to impose strict environmental restriction on automobile producers for fear that they will lose market share. Hence it is no surprise that support for car-sharing is highest in Switzerland and the Netherlands, two countries with no large car industry.

Intermodal travel is most strongly supported by public transport companies that see in these new schemes an opportunity to seize a larger share of passenger travel. In addition, even though people are emotionally and culturally committed to their car, they may want to use public transport at least for part of their trip if this helps to save time. This is the reason behind the growth of train use in the Netherlands, with annual growth rates of 4.7 per cent in the 1990–98 period – well above the growth rate for car travel of 2 per cent a year.[12] It goes without saying that the willingness of users to take part in intermodal travel and to engage in individualized collective transport services, such as self-serviced public vehicles, will be a critical factor. From a user point of view, however, intermodal travel will become more and more attractive, whereas the individual use of cars will become less attractive due to the increasing congestion of roads (which will only be partially mitigated by policy measures to increase the road capacity). This gives us reason to believe that the scenario is indeed a realistic one, perhaps just as plausible as the first scenario in which there are far fewer benefits for individual transport users.

In the second scenario, individual car use will remain the dominant mode of transport for a long time. Mobility will be high, maybe even higher than in the other scenario in which road congestion will restrain further mobility increases. A reduction in mobility demand is conceivable but not likely as it will come from a reorientation to community life, or a shift to teleworking, involving lifestyle and behavioural changes, which is not foreseen, at least not by the authors of this chapter. It does facilitate a learning process in the direction of low mobility and alternative modes of transport, as happened in the large-scale experiment 'grossversuch' with EVs in the Swiss town of Mendrisio (for details, see Harms and Truffer, 1998a and b). Another development which is supporting intermodal travel is local policies to restrict car use, especially in large cities where most of the traffic is due to commuters who live in the suburbs. Such traffic is strongly resented by people living in such cities. Pollution alerts and information about the air quality serve to focus public attention on car exhaust fumes and help to gain support for car-use restrictions. In an attempt to enhance the quality of life, several cities have taken action to restrict the use of cars in city centres, for instance, through pedestrian zones. In April 1998, mayors and chief executives of six major European cities (Athens, Florence, Barcelona, Lisbon, Stockholm and Oxford) launched a plan to boost clean cars by designating special zones closed to conventional vehicles. Apart from promoting the use of alternative vehicles such as EVs, such initiatives encourage the development of social innovations which are important for the wider use of electric vehicles, by altering the logic of travel choices and research and investment policies.

CONCLUDING REMARKS

In this chapter we have sought to sketch the future use of electric vehicles. Instead of extrapolating the current diffusion of EVs, we have placed their development and use in the context of two distinct transport futures, each being the outcome of different interaction processes. The scenarios are based on the interplay of technological innovations in road transport and telematics, social innovations like a change in car ownership, and the policies and strategies of key actors (car manufacturers, public transport companies, transport authorities and local governments).

We describe two scenarios, one based on the optimization of the existing regime of car-based transport in which cars are used to satisfy more or less all travel purposes (commuting, shopping, short trips, long trips), and one based on the integration and convergence of private and collective transport, leading to intermodal travel as a dominant mode of transport such as market liberalization, environmental and social values, belief systems and ideologies.

In the first scenario, the prospects for BEVs are poor: the high purchase price limits their use, as does the limited range. HEVs have the best prospects as they have similar performance characteristics to gasoline cars, while reducing fuel consumption and pollution significantly. At the moment they are the type of EV favoured by car manufacturers, who are investing considerable amounts of money in the development of HEVs. Nevertheless, there are two problems with this technology: first, its complexity requires further R&D, and the costs of production are high; second, there is competition from upgraded versions of internal combustion engine vehicles like the gasoline direct injection Mitsubishi Galant. Fuel cell electric vehicles are a possible long-term option.

Within the second scenario, battery electric vehicles are likely to play a larger role thanks to their attractiveness as a fleet vehicle and the fact that they do not pollute at the point of use, which makes them attractive as urban vehicles. The diffusion of BEVs is connected with social changes such as car-sharing and restrictions to the use of ICEVs in cities. It is also connected with improvements in public transport: for example, dial-a-ride services and transit information systems. EVs are likely to be rented on a short-term basis. Cars will remain dominant for a while but the improvement in public transportation services will make the ownership of individual cars less and less attractive, especially in cities. In this context, BEVs could emerge as a dominant technology for satisfying part of the the mobility needs within large conurbations. HEVs or radically upgraded ICEVs would be the main transport means for making longer trips. HEVs could act as a transitional technology aiding the development of BEVs in the long term through the improvements in the performance in electric drive systems, cost reductions in batteries and helping people to get a better experience of electric driving, which as noted, is different from driving an ICEV.

Which scenario will come true is hard to say. In our view both scenarios are plausible and they are not mutually exclusive. They demonstrate how ongoing developments may add up to distinct futures for EVs and transport at large. The purpose of this chapter is to put the discussion of the future of EVs in a different, less deterministic, perspective. In doing so we try to go beyond the limitations of many future studies that rely on externally specified driving forces, such as the Dutch Central Planning Bureau study *Scanning the Future* (1992).

In the scenarios we do not assume the emergence of an upsurge in environmental awareness or autonomous developments in EV technology, creating a market for EVs. Travel behaviour and vehicle choices are not specified *ex ante*, but seen as something that will co-develop with the overall evolution of the two regimes of car-based and public transport. Technical change is not autonomous, even though it sometimes appears as a juggernaut. The development of EV technology will depend on the size of its market, which will in turn depend on the development of the market for alternative drive trains. In the scenarios, government policies, like the actions and policies of other actors (car companies, public transport companies), are not an exogenous factor but *endogenous* to the process; they build on previous policies, new technological possibilities, and the evolution of demand (the experiences with new technologies) and on other kinds of changes within the socio-technical landscape. We like to note that the co-evolutionary socio-technical scenario combines elements from different futures studies: first of all the method of scenarios but also trends analysis and cross-impact studies (see May, 1996). It is thus not something completely new. What is novel is the special focus on technical change and processes of co-evolution that occur within the context of technological regimes and socio-technical landscape. Special attention is given to the feedforward and feedback processes that give rise to virtuous and vicious circles. A key feature of the CEST is that it combines a top-down and bottom-up approach, through the distinction of three levels: the macro level of the socio-technical landscape, the meso level of regimes and the micro level of local practices.

This chapter is a first attempt to apply the method empirically. It is really a first step; a possible next step is to develop a step plan which is also used to develop more quantitative scenarios based on specified causal relationships and empirically specified trends.[13] In a project for the Dutch environment and economy programme, an attempt is made to develop the CEST scenario method further and to apply it to the problem of future transport and energy.[14] It is useful to develop and relate the scenarios against two ideal types of change: that of system optimization and system renewal or transformation. System optimization involves the use of options that do not involve a fundamental change within the product chain. The fundamental rules or overall guiding principle remain the same. In the case of system renewal there is an important change high up in the rule hierarchy. The fundamental change may reside in a new knowledge base which brings with it a new set of engineering problem-solving approaches (new search heuristics), new product concepts and uses (such as mobility leasing) or the closing of material cycles through the reuse of waste (industrial ecology or symbiosis). The CEST method helps to foresee such changes, and the consecutive steps to it. The latter aspect is important because there will not be a kind of revolutionary change without an evolutionary path to it. The CEST method helps to identify possible paths of co-evolution. This feature also makes it useful for managing multilevel change processes into desirable directions.[15] A good way to develop CEST scenarios is through the use of interactive workshops in which experts discuss techno-economic trends and dynamic outcomes of co-evolution processes in a structured way.

NOTES

1. The costs of air pollution (excluding global warming) are estimated at 0.4 per cent of GDP, those of noise at 0.2 per cent, and those of accidents and congestion at 1.5 per cent and 2 per cent (figures are for the EU, reported in *EU Bulletin* supplement 2/1996).
2. Whitelegg (1993) adds to these problems 'time pollution', the devaluation of time which is lost in travel and in hurrying from one place to another, fuelled by the idea that the next task is more important than the present task. Enjoyment is sought outside local communities, leading to social disruption. There is also the growing immobility of non-automobile owners, especially disabled and elderly people, due to the downsizing of public transport.
3. There is an interesting dichotomy in the perception of public transport between men and women. Whereas men scorn the lack of privacy, women tend to enjoy the company of other travellers.
4. A technological regime is the rule set or grammar that comprises the complex of scientific knowledge, engineering practices, production process technologies, product characteristics, skills and procedures, and institutions and infrastructures that make up the totality of a technology (for example, a computer or gas turbine) (Kemp et al., 1997, 1998; Rip and Kemp, 1998).
5. The term used in the US is intelligent transport systems (ITS).
6. The car-sharing organizations ATG and ShareCom in Switzerland experienced growth rates well above 100 per cent in the first years, and of 50–75 per cent from 1991 onwards. In 1997, when the two organizations joined forces, total membership amounted to 14,000. In the Netherlands in 1997, 25,000 people were involved in organized car-sharing. Dial-a-ride services in Maastricht in the Netherlands, a city of 180,000 inhabitants, increased from 129,000 in 1996 to 230,000 in 1997 and is expected to grow to 450,000 trips in 1998.
7. The trends are not based on systematic research but on a loose scrutiny of evolving trends. More research is needed on this issue.
8. Teleworking and other forms of telecommunications are not considered in the two scenarios. The reason is that telecommunication will develop to a large extent independent from developments in transport: it will be driven by advances in information and communication technology (the creation of the electronic highway with multimedia stations) and social and organizational change (social acceptance of home working, the willingness of people to work at home (or at a telecommuting centre) and the introduction of new management practices for home workers) instead of being driven by developments in transport (such as congestion).
9. These agencies provide a personalized travel plan involving the use of different transport modes (bus, train, taxi, rental car with or without chauffeur). They also take care of the financial and administrative details. Today the main users are business people but once the services become cheaper, private people are likely to follow suit.
10. Another important institutional change is the privatization of public transport companies, which may be necessary for collective transport companies to become more flexible and more tuned to the wishes of individual transport users.
11. Company travel management systems are informational and financial schemes that encourage employees to share rides, and to use bicycles and collective forms of transport instead of automobiles. Such schemes help to reduce company costs of parking space and travel

allowances. Apart from the companies' self-interest, there is often an important social motivation behind the introduction of travel management schemes in companies.

12. The growth rate is for passenger-km. Source: *Centraal Bureau voor de Statistiek* (CBS), (1999).
13. An example of a scenario analysis using a fully specified causal model with empirically specified variables is Bilderdijk et al. (1995). A semi-quantitative scenario analysis for transport is offered by Nijkamp et al. (1995) based on expert opinion about expected and desired developments with regard to a number of transport-relevant variables grouped in four categories: spatial, institutional, social/psychological and economic.
14. See Geels and Schot (1998), who propose the following building blocks for making sociotechnical scenarios: (i) a variety-producing mechanism such as niche creation; (ii) a stability-producing mechanism such as a technological regime; (iii) factors operating at a macro level (socio-technical landscape); and (iv) a mechanism for coupling of changes at all three levels, thus allowing for multilevel development over time.
15. Policy aspects of managing technological regime shifts are described in Kemp et al., (1997a).

BIBLIOGRAPHY

Bass, Frank M. (1969), 'A new product growth model for consumer durables', *Management Science*, **15**, 215–27.

Bilderdijk, Rob, Wim Korver and Cyprian Smits (1995), *Scenario's rond de chipcard in het personenverkeeren vervoerssysteem van 2015* (Scenarios for the chipcard in passenger transport and freight transport in 2015), Apeldorn, The Netherlands: TNO.

Black, Coli (1998), *The Bikeabout Experience: An Automated Smart Card Operated Bike Pool Scheme*, Milton Keynes: Open University.

Centraal Bureau voor de Statistiek (CBS) (1999), *De Mobiliteit van de Nederlandse Bevolking* (The mobility of the Dutch population), The Hague, The Netherlands.

Central Planning Bureau (CPB) (1992), *Scanning the Future. A Long-term Scenario study of the World Economy, 1990–2015*, CPB, SDU: The Hague, The Netherlands.

Cornu, Jean-Pierre (1996), 'La contribution de Saft au développement du véhicule électrique' (The contribution of Saft to the development of the electric vehicle), Internal Paper.

Elzen, Boelie, Remco Hoogma and Johan Schot (1996), 'Mobiliteit met Toekomst – Naar een vraaggericht technologiebeleid' (Mobility with a future: towards a demand driven technology policy), Report to the Ministry of Traffic and Transport (in Dutch).

Electric Power Research Institute (EPRI) (1996), 'Pricing for success: using auto industry models to review electric vehicle costing and pricing'.

European Conference of Ministers of Transport (ECMT) (1993), *Transport Growth in Question*, Paris: OECD.

Financial Times (1996), 'Airing the differences', and, 'Carmakers pay the price of progress' (about the Auto Oil programme), 26 June.

Geels, Frank and Johan Schot (1998), 'Reflexive technology policies and sociotechnical scenarios', Paper for Conference 'Constructing tomorrow: technology strategies for the new millennium', 14–15 September, Bristol.

Harms, Sylvia and Bernhard Truffer (1998a), 'The Swiss large scale experiment with lightweight electric vehicles in Mendrisio', Final Report for Strategic Niche Management project.

Harms, Sylvia and Bernhard Truffer (1998b), 'The emergence and professionalisation of two carsharing cooperatives in Switzerland', Internal Report of Strategic Niche Management project.

Hodge, David C. (1995), 'Intelligent transportation systems, land use, and sustainable transportation', Paper presented at the Intelligent Transport Systems America Alternative Futures Symposium on Transportation, Technology and Society, 13 March.

Hoogma, Remco (1995), 'Towards cleaner cars and transport – country study France', Report for the Dutch Ministry of Transport and Public Works.

Hoogma, Remco (1998), 'Introduction of automated zone access control in Bologna, Italy, case study report of the project "Strategic niche management as a tool for transition to a sustainable transport system",' for Research and Technology Development programme 'Environment and climate' (EU DG XII), University of Twente, Enschede, The Netherlands.

Hughes, Thomas P. (1989), 'The evolution of large technological systems', in Wiebe E. Bijker, Thomas P. Hughes and Trevor J. Pinch (eds), *The Social Construction of Technological Systems: New Directions in the Sociology and History of Technology*, Cambridge, MA: MIT Press, pp. 51–82.

Institute for Prospective Technological Studies (IPTS) (1996), 'The car of the future, the future of the car', Report EUR 17277 EN, Seville: IPTS–IPTS (1997), Special report on Urban Mobility, Seville: IPTS–JRC, February.

Kemp, René (1994), 'Technology and the transition to environmental sustainability. The problem of technological regime shifts', *Futures*, **26** (10), 1023–46.

Kemp, René (1996), 'The transition from hydrocarbons. The issues for policy', in S. Faucheux, D. Pearce and J.L.R. Proops (eds), *Models of Sustainable Development*, Cheltenham: Edward Elgar, pp. 151–75.

Kemp, René (1997), *Environmental Policy and Technical Change. A Comparison of the Technological Impact of Policy Instruments*, Cheltenham: Edward Elgar.

Kemp, René, Ian Miles, Keith Smith et al. (1994b), 'Technology and the transition to environmental stability. Continuity and change in complex technology systems', Final Report of the project Technological Paradigms and Transition Paths: The Case of Energy Technologies for Socio-economic Research on Environmental Change (SEER) research programme of the Commission of the European Communities (DG XII).

Kemp, René, Arie Rip and Johan Schot (1997), 'Constructing transition paths through the management of niches', Paper for Copenhagen workshop on 'Path creation and dependence', 19–21 August.

Kemp, René, Johan Schot and Remco Hoogma (1998), 'Regime shifts to sustainability through processes of niche formation. The approach of strategic niche management', *Technology Analysis and Strategic Management*, **10** (2), 175–95.

Kemp, René and Luc Soete (1992), 'The greening of technological progress: an evolutionary perspective', *Futures*, **24** (5), 437–57.

Kirsch, David (1996), *The Electric Car and the Burden of History. Studies in Automated Systems Rivalry in America, 1890–1996*, PhD thesis, Department of History, Stanford University, Stanford, California.

Korver, Wim (1998), 'Traffic and Transport in the 21st Century. Market chances for new drive concepts', TNO report, Apeldoorn, The Netherlands.

Martin, D.J., and R.A.W. Shock (1989), 'Energy use and energy efficiency in UK transport up to the year 2010', Energy Technology Support Unit (ETSU), Department of Energy, London.

Maruo, Kanehira (1998), *In Search of Signs of a Paradigm Shift in Automotive Technology*, Goteborg: Goteborg University.

May, Graham H. (1996), *The Future is Ours: Foreseeing, Managing and Creating the Future*, London: Adamantine Press.

Meijkamp, Rens (1996), 'Car sharing: consumer acceptance and changes on mobility behaviour', Paper for the 24th European Transport Forum, Brunel University, Uxbridge, London.

Michaelis, Laurie and Ogundale Davidson (1996), 'GHG mitigation in the transport sector', *Energy Policy*, **24**, 969–84.

Molina, A.H. (1993), 'In search of insights into the generation of techno-economic trends: micro- and macro-constituencies in the microprocessor industry', *Research Policy*, **22**, 479–506.

Nelson, Richard R. and Sidney G. Winter (1977), 'In search of useful theory of innovation', *Research Policy*, **6**, 36–76.

Nelson, Richard R. and Sidney G. Winter (1982), *An Evolutionary Theory of Economic Change*, Cambridge, MA: Belknap Press.

Nijkamp, Peter, Sytze A. Rienstra and Jaap M. Vleugel (1995), 'Design and assessment of long-term sustainable transport system scenarios', VU, Amsterdam.

Organization for Economic Cooperation and Development (OECD) (1996), *Prévention et contrôle de la pollution – Critères environnementaux pour des transports durables* (Pollution prevention and control – Environmental criteria for sustainable transport – report on phase 1 of the project on environmentally sustainable transport), Paris: OECD.

Potter, Stephen (1997), 'ASTI case study', Internal Report for Strategic Niche Management project.

Rip, Arie and René Kemp (1998), 'Technological change', in Steve Rayner and Liz Malone (eds), *Human Choice and Climate Change*, Washington, DC: Batelle Press, pp. 327–99.

Rip, Arie, Tom Misa and Johan Schot (eds) (1995), *Managing Technology in Society. New Forms for the Control of Technology*, London: Pinter.

Rosenberg, Nathan (1976), 'The direction of technological change: inducement mechanisms and focussing devices', in *Perspectives on Technology*, Cambridge: Cambridge University Press, pp. 108–25.

Rosenberg, Nathan (1995), 'Uncertainty and technological change', in Ralph Landau, Timothy Taylor and Gavin Wright (eds), *Mosaic of Economic Growth*, Stanford: Stanford University Press, pp. 334–53.

Schot, J.W. (1992), 'Constructive technology assessment and technology dynamics. The case of clean technologies', *Science, Technology and Human Values*, **17** (1), 36–57.

Schot, Johan, Boelie Elzen and Remco Hoogma (1994), 'Strategies for shifting technological systems. The case of the automobile system', *Futures*, **26** (10), 1060–76.

Simon, Benoît (1997a), 'The La Rochelle experiment with electric vehicles', Internal Report for Strategic Niche Management project.

Simon, Benoît (1997b), 'Industrial and institutional barriers to the diffusion of electric vehicles', Stockholm workshop on electric vehicles.

Simon, Benoît (1998), 'The Praxitèle experiment of self-service rented electric vehicles', Internal Report for Strategic Niche Management project.

Smokers et al. (1997), 'Elektrische en hybride voertuigen. Een Quick Scan van de stand van zaken en trends' (Electric and hybrid vehicles. A quick scan of the current situation and trends), Report TNO wegtransportmiddelen, Delft.

Sperling, D. (1995), *Future Drive. Electric Vehicles and Sustainable Transportation*, Washington, DC: Island Press.

Volkskrant (1997a), 'Een auto van gemengde komaf' (A car of mixed origin), 3 May.

Volkskrant (1997b) 'Stimuleren van autodelen doet autodichtheid dalen' (An increase in car sharing reduces car density), 18 June.

Weber, Matthias and Andreas Dorda (1999), 'Strategic niche management: a tool for the market introduction of new transport concepts and technologies', Institute for Prospective Technological Studies (IPTS) Report, February, 20–27.

Weber, Matthias, Remco Hoogma, Ben Lane and Johan Schot (1998), *Experimenting with Sustainable Transport Innovations, A Workbook for Strategic Niche Management*, Seville: Enschede.

Whitelegg, J. (1993), *Transport for a Sustainable Future: The Case for Europe*, London: Belhaven Press.

APPENDIX 6A   REGULATIONS IN EUROPE AND THE US

Table 6A.1   Evolution of emissions standards in the EU (in g/km)

	1993	1996	2000	2005
CO gasoline	2.72	2.2	2.3	1.00
CO diesel	2.72	1.0	0.64	0.50
HC gasoline	1.75*	1.75*	0.12	0.10
HC diesel	1.75*	1.75*	0.07	0.07
NO_x gasoline	2.52*	2.52*	0.15	0.08
NO_x diesel	2.52*	2.52*	0.4	0.19
HC + NO_x gasoline	0.97	0.50	–**	–**
HC + NO_x diesel	0.97	0.7***	0.56	0.30
Part. diesel	0.14	0.08****	0.04	0.02

Notes
   * Standard was already implemented in the 1979 EC Directive.
   ** In the hypothesis voted by the European Parliament, there will no longer be limit values for
      HC + NO_x.
   *** 0.9 for direct injection.
   **** 0.10 for direct injection.

Source: Barbusse (1995).

Table 6A.2   California clean air requirements

			Model			
Year	0.39 HC 7.0 CO 0.4 NO_x	To 50,000 miles 0.25 HC, 3.4 CO, 0.4 NO_x To 100,000 miles 0.31 HC, 4.2 CO, 0.4 NO_x	TLEV 0.125 HC, 3.4 CO, 0.4 NO_x	LEV 0.075 HC, 3.4 CO, 0.2 NO_x	ULEV 0.04 HC, 1.7 CO, 0.2 NO_x	ZEV 0.0 HC, 0.0 CO, 0.0 NO_x
2003				75	15	10
2002				85	10	5*
2001				90	5	5*
2000				96	2	2*
1999		23		73	2	2*
1998		48		48	2	2*
1997		73		25		
1996		80	20			
1995		85	15			
1994	10	80	10			
1993	60	40				
1992	100					
1991	100					

Notes: * These intermediary requirements have been cancelled.
TLEV   Transitional Law Emission Vehicle
LEV   Low Emission Vehicle
ULEV   Ultra Low Emission Vehicle
ZEV   Zero Emission Vehicle

Source: *Automotive News*, 25 February 1991, in Hoogma (1995).

7. Technological innovations in transport: an implementation strategy for underground freight transport

Johan G.S.N. Visser and Harry Geerlings

INTRODUCTION

Since the beginning of the 1990s there has been a renewed interest in the Netherlands in underground transport of freight. Underground transport is expected to be a sustainable way of freight transport within urban areas. The results of recent studies in the Netherlands look promising. There is, however, no clear view on the policy aspects of this technology, especially for the longer term. Important policy questions are:

- How can underground freight transport develop into a sustainable transport mode for freight transport?
- What is the role of the government in the implementation of underground freight transport?

These questions have not yet been answered. The concept of a 'window of technological opportunity', described by Geerlings (1997), is a tool that is helpful in defining public policies for so-called 'mega-technological' innovations. In this chapter, the window of technological opportunity will be used as a policy evaluation framework. We consider this activity to be a starting point for the development of a public policy on underground freight transport.

The content of the chapter is as follows:

- *Transport, the environment and technology* The relationship between environmental problems and transport, and the shift in interest towards the 'technological option' is discussed.
- *Underground freight transport: a promising technology?* The main characteristics of this new technology and the state of the art are defined.
- *The 'window of technological opportunity' for underground freight transport* The concept of a 'window of technological opportunity' is applied to underground freight transport in the Netherlands.

- *Underground freight transport: a technological hype or a new fifth modality?* Conclusions are drawn about the strategy to direct technological innovations. The implications for underground transport are assessed.

TRANSPORT, THE ENVIRONMENT AND TECHNOLOGY

World-wide, the transport sector is characterized by strong growth in both the transport of passengers and the transport of goods. As a consequence of this growth, the negative impact on the environment is increasing. Particular points of attention are the global effects (CO_2 emissions and NO_x emissions), quality-of-life aspects and congestion (EEA, 1995). Other points that need attention are the life-cycle effects related to the production and the recycling of vehicles and the transport system in general. Because of this development, the world-wide impact of transport on the environment will increase in the near future, and continue beyond that. Considering the need for ecological sustainability, it is important that these environmental problems are given priority. From this perspective, it is argued that the transport sector will have no alternative but to develop a sustainable transport system (Gwilliam and Geerlings, 1994).

Technology provides many possibilities to reduce the impact of transport on the environment. Its development and implementation, however, involve several different complexities and, as a result of this, there are great uncertainties and risks. Implementation therefore requires a clear strategy and a multi-actoral approach. The important parts of a development strategy for the technology should be (Geerlings, 1997):

1. distinguishing the right level of analysis (the transport system as a whole, the level of modes and so on);
2. implementation within the transport sector;
3. insight into the development of technological innovations; and
4. the role of the several different actors in the innovation process.

If we focus on the transport sector, we can distinguish between vehicle-orientated technologies and traffic-management-orientated technologies. Several studies indicate that especially technologies that are aimed at management (such as road-pricing, route guidance and enforced speed limitation) can be deployed in the short term. In terms of innovation, these technologies are in the implementation phase. However, the environmental results effects are often disappointing. In the long term, better results for the environment might be achieved by vehicle-orientated technologies (such as new modes, alternative fuels and new engine concepts). This is true in particular for those effects that have been rated a priority, such as the global effects and the life-cycle aspects. In this study, this type of new technology is called a mega-technological innovation. Mega-technological innovations are characterized as technologies which operate on the system level or on a modality level, where the period of research and development (R&D) is distinguished by protracted development, substantial uncertainties (risks) are involved, and the area of application is global.

For a technology in the transport sector that is orientated towards sustainability, it is necessary to pay attention to both the development and the implementation of mega-technological innovations. In this chapter, attention is paid to underground freight transport (UFT), a young and promising technological development. The Dutch Governmental Programme for Sustainable Development (DTO) is a multiyear programme with the objective to define technologies that support sustainable development. The DTO defines underground freight transport as a technological innovation that will lead to a new sustainable way of freight transport (Brouwer et al., 1997a and b). Underground freight transport can also be defined as a 'mega-technological innovation', for the following reasons:

- it operates on the system level;
- its R&D stage is distinguished by protracted development;
- there are many actors involved;
- there are substantial uncertainties (risks) involved; and
- the area of application is global.

UNDERGROUND FREIGHT TRANSPORT: A PROMISING TECHNOLOGY?

In this section, the development of UFT is put in a historical context. We describe why recent underground transport projects are focusing on urban freight transport and what the concept of UFT could look like.

Tube Transportation – the History of Underground Freight Transport

Tube transport has a history which extends back at least two hundred years (USDOT and Volpe, 1994). During this period, systems for both passengers and freight have been proposed. A well-known type of system is the underground subway, also called metro or tube. This transport system for passengers is implemented in most large metropolitan areas of the world. Pipelines for fluids and gases are, of course, also underground transport systems for freight.

These systems have been well developed. Not so well known are freight transport systems in tunnels or large tubes. These types of systems were also built and operated during the same period, but now only a few are still in operation. In this chapter we want to focus on these kinds of systems.

Freight transport systems were already being developed at the beginning of the nineteenth century. The first types of tube transport systems are referred to as pneumatic dispatch systems (USDOT and Volpe, 1994). The original purpose of these systems was to move telegrams and messages from telegraph centres to other offices. The first system that was built connected the offices of Electric and International Telegraph Co. with the London Stock Exchange. This system became operational in 1853. By 1875, London had 33 miles of tubes in operation and the system had been introduced in seven other cities, and by 1909 London had 40 miles of tubes, and 17 English cities also had this type of service. Elsewhere in Europe (Berlin and Paris) and in the United States (New York City, Boston and Chicago) such systems became operational. Le Pneumatique in Paris was in operation until 1984. Due to the rise of modern telecommunications technology, these systems lost their importance.

At the beginning of the twentieth century, another type of transport system for freight was developed. In Chicago, a rail transport system for waste and coal was operational from the beginning of the century until 1959. In London, an underground transport system, called Mail Rail, came into operation in 1927 and is still being used for the transport of mail between post offices within Central London.

In the 1970s, ideas were developed in Europe, Japan and the United States for high-speed transport systems for passengers and freight. Besides the advantage of transport at high speed over long distances, these systems also benefit from the relatively low energy use and limited nuisance to the environment when built underground in low-pressure tunnels.

Historical Overview of Underground Transport Projects in the Netherlands

In 1987, the International System Development and Support (ISDS) foundation developed the integral transport system (ITS) concept, a transport system that consists of a long-distance underground high-speed network for passengers and freight, combined with local short-distance collection and distribution networks, only for freight. Between 1987 and 1993, several projects, financed by the national transport department, studied this concept in more detail (see ISDS, 1993). Although the public and the national authorities showed no interest in the concept as a whole, one aspect – underground transport of freight over shorter distances at low speed – received attention. The reason was that UFT could solve problems of freight transport in congested areas such as cities.

In 1994, the DTO organized several round table discussions with experts and actors concerned about sustainable technologies for transport in the future (Grontmij, 1994). In these meetings, UFT was mentioned as one of the interesting and potentially sustainable technologies for freight transport. Within the framework of this research programme, a definition study (Haccoû et al., 1996) was carried out to determine the feasibility and sustainability of underground transport in more detail, and to define the field of application. The study concluded that in the field of urban freight transport, no alternative sustainable transport modes are available (compared to rail and waterborne alternatives that are available for long-distance transport). This study demonstrated that within urban areas, UFT was potentially a very sustainable and competitive application, and that it could fulfil the role as a sustainable transport mode in freight transport in urban areas.

The next step within the framework of DTO was to design a logistic concept for UFT within urban areas, and to define an implementation strategy. The work was carried out in 1996 and 1997 in a project, called an illustration process, for tube transport of freight within urban areas (Brouwer et al., 1997a and b). In September 1997, the final DTO report was published. The resulting concept was based on small tube networks as a new, sustainable, logistic concept for commodity transport within urban areas. The underground transport system will use small diameter tunnels (at maximum, approximately 2.4 metres). This means that the introduction of such a system needs radical changes in the way freight is distributed today. But on the other hand, it fits within the current logistical trends of 'just-in-time' service with smaller and more frequent delivery.

Meanwhile, in 1995, private companies started two other underground freight projects. The Unit Transport by Pipe (UTP) project was based on a medium-distance underground connection for mini-containers between the seaports of Rotterdam and Antwerp (Lievense, 1995). Another project, the Ondergronds Logistiek Systeem (OLS) project deals with the feasibility of an underground transport network for air cargo and flowers which is to connect Schiphol Airport and the flower auction in Aalsmeer to a new rail terminal in Hoofddorp. The pre-design of this system started in early 1998 (CTT, 1997). A test site for the OLS transport system is planned for 1999.

During 1997 and the beginning of 1998, research was carried out by a special task force of members of the Department of Transport, Internal Affairs, Economic Affairs and Spatial Planning (IPOT, Interdepartmental Project Team on Underground Transport). On behalf of the minister of transport, a memorandum was written about a new national policy for pipeline transport. This memorandum was requested by members of the Dutch House of Commons and was presented in early 1998. The memorandum concluded that the potential transport volume for UFT in the Netherlands will cover about one-third of the total national freight transport volume in 2020, and that it is a potentially interesting development from an economic and environmental point of view. Other conclusions are that more research will be needed before pilot projects can be set up. To this end, a research programme will be developed and implemented by the Department of Transport.

Current Projects Outside the Netherlands

Although there is a strong interest for UFT in the Netherlands at the moment, there are also projects going on in the UK, the USA and Japan. All these projects have in common that they are focused on UFT over short distances with automated transport systems.

In Japan, an investigation was carried out into establishing a dedicated underground infrastructure for freight transport by light trucks that ride through tunnels (dual mode truck). The dual mode truck can move in manned mode on roads, but also in unmanned mode through underground tunnels in Tokyo (see Yamada et al., 1994). This project faces research budget problems due to the economic crises in Japan. L-net Tokyo, another project, a metro-like system for mail-transport underground within Tokyo, was halted in 1994.

In the USA, a company that also produces an ore transport system developed a capsule transport system called Subtrans. A feasibility study started recently on the use of Subtrans for transport of mail and parcels between distribution centres of UPS, TNT and EMS and New Ark Airport near New York.

In the UK, a feasibility study is currently under way to determine whether the underground connections between post offices in Central London used by Mail Rail can be used for the distribution of freight and mail with Metrofreight, a new automated transport system. The large transport volumes to the shopping areas of Central London as well as the congestion problems in London make it very likely that this system will be feasible.

The Need for Underground Freight Transport

UFT is a possible alternative for short-distance road transport in situations where combinations of accessibility problems, lack of space and or environmental problems occur and some concentration of transport flows take place. Situations, identified as possible areas of application, are:

- the distribution of goods within urban areas; and
- freight transport between or within industrial or harbour complexes and intermodal terminals – for instance, in the Schiphol Airport area between the airport, the flower auction Aalsmeer and a rail terminal.

What the two areas have in common is that they deal with transport of general cargo, which is, or can be, transported in relatively small volumes in standardized load units, on pallets or in roll cages, for instance.

In urban areas, freight traffic constitutes a large share of the environmental problems caused by traffic. Most local policies seek to reduce the environmental impact of traffic. Measures taken to control traffic and congestion, such as vehicle and time restrictions, cause accessibility problems for freight transport. In combination with competition from new shopping areas outside of city centres, these accessibility problems endanger the economic and other related functions of the inner cities.

Congestion on the road infrastructure to and from important industrial and harbour complexes is the main driving force behind finding an underground solution in these areas. In the case of Schiphol Airport, new uncongested connections are needed; these cannot be provided above ground. Because these connections will also involve a rail terminal at the airport and at the flower auction, they will also stimulate the use of rail for long-distance transport. In this way, a shift in the modal split in long-distance transport can be provoked. In a study (EAC/TRAIL, 1996) about thirty industrial complexes have been identified where such a collection and distribution system can be implemented.

A third possible area, a long-distance connection between seaports, in this case Rotterdam to Antwerp, seems less feasible. This area has been studied by the Rotterdam Seaport Authorities (Gemeentelijk Havenbedrijf Rotterdam, 1993). Some regional politicians see this connection as an alternative for the new freight railway line between Antwerp and the Netherlands, which was proposed by Belgium.

The Potentials of Underground Freight Transport

The concept of automated UFT through tube networks is based on a particular group of driving forces, characterized as more economy based, as well as social and ecological. These forces were analysed for UFT in urban areas in the DTO programme (Brouwer et al., 1997a and b):

- *The need for a better utilization of city and regional distribution* The efficiency of freight transport can be improved by means of consolidation. City or regional distribution leads to more consolidation and thus to cost reduction. It might also lead to a better transport service with a higher delivery frequency and shorter lead times, which in turn might generate logistics costs savings. Better utilization does not occur spontaneously. Changes in the concept should prod the market, whereby the use would have to increase.

- *Reduction of the environmental costs*   A reduction of noise and emissions and energy consumption in UFT is needed. Running on electric power can reduce the nuisance that vehicles create in the direct environment. Therefore, electric vehicles themselves generate virtually no logistic advantages, except when local restrictions are not applied to electric vehicles.
- *Improvement of local accessibility*   Local accessibility needs to be improved. The general expectation is that a new road infrastructure will generate more car traffic. For this reason, it seems logical to dedicate new infrastructure solely to freight transport. Dedicated lanes for city distribution will increase the average transport speed. The overall time-saving effect will be limited, however. But it might improve the average energy efficiency.
- *Reduction of transshipment costs*   Traditional transshipment is labour intensive. Automation of this activity will decrease transshipment costs.
- *Reduction of transport costs*   The final distribution of goods is very labour intensive because of the slow traffic speeds in urban areas, and the loading and unloading time involved. Considerable savings can be achieved if the transport is automated as well (Clarke and Wright, 1993). Automated transport is not yet feasible with conventional infrastructure due to the conditions in urban areas. It will be feasible, for instance, if automated transport takes place in tunnels.
- *Shorter lead times*   Just-in-time logistics requires distribution of goods in smaller volumes and in higher frequencies with shorter lead times. When transport is automated, it is possible to ship directly from the distribution centre to the delivery destination. Clearly, the costs for personnel are the main reason to consolidate as many parcels in a single vehicle as possible. Making sharp reductions in the shipping costs through automation paves the way for sending shipments directly to the destination instead of making combined trips. When using intermodal transport, the possible loss of travel time as a result of the extra storage and transshipment in the distribution centre is compensated by direct distribution emanating from the distribution centre.
- *Lower investment costs*   Pipeline transport is a logical alternative to automated transport in urban areas when one considers that the size of the shipment will decline in transport automation, while the dedicated lane on the highway would have to be separated and be free of cross-traffic. Partly because of the costs entailed in meeting the needs of dedicated lanes, the choice for pipeline transport seems self-evident. It can be out of sight and is relatively inexpensive (Brouwer et al., 1997a and b). It is expected that the construction costs of pipelines will be lower than the construction costs of roads.

THE 'WINDOW OF TECHNOLOGICAL OPPORTUNITY' FOR UNDERGROUND FREIGHT TRANSPORT

This section describes the application of the theoretical concept of a window of technological opportunity to UFT. This is similar to the application of the concept by Geerlings (1997) to the cases of fuel-cell technology and Maglev technology. This section also describes the Dutch experiences with the implementation of UFT.

In the first part, attention is paid to the general policy requirements, such as the state of development and policy aspects, with respect to:

- robustness;
- prioritization;
- flexibility;
- coherency, consistency, integrity;
- transparency; and
- reliability and trust.

The conditions for UFT are determined and valued in positive or negative terms.

In the second part, the window of technological opportunity concept is applied to underground freight transport. The seven steps distinguished in this concept are described as they are applied to UFT.

An Evaluation of Underground Freight Transport

State of development

The historical overview shows that some examples of UFT exist: one is the Mail Rail system in Central London. There are also some examples of automated freight transport systems that operate on the surface, such as the automated guided vehicles (AGVs) at European Combined Terminals (ECT) in Rotterdam Seaport as well as the internal transport systems used in distribution centres. Automated transport systems for passengers can also be regarded as examples of the technology. In theory, such systems as people-mover systems are suitable for freight transport.

New UFT concepts will most likely be based on existing technology. Challenging innovations such as linear induction propulsion (mentioned as a propulsion technology) are still considered to be a new, futuristic and not yet proven technology, while in fact it has been in use for some years in baggage handling systems and people-mover systems at airports.

At this moment an acceleration seems to be taking place in the development of the technology in the areas of tunnelling and of AGV technology: two important components of underground freight transport.

Actors and activities

A characteristic of 'mega-technological innovations', such as UFT, is that they can hardly be developed by the private sector alone because of the scope of the project. In fact, important actors like manufacturers and users have not even been identified yet. The development of UFT is at the moment initiated by research institutes and individuals who have a social or private interest in the development of such a system, but will not necessarily be the manufacturers or users of the system.

The role of government in relation to the aforementioned projects is less obvious. Table 7.1 characterizes the role of government in four countries where developments are taking place. In the UK and the USA, there is little government involvement. In the UK, researchers at the Centre for Logistics and Transportation at Cranfield University are currently executing the Metrofreight project. In addition to the research team, there is also a consortium of private parties working on the commercial aspects of the introduction of the system. The government is not part of the project: underground transport is primarily seen as a development that has to happen due to market forces. In 1997, a feasibility study in London was subsidized by the government.

In the USA, the US Department of Transportation, in relation to Subtrans, a proposal of Ampower, performed research on the technical feasibility of tube freight transport. The conclusion was that the project was technically feasible, but that there was not enough information to determine the economic feasibility. The public sector has not done any more research. Plans for development, such as the application of Subtrans near Newark, are borne by the private sector.

In Japan, the national government played a leading role in the development of UFT. There, it is the government that initiates and performs research projects: the ministries of post and telecommunications researched the L-Net Tokyo project, and the ministry of construction executed the dual mode truck project. The private sector participated to some extent.

In the Netherlands, the development and construction of infrastructure has,

Table 7.1 The role of the government

Government	Role in the considered projects
UK	No involvement yet. Some R&D funding
USA	No involvement. No R&D funding
Japan	Former leading role of national government
Netherlands	Preparing a national policy, R&D funding, public–private development

for a long time, been a responsibility of the government. This role is changing however. Cooperation with the private sector is necessary because the government is not equipped to fulfil all the roles needed to develop a 'mega-technological innovation'. The government is able to generate the necessary resources and to define goals and milestones, but is not able to develop the necessary skills to produce and commercialize new technologies. These skills are in the hands of the private sector. There is no generic strategy or prescription for setting up such a public–private cooperation. In the Netherlands, the process of initiating a public–private cooperation has started in the OLS project and the DTO programme. In both projects the initial steps, those forming the exploring phase, have taken place. In the DTO and OLS projects, sessions were organized with different parties from the private sector and the national government; this led to an awareness of joint interests. For this reason the Tube Transport Platform was installed in 1998. This platform advises the government in matters related to UFT (as well as traditional transport by pipe). The platform will also be the first step to public–private cooperation in the implementation. The typical image of a win–win situation or a common interest can be decisive.

Despite the great numbers of actors involved in the projects there is still an important role for the government to play. The role of the government in the Dutch situation seems to be twofold: as a 'director' but also as a 'co-actor'.

The following is a discussion of the general policy requirements that have to be fulfilled.

Robustness   There is no policy in the field of underground freight transport yet, but it is certain that a UFT policy will have to deal with high risks, long-term trajectories and the international arena.

The current government efforts are limited to the financing of research, such as the research related to the DTO, and the OLS project of the Centre for Transport Technology, which is financed by the national government. The current developments are almost completely dependent on this research. There is little chance that new (self-developing) processes will be initiated, so that continuity in research can hardly be expected. This means that the development is extremely sensitive to any changes, such as in the current technology policy.

Another point of attention for UFT development is the possibility of the appearance of other, competing, alternatives or the occurrence of opposing developments. It is conceivable, for example, that the current problems could be solved with existing modes, thanks to technical improvements or changing circumstances.

Prioritization   The current developments receive a lot of attention and, consequently, are given a high priority on the political agenda. This priority is not influenced in a negative way by the long-term perspective, which is unusual for development of this type of technology.

Although politicians embraced the concept of UFT, it is remarkable that there are no formal references to this concept as of yet in leading policy documents.

Flexibility   The development of an underground freight transport can be seen as a long-term development. This means that for a long period much effort has to be expended in developing such a system. Long-term efforts are by nature inflexible; especially where the construction of an infrastructure with a dedicated purpose is concerned. It is likely that changes in society and technology will take place in the future. This means that the policy should include a certain degree of flexibility before the project gets to the actual operation stage.

Coherency, consistency, integrity   The potentials of underground freight transport are located in several social policy areas. UFT connects to the policy goals in the areas of environment, transport and economy. The system is seen as positive from both the environmental and the economic point of view. In the Dutch context, several departments are therefore actively involved (the Department of Housing, Spatial Planning and Environment; the Department of Economic Affairs; and the Department of Transport and Water Management) and will probably lead to an integral policy view on this matter.

Transparency   The goal and the area of application of underground transport are quite clear. The way the system is to be applied (in urban areas, between urban areas, or within and between industrial complexes) is, however, still not clear. As underground transport is of interest from both the environmental and the economic point of view, the different parties are starting to line up.

Reliability and trust   No single opinion can be presented in this area. There is a group of believers, and there is a large group of sceptics. The believers attach great value to the potential of underground transport, and see possibilities to initiate large-scale changes both on the environmental and on the logistical levels. The sceptics, on the other hand, see great risks arising out of the high cost of the infrastructure, the limited flexibility and the great uncertainties. These uncertainties are not only the technical and financial risks involved, but also the uncertainties related to the social level. The construction of tunnels in cities has a very negative image, which was created during the construction of the subway train system (metro) in Amsterdam. The construction of tunnels in the city is seen as associated with large-scale demolition of existing buildings and with large open pit construction sites. The drilling of tunnels does not have these negative aspects.

*Table 7.2   Assessment of general policy requirements for underground
                freight transport in the Netherlands*

General policy requirements	
Robustness	−
Prioritization	+
Flexibility	− −
Coherency	++
Transparency	++
Reliability, trust	++/− −

The criteria mentioned above are summarized in Table 7.2. The policy requirements are evaluated and judged with a minus or a plus. Double plus means that
this requirement is fulfilled satisfactorily.

The Strategy Framework

The methodology developed in the window of technological opportunity
model distinguishes seven steps, which will be applied to UFT in the
Netherlands.

1. *Step 1:   Identification of sustainability-sound heuristics*   Underground
    freight transport appeared on the research agenda from the viewpoint of
    sustainability. The advantages to the environment in the projects are there-
    fore clearly identified and, where possible, quantified. The benefits are
    clear in the area of energy consumption (and related emissions), noise and
    severance. In general, positive effects will take place in global pollution,
    non-global pollution and quality-of-life aspects. These are the environ-
    mental advantages that occur in the exploitation phase as a result of the
    changeover from road transport to underground transport or intermodal
    transport (if underground transport is a link in an intermodal chain). There
    is a certain focus on energy savings in the exploitation phase of the system
    and on reduction of environmental nuisance to the immediate surrounding
    area. The environmental cost of the construction and the use of resources,
    however, have not been sufficiently studied. It is partly because of this
    that it is not fully determined whether the system is really sustainable.
        The overall target of the DTO programme was to define technological
    innovations that will increase sustainability by a factor of 20. The studies
    on freight transport in urban areas could only demonstrate an increase by
    a factor of eight to ten. These results, although promising, need some
    consideration.

2. *Step 2:   Defining the relevant 'communities'*
   a.   *The identification of the level playing field*   There is no clear analysis available that identifies the correct level playing field. At least three levels of relevance have been identified.

   The first level of importance is the local level, because UFT to a large extent deals with local accessibility and local environmental problems, but also because local governments will presumably be the ones to make the final decisions.

   The second level of importance is the national level, because it is on this level that the acceptance of the concept as a sustainable mean of transport will take place. It seems to be that the national level is the most suited and best-equipped level to develop a long-term technology policy.

   Currently, the third level, which is the European context, is not of relevance for the implementation of this mega-technological innovation. There are several reasons, however, why the technology and policy development should take place on a European level. Probably the most important reason is that transport problems are more or less 'universal', which means that problems related to transport also occur more or less in the same form as in other (European) countries. This is certainly the case with UFT. But it is also because topics like the setting of standards and legislation prefer an European action. The automotive and telecommunication industries are examples which show that the European level is becoming more and more the right level playing field.

   To determine whether a project is started on the right level is often not easy with a young development such as this. In the case of the OLS Schiphol project, for instance, the project was started at the local level after consultation with Schiphol Airport and the Aalsmeer flower auction. Very soon after the first research efforts, the project initiated contact with the national government.

   The DTO project, on the other hand, was started up on a national level. In this respect, this project may be seen as unusual. During the illustration process, workshops were held with experts, special interest groups, and public and private sector organizations. A point of interest here relates to determining needs, boundary conditions and demands from different community groups.
   b.   *The composition of the strategic consortium*   Several consortia that are interested in working in underground transport are in the process of being organized. The consortium that is executing the OLS project consists of consulting firms, research institutes and industrial corporations.

A weak point in this area is that it is not clear who will deliver underground transport in the future. The current transport and logistics operators have no, or very little, involvement in the present consortium. The same goes for the majority of shippers. As these parties could possibly take on the role of operator, or at least will have to work closely with the operator (as contractee or as competitor), it is essential that they participate in the consortium.

In addition, the local authority is also missing. The local authority is probably the government organization that will be responsible for the decision to introduce UFT in its area of jurisdiction.

The construction sector is incorporating the present plans into its vision of the future of the Netherlands and uses them in their lobbying activities. There is the danger that these activities may provoke negative reactions, and that the current research may be seen in the wrong light.

The installation of the Tube Transport Platform by the government (see above) can be seen as a new strategic alliance between government and the private sector. Although the platform is not involved in actually developing the technology, it has the ability to activate market players and to act as an intermediate between them and the government.

c. *The responsibilities of different actors* By financing research, the government has provided an opportunity to obtain more insight into the potential of underground transport. By financing projects, the government gets the opportunity to fulfil the role of 'director' or 'co-actor. Pilot projects will be initiated for this reason to show the technical and commercial feasibility.

The attitude of the market players at this moment can be described as interested bystanders. The private sector follows the developments with interest but is not yet willing to play a leading role.

The relationship between public and private sector is unclear. The question is: which parts belong to the public domain and which to the private domain? An organizational structure comparable to the privatized national railways is considered. This means a structure where a public/private management company manages the infrastructure and distributes the capacity, with a private development company that has the concession to run the system.

d. *Embodied in – or not in opposition to – the existing policy framework* Underground freight transport is not yet part of present policies in the field of technology development, spatial planning and transport. However, underground transport connects with current policies to improve accessibility and environment in a sustainable fashion.

The current research activities are, in general, characterized as a form of 'techno-centrism', where the activities are particularly geared to scouting for the potentials of underground transport, studying the developments abroad, and determining the economic and technical feasibility. Social and organizational feasibility are aspects that will gain in importance in this process.

The introduction of underground transport itself is still too far in the future to become part of current policy, but the conditions can now be created that will lead to the introduction of underground transport. At the moment, favourable conditions are still insufficiently present. Urban distribution is still not well enough developed. In fact, the current urban distribution centre projects in the Netherlands have not been successful. The organization of present transport is not yet attuned. The logistics are insufficiently in tune, in particular, the needed standardization of load units is insufficiently carried through. At the edge of the city in particular, there is hardly any spatial concentration of logistical activities that can form the feeder locations of the underground transport system.

3. *Step 3: Anticipation of long-term perspectives* There are a number of trends visible, both in and outside of the transport sector, where UFT connects with, for instance, just-in-time logistics, automation and robotization. There is also a need for a 'congestion-free' infrastructure for freight to, from, and within urban areas and industrial complexes. The development of freight lanes and freight freeways is an important policy trend. Intermodality is another important trend in the transport policy. In the policy, the concern is not only about the positive environmental effects that accompany the shift to intermodal transport, but also about the improvement in accessibility as a result of the use of congestion-free modes. There is also a more urban trend present in relation to underground transport in cities: the revitalization of urban centres. In this context, authorities on the local level pay much attention to the revitalization of the inner city.

The following policy areas are currently receiving attention in relation to sustainability: further reduction of local nuisance such as noise pollution and traffic safety, and on a more world-wide level the reduction of CO_2 emissions and the accompanying reduction in the use of energy. In particular, the goals of CO_2 emission reduction seem not to be met in freight transport. That means that much attention will be paid to measures that make it possible to meet these goals.

4. *Step 4: Assessment of technological potentials and limitations* The projects described assume the application of available technology. This is seen as an essential point of departure. From a commercial point of view,

much value is attached to limiting the technical uncertainties. It is for this reason that the application of proven technology is chosen.

However, there are some concerns. The concept is based on down-scaling or up-scaling of existing technologies, but it is also true that these technologies have never been used in this combination. Both aspects might lead to problems or extra costs at the start.

Another important concern is the fact that automated transport has never been implemented on the proposed scale. Tunnelling has never been applied on such a scale in the Netherlands. The constructing costs and time frame of construction, and the operational costs of such a system are uncertain.

5. *Step 5: Identification of the fields of common interest (FCI)* The development and implementation of UFT contributes to the realization of collective policy objectives. A well-thought-out implementation strategy will be a matter of creating a win–win situation when both environmental and economic objectives will be met.

    These common interests were already determined at an early stage and have proved to be successful up till now. This explains also why there is such good cooperation between government and the private sector. The market players became interested at a very early stage. It is remarkable that the participation of the private sector is not motivated purely by financial reasons, but also by strategic considerations. This aspect will certainly require more research.

6. *Step 6: Application of instruments* The instruments currently used by the authorities are consultation and research. There is consultation between the national departments, but not with the provinces. There is also consultation with the municipalities and stakeholders. Consultation is primarily meant to stake out a platform through the provision of information and by brainstorming around the possibilities. It is also meant to develop a vision. Research has to contribute to our knowledge of the system and its potential.

    The following step in the process seems to be the definition of pilot projects. The two goals of a pilot project are testing and demonstrating.

    With respect to legislation and regulation, the areas of automated (underground) transport and underground construction (procedures for decision making, property law) have to be worked on. The area of legislation and regulation will require a considerable amount of work, not only with respect to automated (underground) transport and underground construction (procedures for decision making, property law), but also in regard to the accompanying policies that are of importance to an implementation strategy. This aspect will decidedly require more research.

Table 7.3   The strategy framework

The strategy framework	Netherlands
1. Identification of environmental heuristic	+/++
2. Defining 'communities'	
a. Identification of level playing field	+
b. Composition of strategic consortium	–
c. Responsibilities of different actors	+/–
d. Embodied in policy framework	– –
3. Anticipation of trends	++
4. Assessment of technological characteristics	++/?
5. Identification of FCI	++
6. Application of instruments	+

Each step is evaluated and judged by experts in terms of pluses and minuses (see Table 7.3). From the window of technological opportunity perspective, it can be argued that underground freight transport is off to a promising new start.

The breakthrough of this innovation has become more likely because of the following fundamental differences with earlier attempts:

- there is now a high social appreciation of 'quality of life': this contributes to a priority for environmental solutions, rather than the unthinking realization of an infrastructure that is unfriendly to the environment;
- new technology potentials: automation and robotization have made the building of better transport systems possible; and
- improved logistics: the development of technology has both created and increased the need for more complex logistical structures (for instance, just-in-time logistics).

It is therefore important for both government and private sector to participate in this process.

The application of the window of technological opportunity therefore presents a favourable score on the points of attention. The seven points of attention, identified in the strategy to realize a sustainably-sound policy, are all being dealt with.

In evaluating the strategy framework, it must be noted that the development of underground transport is still clearly in the exploration phase. Characteristics of this phase are:

- the mapping of potentials and uncertainties;
- the sketching of concepts;
- the finding of interested parties; and
- the definition of common interests.

Research is the most important activity at this stage.

The exploration phase cannot yet be rounded off and closed. There are two issues that have to be dealt with in the short term:

- the roles of the actors involved are not clear; and
- the government is expecting active involvement of the private parties, while these parties are afraid to take the initiative.

In addition, a number of issues have not been adequately analysed:

- the uncertainties regarding the potentials: these potentials are clearly there, but underground transport will only be able to facilitate a part of all freight transport, and is therefore no complete alternative for road transport;
- the economical and environmental benefits have not been fully determined;
- there is no clear division of tasks between government and industry;
- the step from exploration to implementation is too big: the change is too large, the investments too high, and the time of development too long; and
- the developments elsewhere in the world are taking place at a slower rate: the question is whether it is wise to take the position of front-runner in the world with the development of such a system.

The question now is how to deal with government policy. To find solutions for contemporary problems it is necessary to create the necessary conditions that fit with the development of underground transport. Underground transport fits within the objectives of government policies, but is not yet part of those policies. A national or Europe-wide policy is still missing.

UNDERGROUND FREIGHT TRANSPORT: A TECHNOLOGICAL HYPE OR A NEW FIFTH MODALITY?

Underground freight transport has certain potentials. It is necessary to understand that there are great uncertainties about the costs and benefits, and that the short-term problem-solving capacity is rather limited. It therefore remains a long-term development. These facts run counter to the recent surge of interest in the subject of underground transport. Calling this a hype, however, is going too far.

An explanation for this interest can possibly be found in the unique conjunction in this system of economic and environmental interests, on the one hand, and the technological challenges of transport automation and underground construction in the Netherlands, on the other hand.

There are, however, a few favourable prospects. The OLS Schiphol project and the Metrofreight project in London can well become reality within ten years. These projects must be seen as pilot projects: they must demonstrate whether UFT has the right to exist. These projects are, in a sense, niche markets, which is favourable for the success of the project.

The development towards a new fifth modality is, however, a long-term process that can only be realized if there is more clarity about the existing uncertainties (financial, technological, enviro-technological and organizational). Application on a large scale can only be expected in the long term, and a carefully designed long-range strategy is necessary for its implementation. A first start in this direction is given in the DTO study (Brouwer et al., 1997a and b).

It is certainly necessary that a clear vision remains in place with respect to the magnitude of the underlying social problem and the resolving capacity of the solution. There is the danger that a shift may occur to the long term (technological fix), or that the machine becomes unstoppable, even after unsatisfactory and disappointing results.

BIBLIOGRAPHY

Brouwer, W., W.E. van Lierop, G.A.A. Erens, A.F.C. Carlebur and J.G.S.N. Visser (eds) (1997a), *Buisleidingtransport (BLT) voor Stedelijk Goederenvervoer, deel A* (Tube transport for urban goods transportation), DTO-werkdocument M9, Delft: DTO.
Brouwer, W., W.E. van Lierop, G.A.A. Erens, A.F.C. Carlebur and J.G.S.N. Visser (eds) (1997b), *Buisleidingtransport (BLT) voor Stedelijk Goederenvervoer, deel B*, DTO-werkdocument M10, Delft: DTO.
Centre for Transport Technology (CTT) (1997), *Ondergronds Logistiek Systeem (OLS), hoofdrapport deel 1: Definitiestudie* (Underground Logistic System (ULS), Main Report Part 1: Definition Study), Rotterdam: CTT.
Clarke, M. and D. Wright (1993), *Metro-freight, a New Direction for Transport: An Introduction*, Cranfield, Bedfordshire: Cranfield School of Management.
Dosi, G. (1982), 'Technological paradigms and technological trajectories: a suggested interpretation of determinants and directions of technological change', *Research Policy*, **11**, 147–62.

European-American Center for Policy Analysis (EAC/)/TRAIL (1996), *Research Plan for an Analysis of Tactics for Underground Freight Transport*, Delft: RAND.

European Environmental Agency (EEA) (1995), *Europe's Environment; the Dobrís Assessment*, Copenhagen: EEA.

Geerlings, H. (1997), 'Towards Sustainability of Technological Innovations in Transport; The Role of Government in Generating a Window of Technological Opportunity', PhD thesis, Erasmus University, Rotterdam.

Gemeentelijk Havenbedrijf Rotterdam, Dienst Gemeentewerken, Dienst Stedebouw en Volks-huisvesting (1993), *Onderzoek ondergronds transport* (Research Underground Transport), Rotterdam: Gemeente Rotterdam.

Grontmij Advies en Techniek (1994), *Verslag van ronde-tafelbijeenkomsten en voorstel voor illustratieprocessen* (Report of the Roundtable Meetings and Proposal for Illustration Process), Zeist: Grontmij.

Gwilliam, K.M. and H. Geerlings (1994), 'New technologies and their potential to reduce the environmental impact of transportation', *Transportation Research A*, **28A** (4), 307–19.

Haccoû, H.A., J.G.S.N. Visser and R.L. Elting (1996), *Buisleidingen voor Goederentransport, Definitiestudie* (Pipelines for Freight Transport, Definition Study), DTO werkdocument M2, Interdepartementaal Onderzoeksprogramma, Delft: DTO.

Raadgevend Ingenieursbureau Lievense, Knight Wendling Consultants en Holec Machines & Apparaten (1995), *Onderzoek naar de Technische en Eeconomische Haalbaarheid van het Transport van Goederen in Units per Pijpleiding (UTP)* (Research at the Technical and Economic Feasibility of Freight Transport in Units by Pipeline (UTP)), Breda: Lievense bu.

Stichting International System Development & Support (ISDS) (1993), *Sustainable Transport, Studying New Dimensions: The Possibilities of Tunnel Transport*, Delft: ISDS Foundation.

US Department of Transportation (USDOT) Research and Special Programs Administration and Volpe National Transportation Systems Center (1994), *Tube Transportation*, Cambridge, MA: USDOT.

van Binsbergen, A. and J. Visser (1995), 'Distributie in stedelijke gebieden ondergronds', in H.J. Meurs and E.J. Verroen (eds), *Colloquium Vervoersplanologisch Speurwerk – 1995 – Decentralisatie van Beleid: Implicaties voor Kennis en Onderzoek*, Delft: CVS, pp. 425–44.

World Commission on Environment and Development (1987), *Our Common Future*, Oxford: Oxford University Press.

Yamada, H., S. Ueda, T. Kono and Y. Tanaka (1994), *Development of the Dual Mode Truck Control Technology for the New Freight Transport System*, Tokyo: Public Works Research Institute, Ministry of Construction.

8. Sustainable underground urban goods distribution networks

Arjan J. van Binsbergen and Piet H.L. Bovy

PROBLEMS RELATED TO GOODS TRANSPORTATION IN URBAN AREAS

Accessibility, Environmental and Traffic Safety Problems

Densely populated urban areas exhibit accessibility, environmental and traffic safety problems and these problems endanger a sustainable development.

Congestion hinders people and goods from entering urban areas. This is no new phenomenon but the notion rises that mass motorization and other (technological) developments undermine the position of urban areas. This could lead to a further urban sprawl, which results in social, economical and ecological problems.

Traffic causes environmental, spatial and safety problems. Goods traffic is responsible for an above-proportional share of chemical emissions and noise and is in some cases the main source of hindrance of all traffic (see Ogden, 1992). Due to their size, weight and manoeuvrability limitations, goods vehicles are relatively often involved in serious accidents (See Table 8.1).

Table 8.1   Problems for and resulting from goods transport

Problems for/imposed upon goods transport	Problems imposed by goods transport
Accessibility and congestion	Accessibility and congestion
Reliability of delivery times	Noise
Entrance time restrictions	Emissions
Restrictions on vehicle size	Damage to infrastructure
Restrictions on vehicle weight	Space use and physical hindrance

In many urbanized European regions the pace of growth in goods transportation is about twice the growth rate of the economic development (GNP) however, the growth rate of goods transportation to and from cities is not that high and relatively low when looking at inner-city transportation. Nevertheless, problems are likely to increase, though to a lesser extent within urban areas than outside those areas.

Technological developments might limit noise and chemical emissions. However, the need for a clean environment also rises in cities. This means that even in the case of a limited objective growth of environmental and accessibility problems, the problems will be perceived as more important than ever.

Goods transportation is indispensable for the prosperity of urban areas; therefore new, sustainable transportation concepts should both accomplish the vital function of goods distribution and limit negative side-effects.

Following this introduction, the chapter describes the base characteristics of underground systems and then elaborates on concepts for underground urban goods transportation in urban areas. After that, the consequences of new transportation concepts for logistics, traffic conditions and the environment are discussed. The chapter concludes with a general assessment of the concept of underground goods transportation in urban areas.

Pipes and Tubes

Underground transportation of goods is common practice when considering the transportation of water, fuels and chemicals. Expressed in transport performance, pipeline transportation is in fact a main goods transportation modality. Water transportation makes up most of the performance, followed by natural gas or crude oil and oil products. Although exact figures are not known, almost all pipeline transportation has to do with the transportation of fluid bulk goods or gases. Transportation of (fluid) bulk goods is an ideal market for pipelines because of the large quantities and relative low unit prices. The fundamental difference between pipe and 'tube' transportation is that in tubes general cargo will be transported, stowed into vehicles. Until now, this type of transportation is used mainly in mines. The only recent urban example is the London Mail System. Other examples are hard to find (see Clarke and Wright, 1993). This is in contrast to underground passenger transportation, which has gained important local market shares in large cities (extended underground or 'metro' systems in New York, London and Paris).

As pipes and tubes are generally located underground, spatial problems and several sorts of direct hindrance (noise, stench, most forms of traffic risks, physical hindrance) are almost non-existent. Due to the nature of the virtually undisturbed traffic flows in underground networks, energy use and related emissions can also be decreased. Therefore, underground transportation can be seen as being sustainable, as long as construction costs (expressed in monetary costs or in material and energy costs) per transported unit can be limited. This is also the biggest challenge for underground transportation concepts.

Underground goods transportation systems will never stand on their own, but will always be part of a larger transportation system. Although underground systems can function in a traditional transport/logistical environment, for optimal results a redesign of the logistic system will be necessary.

Transported Goods

In order to evaluate the potentials of underground distribution systems it is important to know which types of goods can be transported by underground systems. In urban areas a wide variety of goods is transported and the type of goods moved depends on the types of activities located in the urban area. In cities without predominant industrial facilities, most transported goods are related to building activities. Next to that, food products, fuels and consumer goods are important. Expressed in vehicle movements, the transportation of food and consumer goods is by far the most important goods flow in cities (see Ogden, 1992). The concepts of underground goods transportation systems aim at the distribution of this type of goods.

New Logistic Systems

In combined logistic systems, logistic activities of various operators are joined in order to achieve cost or other (economy of scale) advantages. The basis for joining activities is the type of goods to be transported, the type of outlets to be served or the area in which outlets are situated. The main goal of joining the activities is enabling collective use of buildings, infrastructures and/or vehicles. This is displayed in Figure 8.1, where different trade relations are combined by cooperation and by introducing an intermediary.

Urban distribution centres (UDCs) are the physical manifestation of joined, indirect logistic systems. Until now, different management concepts for UDCs have been applied:

- collective and public distribution system in which all relevant distribution activities are performed by a single service provider using a single UDC;
- attuned distribution activities performed by several commercial service providers performed in a limited number of logistic areas around a city; and
- operationally independent distribution activities performed in a limited number of logistic areas, such as the French Garanor system.

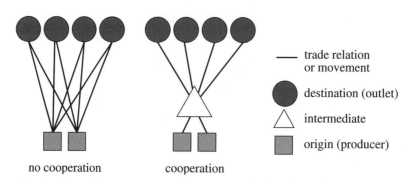

Figure 8.1   Efficiency improvement by cooperation and introducing an intermediary

In all concepts, goods flows are directed via logistic centres close to urban areas. This poses important advantages for future developments in urban distribution activities, such as intermodal rail transportation and also underground distribution.

Combined Transportation for Urban Distribution

Introducing a physical 'break' in the logistic processes of goods distribution to urban areas in an urban distribution area opens the potential for optimizing within city transportation techniques independently from the optimization of transportation techniques outside the city borders. The physical break requires some form of transshipment, which should be as cheap and as fast as possible, thus disturbing the logistic process least.

Developments in city goods transportation aim at lightweight, electric-powered and relatively small vehicles. Improved or newly developed techniques such as hybrid (diesel/gasoline – electric) engines, advanced batteries (sodium-sulphur, lithium, polymers) and fuel cell-powered electric engines can lead to a decrease in energy use, a decrease (in some cases to nil) of local emissions and a decrease of noise.

'Upscaling' is the aim for road-bound goods transportation systems outside cities. For this, the road-train concept is developed, which is a combination of lorries and trailers up to 25 metres (or even more) in length. In future, these combinations may possibly be electric powered and automated guided. In rail transportation traditional (mass cargo) concepts need to be 'downscaled', as is illustrated by the German CargoSprinter concept in which a train consists of up to five carriages only. Technical characteristics such as rate of acceleration and maximum speed allow these trains to mix with intercity (passenger) train operations. This opens the perspective of short-interval train services. Both advanced, upscaled road transportation systems and downscaled rail transportation systems can be used for the transportation of consumer goods over larger distances (from 50 kilometres upwards) outside urban areas.

CHARACTERISTICS OF UNDERGROUND SYSTEMS

Underground infrastructure has some typical, functional and technical characteristics that largely determine the way the infrastructure can be used.

Functional Characteristics

The main functional characteristics of underground infrastructure are underground location and encasement (see Figure 8.2). An underground position allows multiple space use and thus leads to space savings (at the surface level). Furthermore, an underground position allows more freedom in network design in three dimensions. A negative side-effect is the need for vertical transport (to overcome height differences between the tunnel and the surface).

Encasement offers advantages for the application and operation of transportation systems. Encasement protects the system against climatic influences and allows the system to be entered only through a selected number of entrance points (hence limiting the risk of accidents, theft and so on). Encasement also protects the surroundings from influences generated by the

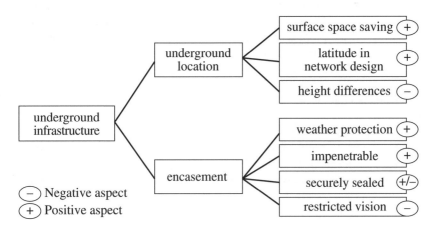

Source: Van Binsbergen et al., 1995.

Figure 8.2   Fundamental characteristics of underground infrastructure

transportation system, such as noise and emissions. As a drawback, encasement limits the accessibility for emergency services.

In most cases, underground transportation will be designed as an autonomous system, which means that other traffic cannot disturb the underground traffic process. However, this is not a specific advantage for underground transport, since autonomy may also be realized with surface transportation.

Functional characteristics determine the user friendliness of the system as is expressed in accessibility and costs.

Technical Characteristics

Technical features of the underground infrastructure include the depth of the tunnel (the depth below surface), the tunnel diameter and the construction method. The construction method largely determines the alignment of the underground system and also the impact of the construction phase on the surface activities.

Other technical characteristics relate to the way vehicles are guided through the tunnel. In electronic guided systems, sensors detect the exact position of the vehicle and computers determine the path. This gives 'free-ranging' capabilities in terminals – a vehicle can go anywhere as long as a positioning system is in place and computers allow access. In physical guidance, infrastructural provisions, such as rails, guide the vehicles. Computers are used only to determine the speed, accelerations and decelerations. The lateral position of vehicles is fully determined by the infrastructure. This is a fail-safe system, but is costly and requires special attention to the design of terminals.

Moreover, the propulsion system of the vehicles determines which additional technical features are needed. Dedicated vehicles will probably make use of electric propulsion, provided either by wires or by internal batteries.

Interdependency between Characteristics

Those characteristics are interdependent. The cut-and-cover construction method limits the depth of a tunnel, but allows large diameters and various shapes. Boring methods demand a greater depth because of the necessary ground cover. Only relatively limited tunnel diameters and only a restricted variation in shape can be bored.

The main characteristics of underground transport, namely autonomy and encasement, allow for and sometimes demand specialized vehicles. Autonomous infrastructure is very suitable for operating automated vehicles. Thus in most plans for underground goods transport, vehicle automation is a key issue. Encasement is disadvantageous for the traditional combustion driving techniques because of the exhaust fumes. Electric drive is a far better alternative.

The depth of the tunnel, the tunnel diameter and the construction method that is chosen are interrelated and have a strong impact on investment costs. Cost can be regarded as the main influencing factor – it determines the willingness to invest and tariffs determine the willingness to use the system. Therefore underground systems will generally consist of relatively coarse networks with a low spatial density of access points and will thus need a high degree of spatial bundling to operate effectively.

INNER-CITY UNDERGROUND NETWORK ALTERNATIVES

Underground Concepts

For goods distribution in urban areas, four underground concepts can be distinguished:

- underground objects (cellars, depots);
- underground sections (tunnels);
- underground links; and
- underground networks.

In many urban areas underground facilities are in use, especially for storage (cellars). Some of these facilities have direct access to roadways using ramps or elevators. Often, goods need to be 'transferred' to be transported to the underground facilities, but because these are often storage facilities, vehicles should be unloaded anyway. Figure 8.3 shows schematically the solitary function of

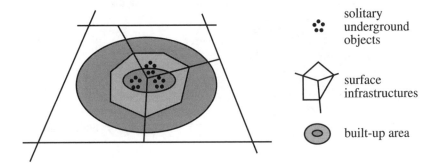

Figure 8.3   Underground objects

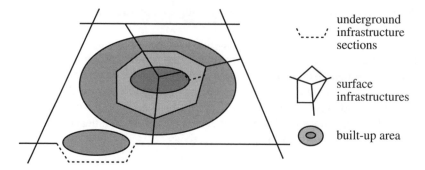

Figure 8.4   Underground sections linked by ramps to surface infrastructure

these underground objects. Those objects have no specific traffic or transport function, but may help to overcome local spatial problems regarding storage.

To cross waterways, other roads or vulnerable (urban) landscapes, parts of the urban infrastructure can be put partly underground in tunnels, as is shown schematically in Figure 8.4.

Underground links resemble underground sections (see Figure 8.5), but differ in that only dedicated vehicles may use the infrastructure. Underground links can be used to interconnect important activity centres, without interference by other (transport) activities. Underground links underpass congested areas, such as inner-city areas. Although dedicated 'underground' vehicles can be used, another option is to use vehicles that can be used both on the surface (traditional infrastructure) as well as at the underground link. An example of such a concept is the dual mode truck as developed in Japan (Koshi, 1992). Even traditional vehicles can be used, although this requires specific adaptations to the underground infrastructure (lighting, air conditioning).

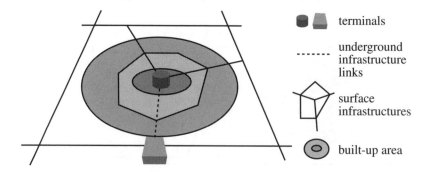

Figure 8.5   Underground links with start and end terminals (transshipment points)

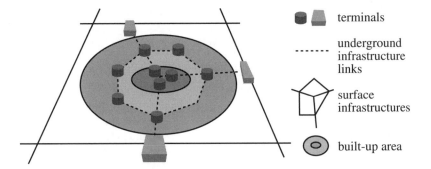

Figure 8.6   An underground network with terminals

Full underground networks connect multiple activity centres (see Figure 8.6). A full underground network provides an independent (autonomous) service that is not hindered by other traffic. The full autonomy again allows the use of dedicated vehicles.

The underground network consists of a limited number of main access points, situated at the border of the urban area, a number of neighbourhood distribution centres and the underground links. The goods are then transported through the tube network to a neighbourhood distribution centre near the final destination. From that centre, goods are delivered directly to main final addressees (having their own servicing point) or are transported, at surface level, to the other addressees. In the latter case, goods may have to be trans-shipped again.

The underground network requires an adapted logistic system, mainly because goods need to be transshipped at the main service centres. Also the rather complex organization of (very) short-distance intermodal transportation requires adapted logistic systems (see also Clarke and Wright, 1993). In contrast to 'traditional' urban distribution, for underground distribution there is no need for consolidation since in the underground system rather small vehicles are used.

Vehicle Use in Combined Surface/Underground Systems

In the case of underground 'sections', ordinary road vehicles can be used, so transshipments are not necessary. Ordinary vehicles require special provisions, such as lighting, air-condition and safety systems. In sections of limited length, the costs of these provisions are regarded as acceptable. This is often not the case with long stretches, where trains on which the road vehicles can be placed are often used (Channel Tunnel, several Alpine crossings). In fact, the 'section'-type tunnel then changes into a link-type tunnel.

Table 8.2   Provisions for underground use of different types of vehicles

	Provisions for vehicles	Infrastructural provisions
Traditional road Vehicles	(Driver's cabin) (Combustion engine)	Large tube diameter Lighting Air conditioning Safety measures
Multipurpose vehicles	Driver's cabin Guidance system Combustion engine Electric drive	Guidance system
Dedicated vehicle	Guidance system Electric drive	Guidance system

In lengthy underground 'link' and 'network' systems, preferably special-ized (dedicated) vehicles should be used. The characteristics of the vehicles should allow some of the expensive provisions to be omitted.

To make use of the underground links or networks, either transshipments or the use of multipurpose vehicles will be necessary (see Table 8.2 for a compar-ison). By using transshipments, costly and time-consuming processes are introduced, but the traffic flows inside the tunnel are not (directly) influenced by surface operations. This enhances the reliability of the system.

Multipurpose vehicles can operate both as 'ordinary' road vehicle and as 'dedicated' vehicle. For example, dual propulsion systems (electric/combus-tion) and steering (automatic/human driver) devices will be used. The vehicles are more expensive than either ordinary road vehicles or dedicated under-ground transport vehicles. Because transfers are not needed, there will be no transfer costs (see Koshi, 1992).

Investment Costs

In the Netherlands thus far about twenty main tunnels for road and rail trans-portation have been built. These tunnels are of the 'underground section' type. There are no examples of underground networks for goods transport vehicles. Therefore, except for the underground section type of tunnels, only estimates can be made about the construction costs of other types of tunnels or networks.

Of the underground section type, 13 tunnels for road traffic and three for rail transportation were built to cross waterways and one for road and one for rail to pass under Amsterdam's Schiphol Airport. Four stretches of metro-tunnel have been built in Amsterdam and Rotterdam. Thus far, all traffic tunnels were constructed by the cut-and-cover method.

In 1999, two main 'underground section-type' tunnels are under construction. In the city of The Hague, a 1250 metre tramway tunnel combined with a parking facility will be realized. For the tramway tunnel, a budget of about HFL 195 million is reserved, coming down to HFL 156 thousand (approximately $80 thousand) per metre. The tunnel will be built in an excavation ('cut-and-cover method'), allowing a rather complicated construction that incorporates the tramway tunnel, stations and an underground parking facility. The other project is a bored tunnel (second 'Heinenoordtunnel') passing a waterway. It consists of two tubes of 7.5 metre diameter each with a combined length of about 1900 metres. As it functions as a cross-river link, it has no stations, but it has complicated entrance facilities. The total costs are estimated at HFL 300 million, thus about HFL 160 thousand ($80 thousand) per metre.

One may assume that the costs of an 'underground link-type' tunnel of a diameter of about 7.5 metres will be comparable to or lower (scale-effects) than the 'section type'. Tunnels with smaller diameters are significantly cheaper. The estimated costs for a 4.8 metre diameter tunnel are HFL 40 thousand ($20 thousand). When looking to tube networks for goods transport, these costs are much too high to be acceptable. Therefore, research aims at logistic concepts that are able to use tubes with smaller diameters. These tubes are again cheaper: an estimated HFL 10 thousand ($5 thousand) per metre for a 2.2 metre diameter tube and about HFL 5 thousand ($2.5 thousand) for a 1.2 metre tube. The latter will be constructed by pressing tunnel segments into the soil ('pipe-jacking'). The costs of access points range from HFL 6 million for a small unit (servicing a neighbourhood), HFL 12 million serving a district, and up to HFL 90 million for a centre serving a substantial part of an urban area (50,000 to 80,000 inhabitants).

Investments for an underground network serving Utrecht, a city of about 250,000 inhabitants, would be about HFL 2 billion ($1 billion). Such a network consists of three large service centres, six district service centres, about 70 small neighbourhood service centres, and a total network length of 123 kilometres. More than 7800 small, specially designed, vehicles transport 3.2 million tons of goods annually (see Brouwer et al., 1997 and Visser et al., 1998). Table 8.3 compares the different characteristics of the four underground concepts.

CHANGES IN LOGISTICS

Changes in Logistic Performance

The introduction of underground distribution concepts will change logistic performance, for example, average delivery times and reliability of deliveries.

Table 8.3 Comparison of underground goods transportation systems

	Adapted logistic system necessary?	Specialized vehicles necessary?	Inter-modality?	Typical tube diameter (m)	Typical cost per metre ($ thousand)
Section	No	No	No	7.5	80
Link*	No	No	No	7.5	80
	Possibly	Possibly	Possibly	4.8	20 +
	Yes	Yes	Yes	2.2	5
Network*	Yes	Yes	Yes	4.8	20
	Yes	Yes	Yes	2.2	5
	Yes	Yes	Yes	1.2	2.5

Note: * Describes different options.

Underground distribution is not the only possible way to improve urban goods distribution. To compare possible alternatives, we distinguish five distribution models:

- I. direct distribution;
- II. round trips;
- III. direct distribution originating from a UDC;
- IV. round trips originating from a UDC; and
- V. underground systems.

In model I (Figure 8.7), goods are directly transported from their origin address to the addressee. No consolidation takes place, no transshipments are necessary and fewest detours (only imposed by the physical network structure) are needed. The model is often used for distributing larger shipments.

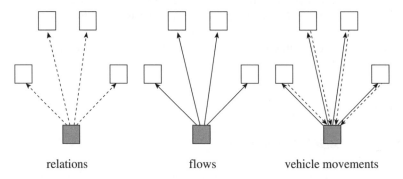

relations   flows   vehicle movements

Figure 8.7 Direct distribution (I)

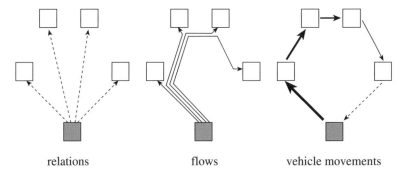

relations   flows   vehicle movements

Figure 8.8   Round trips (II)

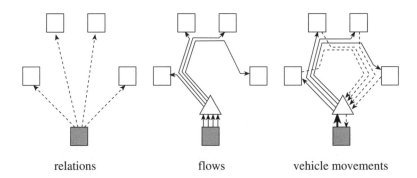

relations   flows   vehicle movements

Figure 8.9   Underground system: direct distribution (V)

In model II (Figure 8.8) goods are distributed by round trips. The system is often used to distribute small shipments in a cost-efficient way. The model requires both transshipments and some form of consolidation.

Models III and IV are based on the urban distribution concept which uses one or more central distribution centres for an urban area in which goods are consolidated prior to be further distributed. The underground alternative model V refers to a full underground distribution system (see Figure 8.9).

Table 8.4 shows estimates for average speeds which are based on a maximum speed[1] on the one hand (determined by the type of infrastructure) and an average stopping distance on the other hand.[2] Because in underground networks the stopping distance is significantly larger than in surface operation, the average speed will be considerably higher at a given maximum speed. To obtain a certain operational speed, in underground systems we need lower maximum speeds than in surface operations.

The average speed does not give the complete picture since the logistic models III, IV and V require transshipments, while IV also requires consolidation.

Table 8.4   Logistic concepts with average speeds at links

		Urban through-roads (km/h)	Narrow urban roads (km/h)
I + II	Traditional surface distribution	27	20
III + IV	UDC (surface) distribution	27	20
III	UDC + direct distribution	30	21
IV	UDC + round trips	30	21
V	UUFT + direct distribution	35	25

Note: UDC: Urban distribution centre or urban logistic park; UUFT: Underground urban freight transport.

Transshipments and consolidation are time-consuming, so the travel times will increase. Table 8.5 shows the results of rough calculations of logistic performance for the city of Delft (about 100,000 inhabitants). In this calculation no waiting times are included. The standard deviation indicates the difference in transportation times between earlier and later deliveries in round trips. Large differences may pose problems for addressees since they cannot be sure when consignments will arrive. This uncertainty in delivery times can be resolved

Table 8.5   Logistic concepts with delivery times

		Average delivery time (minutes)	Standard deviation (minutes)	Delivery time, index I = 100	Delivery time, index V = 100
I	Direct distribution	7.2	0.4	100	85
II	Round trips	14.6	5.5	203	173
III	UDC + direct distribution	8.9	0.3	124	106
IV	UDC + round trips	22.4	5.5	310	265
V	UUT + underground direct	8.4	0.2	117	100

partly by introducing smart planning systems: better estimates of planned delivery times can then be made. Nevertheless, round trips will lead to higher mean transportation times than direct distribution.

From Table 8.5, we may conclude that direct distribution will be faster than the other possible distribution methods, including underground transport: transshipments and round trips increase transportation time too much. When comparing alternatives II to V we may conclude that underground transportation is the best alternative for direct distribution.

Note that consolidation makes sense if cost reductions or other (societal) benefits can be achieved; for example, a reduction in vehicle-kilometres or smaller vehicle fleets. In the proposed underground system, consolidation is not an issue due to the small vehicles that are used. Because the operation of these vehicles is relatively cheap (there are no drivers) and the possible negative side-effects are largely 'encapsulated' (underground infrastructure), this poses no real problems.

Adapted Logistics: Prerequisite or Spin-off?

The above sketched 'underground link' and especially 'underground network' alternatives may need adapted logistic systems to operate efficiently. This adaptation comes down to a higher spatial consolidation of goods flows: the flows have to pass through a limited number of service centres and use a low-density network.

The underground system may look like an urban distribution system, but there are important differences. In a typical urban distribution process incoming goods in the UDC are taken out of delivering vehicles (decomposition) and redistributed over UDC vehicles (recomposition) so goods for the addressees in a round trip are combined (consolidated distribution). In a typical underground distribution process incoming goods in the urban underground freight transportation system (UUFT) are also taken out of the delivering vehicles and then directly transferred to small underground transportation vehicles. The only time when recomposition takes place is if small consignments for one addressee are combined. See Table 8.6 for the characteristics of both concepts. These decomposition/recomposition activities seem to interfere with 'modern' logistic concepts which aim to skip as many intermediaries as possible. However, these activities also allow the introduction of new transportation concepts outside the urban areas.

Remarkably, two strongly opposing developments can take place. On the one hand, if short-term storage is accepted at the service points, consolidated transportation at the inter-city links can take place. This development allows a redesign of the logistic chains in the way consignments coming from factories are 'recomposed' near their final destinations. Visser et al. (1998) show that

Table 8.6   Comparison of surface and underground goods distribution

	Urban (surface) distribution (UDC)	Underground distribution (UUFT)
Vehicle size (load capacity)	2–5 m^3	1 m^3
Distribution system	Round trips	Direct distribution
Ingoing flows*	Decomposition	Decomposition
Outgoing flows*	Consolidated	Individual shipments

Note: *Relative to the distribution centre or terminal; all city inbound goods flows.

this can reduce transportation costs significantly. On the other hand, in the future the local urban systems can be combined to regional or even national automated systems. In these systems, direct, fully non-consolidated transportation takes place. Although this last perspective is achievable only in the distant future, it can strengthen the tendency of less 'batch-processing' and more 'continuous processing' in the entire logistic chain.

CHANGES IN TRAFFIC CONDITIONS

Discrete Improvements in Accessibility

Surface infrastructure offers a seemingly unrestricted number of entrance points to the system: in urban areas every stretch of a road theoretically can act as a loading/unloading point. In practice, the number of access points is restricted by legislation, although often this regulation is abused on a regular basis. In underground transport, the number of access points is physically limited to the built entrance facilities. Therefore, the access-point density of underground transportation systems is lower than that of surface, road-bound systems. These access points and their vicinity offer a considerable improvement in accessibility, while points at a larger distance can only benefit in a limited way. Therefore, underground transportation systems improve accessibility in a discrete way, for example, only in the vicinity of access points (see Figure 8.10).

Better Traffic Performance of Underground Goods Distribution

A main difference between a mixed traffic surface distribution system and a dedicated underground distribution system is the traffic condition. In mixed

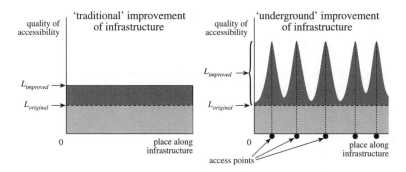

Figure 8.10   'Discrete' improvement in accessibility

traffic in a surface (road) network, vehicles have to stop regularly to give way for traffic lights, pedestrian crossings and so on. In an underground system the number of 'unplanned' stops is very limited.

Stop-and-go traffic limits the average speed drastically. In a typical urban situation the maximum speed is 50 km/h and on average every one-third kilometre there is a 'full stop', giving an average speed of about 30 km/h. In an underground system the assumed average stopping distance is about one kilometre. Given a maximum speed of 40 km/h, the average speed is still 35 km/h. To compete with surface systems (in mixed traffic conditions), for underground systems a maximum speed of 30–40 km/h will suffice.

Next to average speed, intensity (related to road capacity) is an important issue. Alas, little is known about the exact capacity of mixed traffic situations, especially if we want to 'assign' capacity to a certain user group.

The capacity of a linear stretch of road can be calculated using a vehicle-following model that describes the behaviour of vehicles that drive in succession. In the 'prudent follower' model, a driver following a preceding vehicle assumes that the preceding vehicle cannot come to a full stop instantly. Therefore, the distance between the vehicles is not too large. Based on this model and assuming realistic maximum deceleration rates of 3.5 to 4.0 m/s^2, a capacity of about 1880 vehicles per hour is estimated for a main artery. If at maximum 20 per cent of this capacity can be used by goods vehicles, a figure we can derive from practice, the effective capacity is about 380 goods vehicles an hour. Automated systems will use a safer model, based on the assumption that the vehicle cannot anticipate all possible traffic conditions. The model therefore assumes that a preceding vehicle (or a falling object) can block the road instantaneously. Based on this 'brick wall' model, the capacity is only 1200 vehicles per hour, but in dedicated underground links, the full capacity is available for goods transport.

If an advanced, automated system could use an anticipating vehicle-following strategy (prudent follower), a capacity of 2500 vehicles per hour is achievable. This means that an underground, autonomous, dedicated link has an effective capacity that is up to seven times larger than the effective capacity for goods vehicles of a surface, mixed traffic road. Therefore an underground network has large consolidation opportunities which partly justifies the high costs of underground infrastructures.

Lower Goods Traffic Densities at Surface

An underground system designed to transport goods may theoretically replace about 80 per cent of the trips of goods transportation vehicles in an urban area. In practice, because of measures of load, specialized goods and logistic reasons, this share will be lower. Nevertheless, a large share of total urban goods transportation will 'disappear' into tunnels. To obtain exact figures, an in-depth profound study of business behaviour, urban legislation and urban characteristics is needed.

We estimate a modal shift somewhere in the range between 50 per cent and 80 per cent of goods transport trips in a city – and for such a modal shift a complete underground distribution network will be necessary. If goods transportation comprises 20 per cent of total capacity at a goods transport peak period, effective overall capacity gains of 10–15 per cent in those periods will be achievable. A decrease in goods vehicle-kilometres on the surface will have an important positive impact on traffic safety, although it should be noted that the underground system replaces just a minor share of the heaviest lorries.

CHANGES IN ENVIRONMENTAL CONDITIONS

Less Local Pollution

In operation, underground transportation systems cause less local environmental damage than their surface counterparts. Since goods vehicles are responsible for a large share of noise pollution, an underground urban distribution system will decrease noise levels. For vehicles that are replaced by the underground transportation system, the noise pollution is reduced to a minimum. However, massive changes must not be expected: underground transportation alternatives as sketched above replace mainly light vehicles such as vans and small lorries. The system does not eliminate heavy goods vehicles (for example, transporting building materials).

A noise-associated problem may be slight tremors in the soil resulting from running vehicles in underground infrastructure. This problem can be resolved by using rubber tyres or, in the case of steel rails and wheels, rubber mountings of the rails and sleepers and other types of dampers.

Local air pollution can be controlled or reduced because underground-produced emissions can escape the underground infrastructure only through specially designed conducts. Furthermore, electric-powered vehicles, which do not produce local emissions at all, will probably use the underground network. Of course, physical hindrance and visual intrusion are eliminated.

Less Energy Use in the Operational Phase

Energy use for propulsion in underground networks or links is significantly less than in surface situations, that is: underground autonomy (so independent, undisturbed) requires significantly less energy than surface mixed stop-and-go traffic. An average speed of 30 km/h in stop-and-go traffic requires 0.81 MJ of net energy or gross 18.3 litres of gasoline per 100 km for a van. The same vehicle uses only 0.37 MJH (net) or 10.7 l/100 km fuel (gross) when driving at a consistent speed of 30 km/h. This means that gains of about 40 per cent can be achieved. In practice, gains may be less due to lower average load factors and detours in underground networks. Note that contrary to what may be expected, the energy use for vertical transportation is negligible compared to the energy use of 'horizontal' transport.[3]

Uncertain Overall Effects

The environmental effects stated above refer to the operational phase and to local effects. The overall effects of underground transportation may be less positive. The construction of the infrastructure not only requires an investment in capital, but it also needs 'investments' in energy for excavating soil and constructing the actual underground infrastructure. In traditional (surface) road infrastructure this so-called indirect energy use ranges from about 0.2 up to 1.3 MJ/ton km (Bos, 1998a and b), of which the higher estimate is more than 20 per cent of the direct energy use of 6.0 MJ/ton km.[4] One may expect that the energy required to construct underground infrastructures is higher than for surface infrastructure, so the indirect energy use could easily mount to about 2–3 MJ/ton km.[5] Like monetary investments, the lower direct energy use must first recoup this 'energy investment'.

Looking at the figures, a net positive result will eventually be achieved, but the 'return of ecological investment' period can be years or even decades. With respect to local pollution, the total effect also relates to the share and type of traffic that is replaced by underground transport. Although in absolute figures a lot of progress is expected, in relative figures the effects may be somewhat

disappointing since passenger traffic and heavy goods traffic (building materials) still run in urban streets.

CONCLUSIONS

From the above we may draw conclusions with respect to investment costs,
efficiency gains and effects on the environment.

Costs and Logistic Efficiency

The required heavy investment costs play a prominent role in discussions
about underground transport. Given the fact that surface infrastructure is
provided by public parties, there will be no big urge by private parties to
wholly finance and exploit a competing underground system. Therefore, at
least a public–private partnership will be necessary. The investment costs
strongly depend on the tube diameter, the construction method used and the
local circumstances. Therefore, estimations of investment costs and related
user costs vary widely. Compared to surface operations, operational costs will
be lower, because in the underground network automated vehicles will be
used. The level of total variable costs (user costs and operational costs) will
vary according to the investment costs and public policy. If public parties take
care of a reasonable part of the initial investment costs, the systems could be
economically feasible (Visser and van Binsbergen 1997).

Underground networks will provide a new way of distributing goods, but
will at the same time need completely new logistic concepts. In these new
concepts, the intermodal transfer (from surface to underground transport vehicles) is not necessarily an additional transfer, but is embedded in the logistics
system of consolidation and deconsolidation. Direct (surface) distribution will
mostly stay the fastest mode of transport, but underground distribution will be
significantly faster than combined distribution concepts.

Environmental and Other Gains

Underground networks can release 10–15 per cent of capacity at surface roads,
so initially road intensities will decrease. Without further actions, these gains
may be 'lost' to other traffic that fill the gap, but economic theory shows that
this is also beneficial for society.

Underground networks will reduce the number of trips of light- to medium-
goods vehicles significantly, but only marginally the number of trips of very
heavy vehicles. The system limits the number of trip ends in inner cities significantly and therefore helps to solve one important spatial problem.

Transportation by underground systems causes much less hindrance than transportation at surface level due to encapsulation, underground situation and autonomous transport operations. It also results in energy gains (up to 40 per cent) in the operational phase that is to be attributed mainly to the homogeneous traffic flow. It must be noted, however, that the energy requirements in the construction phase are significant.

Sustainability

From social, economical and environmental perspectives, underground goods distribution systems could be a really sustainable transportation means. If the system is designed and used properly, the investment costs can be recovered (especially if societal gains are taken into account), and energy use, emissions, noise problems, physical hindrance and traffic safety problems will be reduced. Nevertheless, underground goods distribution systems will certainly not solve all goods transportation problems, since a major share of goods transportation cannot be handled by the underground system. Also, building the system can cause major disruptions that may not be acceptable. Therefore, the advantages and disadvantages of the system for a specific situation must always be determined, but all in all, underground goods distribution is a promising way of efficiently transporting goods into urban areas while at the same time limiting the negative side-effects related to goods transport.

NOTES

1. The speed a driver would maintain in a free-flow situation.
2. A calculation method in which all deceleration (braking) instances are modelled to a certain number of instances a vehicle comes completely to a halt.
3. Lifting a weight of 1000 kg over 20 metres requires about 0.2 MJ net energy, equivalent to about 200 metres of 'horizontal' driving; of course, in underground networks the horizontal driving distance is far more than the vertical distance – in an average 'horizontal' intra-city trip of 15 km (Visser et al., 1998), a maximum vertical lifting height of 2×20 m is needed, a ratio of 375 to one.
4. Note that the energy requirements depend strongly on assumptions about speed, average loading and so on; the direct energy requirement calculations are based on a van (GWT 3500 kg, payload 1000 kg), the high estimates for indirect energy use in traditional transport are based on a light truck.
5. On this aspect thus far no exact calculations have been made but it must be noted that in traditional infrastructure construction also, large quantities of soil are displaced – therefore the estimate should not be exaggerated.

REFERENCES

Bos, A.J.M. (1998a), *Direction Indirect, the Indirect Energy Requirements and Emissions from Freight Transport*, Groningen: Rijksuniversiteit Groningen.

Bos, A.J.M. (1998b), Interview.

Brouwer, W., W.E. van Lierop, G.A.A. Erens, A.F.C. Carlebur and J.G.S.N. Visser (1997), *Tube Transport for Urban Goods Transportation* (in Dutch: *Buisleidingtransport (BLT) voor stedelijk goederenvervoer deel A/B*, DTO-Werkdocument M9/M10), Delft: DTO.

Clarke, M. and D. Wright (1993), *Metro Freight, a New Direction for Transport*, various reports, Cranfield, Bedfordshire: Cranfield School of Management.

Koshi, M. (1992), 'An automated underground tube network for urban goods transport', in *IATSS Research 16*, no. 2, Tokyo: International Association for Traffic and Safety Sciences (IATSS), pp. 50–56.

Ogden, K.W. (1992), *Urban Goods Movement, a Guide to Policy and Planning*, Cambridge: Cambridge University Press.

van Binsbergen, A.J., Th.J.H. Schoemaker and C.D. van Goeverden (1995), *Underground Transportation Opportunities, A Systematic Survey* (in Dutch: *Ondergrondse transportmogelijkheden doorgrond, een systematische verkenning*), Projectbureau IVVS/TRAIL Research School, Den Haag/Delft.

Visser, J.G.S.N. and A.J. van Binsbergen (1997), 'Underground networks for freight transport. A dedicated infrastructure for intermodal short-distance freight transport', in Third TRAIL Year Congress 1997, *Transport, Infrastructure and Logistics, New Times and Innovative Solutions Offered*, October, Delft: TRAIL Research School.

Visser, J.G.S.N., A.J.M. Vermunt and A.J. van Binsbergen (1998), *Spatial Concepts for Underground Transportation* (in Dutch: *Ruimtelijke concepten ondergronds transport*), Delft/Hoeven: TRAIL Research School.

PART III

Spatial Aspects

9. Public transport-orientated urban design: plans and possibilities

Stephen Marshall

INTRODUCTION

Transit-orientated development, transit corridor districts and transit villages are all manifestations of public transport-orientated urban design, or the use of urban design and physical planning to facilitate public transport use. In the context of the drive towards sustainable solutions to transport provision, public transport-orientated urban design relates sustainable modes of transport to the design of the built environment.

The justification for promoting public transport has generally been derived from reasons of operational efficiency (high-capacity systems able to move large numbers of people) and equity (providing a service for those who do not have access to private transport), and has been given particular contemporary significance by the increasing concerns for the environment and the desire for achieving sustainable mobility.

Settlement forms have traditionally been associated with particular forms of mobility: from cities of the pre-motorized age based on movement on foot, through public transport-influenced development patterns (railway and street-car suburbs) to forms geared to use of the private car. With renewed interest in public transport, the forms orientated towards rail- and bus-based travel have become the object of various works of speculation and evaluation.

Public transport systems can be influential in the design of urban areas at a variety of scales. At the macro scale, the main public transport routes may act as 'structural axes' or 'spine routes' which help shape the structure of settlements as a whole. At the micro scale, the location and detailed design of public transport stops can influence local accessibility and environmental amenity, both of which can boost the attractiveness of travelling by public transport.

Public transport-orientated urban design contrasts with 'conventional suburban' design which is considered to be car orientated, typically featuring a hierarchical system of roads, circuitous loop roads and culs-de-sac, generally impermeable to public transport penetration and direct pedestrian connectivity, and low density, mono-use development which tends to create long distances between points of activity and demand.

For the purposes of this chapter, public transport-orientated urban design is taken to include access by non-motorized modes (walking, cycling) but not access by car (park and ride). While promotion of access by car might boost patronage, the maximization of public transport use *per se* is not taken here as the overriding objective of public transport-orientated urban design. Rather, the objective is the pursuit of an integrated planning policy that promotes both sustainable mobility and sustainable urbanity as a package.

As will be demonstrated in this chapter, the acceptance and advocacy of public transport orientation is widespread. However, public transport-orientated urban design has to overcome several obstacles. The first is whether the form of urban development can actually encourage public transport use. For example, Berman (1996) describes the 'myth of neo-traditional development', in effect questioning the belief that development which replicates traditional urban forms will give rise to traditional patterns of travel, such as public transport use. Second, there is the question as to whether public transport (particularly rail-based transport) is a worthwhile solution in the first place (Pickrell, 1992; Richmond, 1998), and the related question as to whether it is properly 'sustainable'. Finally, there is the question as to whether the design solutions devised and promoted as being 'public transport-orientated' actually possess the desired properties that are understood to be supportive of public transport use.

This chapter is principally concerned with the last of these, and therefore sets out first to investigate those properties understood to support public transport use, and then to explore possibilities for further developing public transport-orientated solutions for urban layouts. The chapter does not, however, attempt to evaluate the effects of different urban forms on actual travel behaviour, which is a distinct exercise in its own right, evaluated for example by Cervero and Gorham (1995), Transportation Research Board (1996), Stead and Marshall (1998), Stead (1999), Williams et al. (2000).

THE RATIONALE FOR PUBLIC TRANSPORT ORIENTATION

The transport structure of a settlement can be a key determinant of overall urban spatial structure and settlement form, and can be a significant influence on patterns of movement. The integration of public transport routes, land uses and activities is regarded as being crucial for the efficient functioning of the settlement and for promoting sustainable mobility (DETR, 1998a, 1998b, 1998c).

Possible influences of urban form and layout include the use and distribution of buildings, which can influence overall patterns of travel, and the patterns of connection to the transport network, which can influence modal split. Moreover, the design of built form itself can provide orientation, visual interest, security and shelter, all of which can render the environment more amenable for people accessing public transport by foot or other non-motorized means.

These considerations are proposed or recommended in a variety of sources. For example, the design guide *Sustainable Settlements* argues that the viability of public transport can be effectively predetermined by layout considerations, where achieving the most effective public transport configuration is given high priority for the design of the settlement as a whole (Barton et al., 1995). As Punter and Carmona (1997, p. 179) point out, 'Clearly, layouts cannot themselves ensure provision of public transport, but the disposition of roads and footpaths and the densities created can establish the necessary preconditions for such provision'.

This element of providing options is echoed by Calthorpe (1989), whose 'pedestrian pockets' aim to create an environment that offers choices. Cervero and Gorham (1995, p. 210) observe that, in contrast, 'many modern suburbs limit travel choice by physically designing out all but the automobile option'. Although the main point of the discussion here is referred to as public transport orientation, the whole rationale for public transport orientation in urban design – the aspiration to design development and locales which promote public transport use – necessarily includes more than the public transport system itself, but is innately concerned with the question of access: 'The attractiveness of public transport is determined as much by the quality and convenience of access to and from it as by the quality, frequency and reliability of the services themselves' (DoE/DoT, 1995, p. 11).

This means consideration of other modes – normally, at least, the pedestrian. Walking and public transport can be seen as 'two sides of the same coin' (Garbrecht, 1997). Indeed, it has been suggested that while 'a healthy walking environment can succeed without transit . . . a transit system cannot exist without the pedestrian' (Calthorpe, 1993, p. 42). Public transport orientation can therefore be seen both as an intermodal strategy (integrated transport) as well as one uniting transport with land use and built form (integrated planning).

The concept of public transport orientation is therefore arguably as much to do with the attributes of the pedestrian mode (or more properly any non-motorized modes used for access, including cycles and access by wheelchair) as it is with the detailed attributes of the public transport mode itself, which for the purposes of the present discussion may almost interchangeably be assumed to be bus, tram or rail, or indeed any high capacity public service accessed at discrete points.

Accordingly, public transport orientation becomes concerned with urban design issues such as density and layout. Higher density is equated with encouraging walking and cycling, and hence supporting the viability of public transport (Houghton and Hunter, 1994). In terms of layout, it is arguably the location of stops or stations that is critical. According to Baker (1977, p. 205), 'It is the station, alone, which makes the system accessible to the public. Routes serve simply to join up the stations. There is little point in considering the route before likely station locations can be found'.

Although the pedestrian role is important for access, the requirements for transit-friendly design do not, however, wholly overlap with those for pedestrian-friendly design. This is not only because not all public transport users gain access on foot, but because those pedestrians who do access public transport will have slightly different requirements compared with those walking for other purposes (Ewing, 1996). Nevertheless, in general it is reasonable to argue, at least, that good design for pedestrian movement in general should also favour pedestrian access to public transport.

The support for public transport-orientated urban design may now appear to be a consensus with a gathering momentum. However, it has not always been this way. In the past the seemingly obvious idea of laying out development around public transport stops was often absent from town plans, and public transport in general was often overlooked or positively disadvantaged (White, 1995).

This was particularly so in the 'modernist' era of town planning. As an example, it could be noted that the British new towns – supposedly at the vanguard of town design at the time – were often established with road layouts considered inconvenient for the provision of bus services and in some cases had only peripheral railway stations (for example, Glenrothes, Livingston) or no stations at all (for example, Washington, Skelmersdale).

Of course, nowadays, not only is public transport taken into due consideration, but may actually be prioritized: 'While most modern development planning uses the road network as the key structural element, a sustainable design takes the circulation of people on foot and bike, and the effectiveness of public transport as starting points' (Barton et al., 1995, p. 105). Strategic land-use planning and the location of new development are now routinely considered in terms of their public transport accessibility (Maat, 2000), while the detailed layout of housing areas also requires consideration of access by public transport (DETR, 1998b). Public transport may be prioritized both in terms of space (bus lanes and bus gates) and time (precedence at traffic signals), and may be elevated, in principle at least, above the car and other traffic in more progressive road hierarchies (or 'hierarchies of users') (Hanna, 1997). Finally, public transport strategies of many varieties may be used as part of a policy package to reduce the overall amount of travel (Banister and Marshall, 2000).

It is to those particular means of promoting public transport through urban design and layout that we now turn as we investigate the 'emerging consensus'.

THE EMERGING CONSENSUS

Public transport-orientated urban design has been in existence for a long time, albeit appearing in various different forms and contexts over the years. The revival of interest in public transport orientation in Western countries which had previously rather neglected it as a priority effectively represents an emerging consensus, which can be regarded as a baseline from which to consider possibilities for further development.

The persistence of the ideals of public transport orientation, and advocacy for their forms, is notable both from a historical perspective and in terms of their current manifestation in the pursuit of sustainable settlements. Calthorpe's pedestrian pockets have been described as 'nothing more or less than a railway suburb for the 1990s' (Hall, 1992, p. 9), while transit villages have been related back to the ideas of Ebenezer Howard (Cervero, 1994). Ebenezer Howard's ideas for the Garden City included the proposal that 'no inhabitant of the city is more than 660 yards from the railway' (Howard, [1904] 1998, p. 17). Public transport orientation can also be traced through plans for linear cities (Houghton-Evans, 1975) and streetcar suburbs, and concepts of public transport orientation are nowadays suggested for the retro-fitting of existing urban corridors (Loukaitou-Sideris, 1993).

While there are numerous stylistic varieties of public transport orientation, these tend to follow the same basic configurational theme (Figure 9.1).

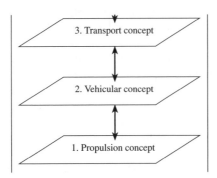

Note: See Tables 9.1 and 9.2 for examples.

Figure 9.1   *'Beads on a string': the classic proforma for public transport orientation*

Table 9.1   The emerging consensus in public transport orientation

Examples of public transport orientation

Sustainable Settlements: public transport magnets situated on a public transport 'spine'; development forms: 'beads and spacers', 'beads on a string', 'overlapping areas' (Barton et al., 1995).

Transit Corridor Districts (TCDs): would separate transit- and auto-orientated land uses. Such areas would have a mix of land uses with higher densities located near a transit route (Beimborn and Rabinowitz, 1991).

Transit Villages: moderately dense, mixed-use communities encouraging greater transit use (Bernick and Cervero, 1997).

Pedestrian Pocket: a balanced mixed-use area within a quarter mile or a five minute walking radius of a transit station (Calthorpe, 1989).

Transit-orientated Development (TOD): moderate and high-density housing, along with complementary public uses, jobs, retail and services, are concentrated in mixed-use developments at strategic points along the regional transit system (Calthorpe, 1993).

Corridors and Nodes: 'string of catchment areas'; major travel-generating development where routes terminate, meet or cross' (DoE/DoT, 1995).

Sociable Cities: new settlements focused on railway nodes, forming corridors, after Ebenezer Howard and others (Hall and Ward, 1998) .

Sustainable Urban Neighbourhoods: 'development concentrated in a string of compact centres along public transport routes' (SUNI, 1997).

'Stars and Stripes': 'stars' are the radial cycle or pedestrian routes feeding the linear 'stripes' of the bus or rail routes. Cycle stores, cafes, shops, shelters and gardens are located at the centre of the 'stars' (Turner, 1996).

Plan for North Bucks New City: townships to be placed along the overhead monorail, like 'beads on a string' (Bendixson and Platt, 1992).

Activity Centres (Milton Keynes): bus stops, shops, pubs and schools to be grouped at 'activity centres' (MKDC, 1970).

Table 9.2 Examples of catchment area attributes

Case	Land use or activity within catchment area	Distance	Walk time
Barton et al. (1995)	Public transport 'magnets' set along public transport spine	400m (or 300m radius)	
Beimborn and Rabinowitz (1991)	Separation of transit corridors and highway arterials	¼ to ¾ mile	
Bendixson and Platt (1992)	Maximum walk time from house to station		7 mins
Calthorpe (1989)	Radius from transit station	¼ mile	5 mins
Ewing (1996)	What transit users will walk	¼ mile	5 mins
IHT (1999)	Walk distance within corridor either side of bus route	400m (300m preferable)	
MKDC (1970)	Walking distance from activity centre	500m	
SUNI (1997)	Area of circle drawn round bus stops (on example plan)	160m (diameter)	2 mins (straight line) or 5 mins
SUNI (1997)	'Optimum' or 'comfortable' walk	800m	10 mins
SUNI (1997)	Distance people will walk with shopping	400m	
White (1995)	Likely walk distance based partly on journey purpose (less for shopping, more for commuting) and mode (higher for railway)	Probability distribution, max. 1km (railway)	

Indeed, the form of development which is 'concentrated in a string of compact centres along public transport routes' is now widely accepted (SUNI, 1997, p. 4).

Examples of public transport orientation are described in Tables 9.1 (over-all form) and 9.2 (catchment area characteristics). The recurring themes which appear to demonstrate the emergence of a consensus may be summarized in eight key principles of public transport orientation as follows:

1. Each public transport stop has an associated catchment area, within which the activities that are supposed to be served by the stop are located.
2. The size of this catchment area is usually determined by a desirable maximum walking distance. This is normally based on about half a kilometre or 5 minutes' walk, but may vary with assumed journey purpose and public transport mode (White, 1995).
3. The shape of the catchment area is often equated, at least theoretically, with a circular locus around the public transport stop.
4. The loci for adjacent stops may overlap, forming a corridor, or there may be clear green space between loci.
5. A succession of loci situated along the transport route, each focused on a public transport stop, form the characteristic 'beads on a string' pattern.
6. Street patterns tend to 'focus' movement on public transport stops, often suggesting access routes 'radiating' from the stop.
7. There should be greater densities and intensities of use nearer to the public transport stop.
8. Particular types of land uses should be formed around the stop – typically retail or community services – to create a mixed-use focal point.

Additional features present in some examples – while not explicitly excluded from the remainder – may be identified as follows:

*   the presence of less-intensive, probably car-orientated land uses beyond the immediate loci of the stops, sometimes separated from the rest of the development by the transport route itself (for example, 'secondary areas' – Calthorpe, 1993);
*   the possible separation of the arterial highway system from the public transport route (Beimborn and Rabinowitz, 1991);
*   grid-like street patterns may be favoured as they allow direct routes for pedestrian access and minimize the need for turning and backtracking for public transport vehicles (Ewing, 1996; Beimborn and Rabinowitz, 1991). However, there is not unqualified approval of grid patterns to the exclusion of other forms, and hybrid networks have also been suggested (Ewing, 1996);

- short block lengths can create the potential for more direct routes and a greater choice of routes which are regarded as being desirable to the pedestrian (Ewing, 1996). Small block sizes also allow for greater permeability and activity at central locations (TRL, 1997).

The general principles of public transport-orientated urban design as outlined above feature in numerous specific works of advocacy such as design guides and illustrative prototypes, and can also be seen built out on the ground, as discussed in the following sections.

Design Guides and Illustrative Prototypes

In *Pedestrian- and Transit-friendly Design*, Ewing (1996) notes that about 40 manuals relating to transit-orientated developments are available in North America alone. Synthesizing the results of a review of these with findings from empirical investigations, Ewing has identified a list of 'essential' and 'highly desirable' characteristics which would ideally feature in areas served by public transport. These are compiled (together with less essential 'nice additions') in Table 9.3.

Calthorpe's transit-orientated development (TOD) aims not only to support the public transport service, but to encourage walking and cycling while reducing car dependency, and also to create distinct, identifiable neighbourhoods. Transit corridor districts (TCDs) as formulated by Beimborn and Rabinowitz (1991) would use zoning to designate transit- and auto-orientated land uses; the 'transit-sensitive' land-use design would feature a mix of land uses with higher densities located near the transit route. TCDs encourage direct connection of activity centres by transit, while TODs allow for a system of trunk lines and feeder routes.

Bernick and Cervero (1997) suggest that transit villages can, by design, invite greater use of transit and less car use. Owners (1996, p. 287) relates the walkability of the urban locale to the transportation system: 'The *quarters*, of walkable dimensions, are then seen to link to form a mosaic, overlaid on the city *mesh*, (of infrastructure)' (original italics). Meanwhile Morris and Kaufman (1998) refer to the walkable catchments as 'Ped Sheds' – loci analogous to the 'watersheds' of pedestrian flow.

In *Sustainable Settlements*, the authors take the 400m walking distance and equate this with a theoretical circular catchment of radius 300m, allowing for a maximum route deflection of 15 to 20 per cent (Barton et al., 1995). They also demonstrate the implications of different stop spacings for the resulting urban forms, characterized as 'beads and spacers', 'beads on a string' and 'overlapping areas' for stop spacings of 800m, 600m and 400m, respectively.

Table 9.3   Checklist of pedestrian- and transit-friendly features

Category	Features
'Essentials'	1. Medium-to-high densities
	2. Mix of land uses
	3. Short-to-medium length blocks
	4. Transit routes every half-mile
	5. Two- or four-lane streets (with rare exceptions)
	6. Continuous sidewalks wide enough for couples
	7. Safe crossings
	8. Appropriate buffering from traffic
	9. Street-oriented buildings
	10. Comfortable and safe places to wait
'Highly Desirables'	1. Supportive commercial uses
	2. Grid-like street networks
	3. Traffic calming along access routes
	4. Closely spaced shade trees along access routes
	5. Not much 'dead space' (or visible parking)
	6. Nearby parks and other public spaces
	7. Small-scale buildings
	8. Classy looking transit facilities
'Nice Additions'	1. 'Streetwalls'
	2. Functional street furniture
	3. Coherent, small-scale signage
	4. Special pavement
	5. Lovable objects, especially public art

Source: Compiled from Ewing (1996).

In addition to these specific intentions of public transport-orientated devices, many of the individual principles are espoused independently in other circumstances. For example, White (1976) depicts bus routes with their theoretically circular catchment areas skewed according to the direction of travel; Lynch (1991) advocates higher density clusters of development around transit stations; Llewelyn-Davies (1968, p. 45) describes natural towns growing 'like crystals on a thread, around pre-existing transport routes'.

Implemented Plans

The principles of public transport orientation have been successfully applied in practice, in the design and retrofitting of many settlements.

Notwithstanding the earlier examples to the contrary, the British new towns are often (in theory at least) public transport-orientated. These cases include quite explicit examples, such as Runcorn with its dedicated busway – taken as the principal 'structural' feature of the town plan – around which housing development is laid out like beads on a string (RDC, 1967) or Irvine with its 'community routes' where shops and services are aligned along bus-only links (IDC, 1971). They also include less obvious examples like Milton Keynes, which despite its car-orientated image was similarly conceived along the lines of 'activity centres' focused on bus stops (MKDC, 1974). Of course, the final physical form of Milton Keynes as-built contrasts strongly with the original plans for North Bucks New City, which were very heavily structured around the concept of the (monorail) transport node and its walk-in catchment, laid out quite explicitly like beads along a string (Barton et al., 1995).

Explicit public transport orientation is noted in examples of 'planned' settlements elsewhere. Almere, a new town in the Netherlands, has a network of bus-only links which provide more direct connections between adjacent neighbourhoods than the highways routes (DoE/DoT, 1995). Another Dutch new town, Houten, has a central railway station with direct cycle and bus connections radiating from it, while the road network is more indirect, requiring the more circuitous negotiation of a ring road (Kraay, 1996; Maat, 2000). Curitiba in Brazil is often cited as a 'model' public transport-orientated city, based along 'structural axes' served by high capacity express bus lanes (see, for example, TRL, 1997).

Critique

From consideration of a range of both prototype plans and examples on the ground, it is possible to discern a number of issues regarding points of detail which tend to detract from their public transport supportive intentions, or otherwise prompt caution over general desirability. These are itemized as follows:

1. *Radial focus of access routes* The use of a contrived, quasi-radial pattern of access routes to 'focus' movement around the public transport stop may not in fact provide optimal accessibility (Figure 9.2). Routes which in the abstract trace out radial axes, but which are actually staggered, interrupted or otherwise circuitous on the ground may be less direct than other patterns, such as a straightforward grid, and may therefore disadvantage

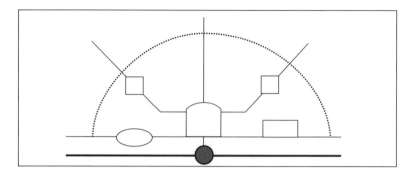

Source and note: Based on proposal for transit-orientated development in Calthorpe, 1993. However, the routes are not particularly direct, compromising accessibility. While the abstract radial axes are implicit, the actual paths are interrupted by small parks, requiring the pedestrian to make several deviations over a short distance.

Figure 9.2   A 'quasi-radial' pattern of access routes which appear to 'focus' on the public transport stop

pedestrian accessibility to the stop. Without compromising distance to the stop, alternative patterns could be employed, such as grids, which would be more flexible in terms of serving abutting land uses and in connecting a wider range of areas in a way that is more direct for desire lines not centred on the public transport stop.

2.   *Adverse differentiation*   In some cases excessive segregation by density may be counterproductive. This might happen if there is too strict a correlation of high density development next to public transport routes and low density development next to highway arterials, which may polarize the urban area into segregated zones. While from a public transport point of view this arrangement maximizes 'transit friendliness' for high density dwellers, at the same time it equally can be seen to countenance or even promote low density development for auto owners. Indeed, Maat (2000) notes that with the ABC location policy in the Netherlands, some businesses may prefer the car-accessible 'C' locations, and authorities the most flexible 'B' locations, rather than the dense, public transport-orientated nodes of the 'A' locations.

3.   *Viability and vitality*   Attempts to focus retail development at public transport nodes may be hindered if such nodes are (deliberately) remote from competing highway arterials. This may diminish the overall accessibility and hence viability of commercial development and perhaps favour competing development growing up along highway arterials remote from public transport. In general, the aspiration to create activity around a public transport stop is not sufficient in itself to establish a successful

transit-centred development. A supportive context will be crucial. Two key factors for successful development are a healthy local economy and planning policies which positively favour public transport related development (Walmsley and Perrett, 1992; Cervero, 1998; Banister and Berechman, 2000).

4. *Proximity of relevant land uses* The absolute scale of distances should be borne in mind – having facilities like shop fronts immediately by the stop are more likely to have the desired impact than situated at some remove albeit on a 'direct' route. The importance of proximity is also used as an argument for the success of bus orientation in Almere as opposed to in Runcorn or Milton Keynes. In Almere the bus gains closest access to the dense development of the central core without being isolated from it by a 'ring of car parks' (DoE/DoT, 1995).

5. *Pedestrian network context* The intention is that public transport stops should be located to serve the natural foci of pedestrian accessibility. In settlements where arterial traffic routes do not discourage pedestrian use, the most accessible nodes in the pedestrian-accessible network may well be the nodes of the arterial network, rather than any consciously devised nodal points in the dedicated pedestrian network. If on the other hand pedestrians are confined to an 'insular' network of dedicated pedestrian routes, which has poor overall connectivity relative to the traffic network, this may be sufficient to discourage pedestrian movement in the first place (Figure 9.3).

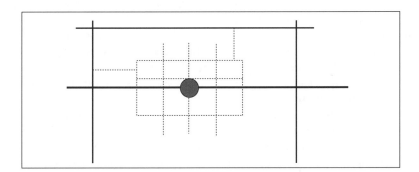

Note: The public transport stop is sited at the central node of the dedicated pedestrian network (dotted lines). However, the main system of arterial roads is the best connected large-scale grid, suggesting that these might become the most accessible and highly used pedestrian routes. Then the transit stops in the interior would suffer from being somewhat isolated.

Figure 9.3   Pedestrian network context

6. *Continuity*   As noted above, it is important that pedestrian networks are
    continuous and pedestrian routes connective in order to encourage move-
    ment on foot. Ewing argues that it is not sufficient to provide isolated
    'oases' for pedestrians, but rather that continuous networks should be
    provided (at least in the form of sidewalks along vehicular routes).
    Nevertheless, such routes can link any 'oases' that do emerge, which may
    also be coincident with nodal points in the pedestrian network.
7. *Access time and speed*   Access time to the public transport system may
    in some cases be more important than having a high running speed of the
    public transport mode itself. For example, while a high-speed busway
    'may reduce the in-bus journey time and the operating costs, high speed
    requires segregation from pedestrians which may itself reduce the acces-
    sibility of the system' (CBRPT, 1981, p. 38) An example is seen in the
    case of Runcorn's busway, where the 'railway like' busway is segregated
    and grade separated from the surrounding area, requiring ramps and
    access ways that make the bus stop somewhat remote from the adjacent
    demand (Lemberg, 1977). That said, in other circumstances, especially for
    longer-distance interurban travel, high speed may be a necessary part of a
    competitive public transport package.
8. *Degree of branching and angularity*   The overall accessibility from the
    stop (in the sense of the product of number of people times distance)
    depends on the density of activity per unit length of access route and the
    degree of branching of the access route pattern. In this sense a public
    transport stop located at a crossroads has greater potential than one at the
    end of a cul-de-sac access road. However, while branching boosts the
    number of routes on which demand-intensive land uses can be situated,
    the overall scale should be borne in mind, as the branching has to occur
    within the target locus in order to fulfil its potential. Also the degree of
    branching should not negatively influence density by creating angular
    plots which may be unsuitable for building on.
9. *The divisive artery*   The physical presence of public transport infrastruc-
    ture – particularly systems segregated or above or below grade – can be
    divisive to the detriment of local accessibility, although, assuming careful
    design, stop location can mitigate effects of route location. There is effec-
    tively a tradeoff here between local and settlement-wide accessibility. For
    example, a railway station served by several branching rail lines may
    isolate itself locally through severance of the urban fabric, while having
    good regional accessibility.

A key point emerging here is that settlement forms not planned specifically
for public transport orientation may often be suited for supporting public
transport use. When developing plans for public transport orientation,

therefore, designers must take care not to overlook successfully functioning *de facto* transit-orientated developments.

Thus, while the plan form of North Bucks New City plan (see, for example, Richards, 1969) is a literal interpretation of the configuration that we would now call a transit-orientated development, of course, there is no guarantee that it would function any better than later manifestations of public transport-orientated development, such as Milton Keynes's grid-based network with bus stops at 'activity centres'. For example, the North Bucks New City plan lacks some features often associated with existing transit-served areas, such as a retail corridor, or a public thoroughfare lined with shops.

In other words, a traditional gridlike townscape can behave just like a public transport-orientated node in practice. Indeed, Southworth and Ben-Joseph (1997) have demonstrated that traditional streetcar suburbs may perform better as pedestrian-orientated environments than supposedly pedestrian- and public transport-friendly neo-traditional developments.

A NOTE ON DETERMINISM

Any criticisms of plans and suggestions for improvements should bear in mind the possibility that 'public transport-orientated' design details may not turn out to be effective in promoting actual public transport use.

For example, as mentioned earlier, Berman (1996) questions the 'myth of neo-traditional development'. Similarly, Cervero and Gorham (1995) imply that the kind of detailed design used to create transit-orientated neighbourhoods may be ineffective in a car-dominated region. From another angle, Ewing (1996) suggests that if a transit-served area has enough potential riders, the precise layout of the area may matter only a little.

On the other hand, the local sensitivity may matter from another point of view: 'a broad structure designed to reduce the need to travel . . . can easily be undermined by poor layout and design at the local level' (DoE/DoT, 1995, p. 8). Accordingly, the pursuit of appropriate design should not be discouraged, not least because having an attractive walkable environment may be considered desirable in its own right – irrespective of its influence on public transport use.

From Ewing's analysis, it is concluded that having a grid form of street pattern is a 'highly desirable' but not essential characteristic of a public transport supportive design. Yet it must also be pointed out that street pattern does have a role to play in supporting some of the 'essential' attributes of public transport orientation, such as (i) ensuring that sufficient density is achieved within the requisite distances; (ii) achieving short to medium blocks; and (iii) delivering a network which supports transit routes every half mile (derived from Ewing, 1996). Therefore, patterns such as grids can be supportive of 'essential' characteristics as well as being 'highly desirable' in their own right.

In fact, the study of the effects of different types of street pattern on travel patterns is ongoing (Stead and Marshall, 1998), but this testing requires better definition and characterization of street pattern types. For example, the distinction between different types of grid structure and 'tree' structure, the differentiation between macro and micro structure, and the characterization of different forms of route continuity, connectivity and hierarchy may all be used to characterize street pattern at a higher resolution than conventional descriptors such as 'traditional/public transport-orientated' versus 'suburban/car-orientated' neighbourhoods (Marshall, 2001).

POSSIBILITIES

The development of appropriate urban design for public transport orientation is interwoven with empirical research into the effects of different urban forms and land-use patterns on actual travel behaviour. Design ideas or plans (often envisaged by urban planners or architects) are tested for their efficacy in achieving the desired travel outcomes (typically by transport analysts) hence leading to refined design ideas. This is an ongoing iterative process.

The intention here is to develop further possibilities for public transport-orientated urban design, emerging from the foregoing exploration and critique of established plans and principles. In due course these possibilities would require to be subjected to further rounds of empirical testing and refinement.

Pedestrian Orientation

First, let us start with consideration of the pedestrian, whose importance to the public transport mode has earlier been demonstrated. Public transport orientation should pay due attention to the design of the pedestrian's environment. According to Rapoport (1987), the public's use of streets is determined largely by cultural factors. Therefore, design must take into account not only the traditional concerns of infrastructure and the purely quantitative concerns of time and distance to access public transport stops, but also the qualitative and 'human' characteristics of the locale.

The pedestrian is a 'sensitive mode' in two senses. First, the pedestrian has a greater sensory awareness and appreciation of the environment. Second, the pedestrian mode is sensitive in the sense that demand for walking may be more susceptible to influence by a wider variety of factors than other modes – in other words, one may easily be deterred from walking by relatively small adverse changes in the environment (for example, closure of a short-cut, rain). Both of these considerations should be borne in mind when considering public transport orientation, which translates to providing an attractive environment with as direct routes as possible.

Overall, design for the pedestrian is arguably more a case of design of the pedestrian 'landscape', rather than a mechanistic configuration of a pedestrian 'network'. It may best be approached from the ground, taking into consideration the existing site features and patterns of use, rather than proposing an abstract solution contrived on the drawing board (Marshall, 2001).

Activity Interfaces

A holistic approach can ensure that travel is integrated with non-transport activities, and not seen as a separate issue requiring separate solutions. The attractiveness of public transport is not merely a matter of level of service. Walk time and wait time are significant components of a public transport journey. Accordingly, any steps taken which can enhance the 'quality' of this time (that is, through creation of an attractive environment for walking – or cycling – and waiting) can assist the attractiveness of public transport use as a whole. For example, the snack bar and newspaper stall next to the bus stop can enhance the attractiveness of travel by bus. The integration of transport and non-transport activities can also aid trip chaining and hence reduce vehicle-kilometres.

In other words, if the urban street is conceptualized in its role as a linear public transport interchange, involving not only movement and boarding possibilities, but also information provision, seating, waiting, other forms of urban activity and occupation, then it should be possible to fulfil the potential both of the street-as-interchange and the interchange-as-street.

The use of the street as an activity interface supports the idea of shared surfaces and integration, where immediate accessibility to vehicles is regarded as being more important than achieving a high running speed. This implies an arterial-type 'street as interchange', which would be correlated with some kind of connective qualities.

That is, there should be a correspondence between streets used for public transport access and interchange and those streets liable to serve as natural foci for pedestrian activity, due to their spatial structure (as, for example, investigated by Hillier, 1996). This may appear to be stating the obvious, but examples of bus stops and bus stations in isolated or back-street locations which require a special effort to reach are all too common.

Use of Grid Forms

Since pedestrians are particularly sensitive to distance, access to public transport should be as direct as possible. In this respect, conventional grid patterns may serve as well as quasi-radial street patterns where imaginary axes radiate from the public transport stop but fail to provide a direct route on the ground. In particular, where a public transport stop is near to a crossroads, then one can naturally take advantage of access from four directions. The rectilinear form is also practical and convenient for laying out abutting plots with buildings which can assist in providing a high concentration of activity generators near the stop. Naturally, other street patterns may also be used to suit local circumstances; the point is that grid forms are likely to be at least as good a solution as any other, and should not be arbitrarily ruled out.

The 'Tartan' Grid

It is suggested here that laying out a settlement in the form of a differentiated, 'directional' or 'tartan' grid can assist public transport orientation by interweaving different corridors based on different modes – principally, routes for pedestrians, for public transport and for general traffic (Figure 9.4). Basically,

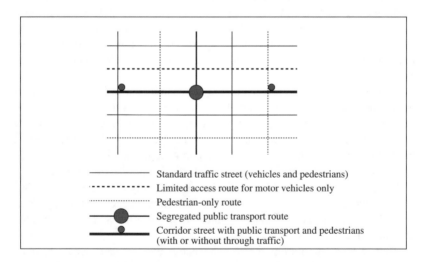

Note: Each route type is continuous and can intersect and/or interchange with any other. Integration of coincident routes on a corridor street, or segregation and limited access, are equally possible. The strands can also reflect corridors of different land use or density.

Figure 9.4   Example of a tartan grid (diagrammatic only)

the tartan grid uses a variety of different street or corridor types formed into a more or less continuous grid (as opposed to a supergrid of one type of route with micro-grid enclaves of other types nested within).

Thus denser corridors could accompany public transport routes while being permeated with pedestrian routes linking out to the lower-density areas around highways for general traffic. The arrangement in a grid (rather than a purely linear form) would allow intersections between all route types, allowing, for example, particularly high densities at crossing points of two public transport routes and commercial activities where public transport routes crossed highways (maximum intermodal accessibility). Indeed, the logic of the 'ABC' type of nodal policy is ideally suited to the tartan grid.

The tartan grid has the advantage that each type of corridor can be more or less continuous, with the advantages that continuous networks bring, and yet would be near to the other types of corridor, thus avoiding overly polarized corridors of high density and peripheries of low density. The use of such a grid also solves some of the problems of linear settlements – long distances and the temptation to build laterally – by allowing more compact forms where lateral expansion is structured and integrated.

As well as catering for different transport arteries, the tartan grid also allows variety in land-use disposition, allowing continuity of land use along corridors, while mixed in close proximity to different land uses in parallel or perpendicular corridors. This creates a framework that combines linear consistency with lateral (and areal) diversity, and can be related to MacCormac's (1996) ideas of homogeneous streets backing on to heterogeneous blocks. The tartan grid therefore embodies the integration of mixed-use land-use zoning as well as a mix of route types.

Overlapping Catchments

The idea of overlapping catchments can be developed to allow recreation of 'strings of high streets', such as Risemberg's 'multiple main street' model (1997) or Simmonds's 'A-road high streets' model (1993). This would allow a more integrated urban fabric – which appears in many traditional, de facto public transport-orientated settlements – rather than the somewhat dislocated pattern of the abstract 'beads on a string' form.

These linear corridors may be arranged in a grid or radial form at the macro level, while retaining a grid structure for the pedestrian network at the micro level. Either way, it is possible to have continuous corridors of urban streets lined with shops and traversed by street-based public transport (bus or tram). The continuity of the grid-based minor road structure (side roads) allows catchments to be overlapping. This avoids the discontinuity (and some might say disurbanity) of discrete 'beads' or 'pods'.

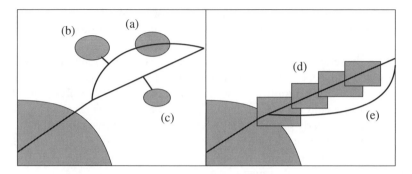

Note: Development may be centred on a public transport route (a) though this may itself be a loop road off the nearest through-route. In other cases, the development may take the form of discrete 'pods' lying off the public transport route (b), or even off a route with no local public transport (c). Alternately, development can be arranged along a street-running public transport corridor, with a series of grid-based, overlapping catchments (d). This follows the existing radial route and can be contiguous with the existing urban area. Through-traffic might be diverted to a segregated arterial (e) whose form might reflect a traditional railway alignment.

Figure 9.5   Extension of a public transport corridor at the urban periphery

Such a system of 'high streets' would feature significant pedestrian and public transport functions in combination with a moderate traffic function. However, the majority of through-traffic could be accommodated by segregated arterials running in parallel with the 'high streets'. Such an arrangement could be applied to a radial corridor extending out from an existing urban area (Figure 9.5).

The point here would be that both the public transport and pedestrian environments would be contiguous with each other and with the rest of the urban environment, in contrast to modern practice where existing major roads are upgraded to high-capacity vehicular routes, and all development takes place off-line, in discrete 'pods' of development. Such an arrangement is not normally amenable to service by public transport, or the creation of an integrated pedestrian environment.

Instead of the existing radial route being reserved as a vehicular highway, it would be retained as the major public right of way for all modes, but with the main through-traffic flows being filtered off-line on to a dedicated distributor route.

An advantage of this arrangement is that the corridor can be built up in a progressive, incremental fashion, adjusted to the immediate needs of the locales concerned, and does not require an all-or-nothing commitment to a particular form of public transport that is dependent on a particular form of development, or vice versa.

Public Street-running Transport Options

Given the earlier points about accessibility to the public transport stop, there will be clear advantages, in some circumstances, for street running (of buses and light rail). In this sense, street running is more orientated to the combined public transport–pedestrian system than the provision of segregated routes. Segregation seems to be most appropriate for those modes which need have least contact with the public realm. This includes through-traffic which not only has no need for interaction with the public street but is positively harmful to that environment.

Taken together, it is possible that in some circumstances it might make sense to (re)instate street running of public transport while diverting through-road traffic to a parallel route – such as a disused railway line (Figure 9.5 d, e). Such a scenario could even involve a straight 'swap' between the through-road and an existing public transport route. This would need to be done sensitively to be compatible with other urban and transport policies, for example, to ensure that road capacity overall was not increased. By switching routes, the public transport would be where it was appreciated, while traffic would be rerouted away from the public street.

Road Hierarchies and User Hierarchies

Conventional road hierarchies can be criticized for their inflexibility and for their disadvantageous disposition towards the public transport–pedestrian systems. Where such hierarchies segregate routes for traffic (on which the buses would travel) from those used by pedestrians and for access to buildings, they effectively separate public transport from its users (that is, pedestrians) and their destinations (that is, urban 'streets', shopping areas, houses and so on) (Marshall, 1998).

CBRPT (1981) has also argued that 'Radburn'-type layouts, which are often associated with such hierarchical systems, are difficult to serve by bus, not only due to pedestrian–vehicle segregation, but also due to the 'long circuitous perimeter roads'.

It is suggested that a more flexible hierarchy could be used to allow for a more public transport-orientated road network. Such a hierarchy could allow the recreation of traditional street types which could be served by buses or trams, as well as being the natural conduits of pedestrian movement. Conceptually, this could be achieved by dislocating public transport function as a separate 'dimension' of the hierarchy, independent of the road hierarchy allocated for general traffic, but allowing it to be overlaid as appropriate on a variety of street types (Marshall, 1998).

The use of such a hierarchy would allow both pedestrian and public transport routes to be devised to optimize the public transport–pedestrian system, rather than being constrained within a hierarchy which in practice tends to favour private vehicular traffic. For example, public transport routes and nodes could optimally be located with respect to points of pedestrian concentration (as noted earlier). It would allow traditional arterial routes to be developed as corridor streets lined with shopfronts – the 'string of high streets' model – to be retained as the most direct and connective routes. By means of layout solutions such as these, it should be possible to properly realize a user hierarchy placing pedestrians and public transport near the top, which may in other circumstances remain little more than a wishful intention.

CONCLUSIONS

Public transport-orientated urban design is a widely accepted principle which can play a role in an integrated transport system and towards a more 'sustainable' urban environment. This chapter has demonstrated the extent to which there is an emerging consensus in the design of settlements for public transport orientation.

The existence of a consensus may merely reflect that most people would like good access to good public transport – even if they do not actually use it themselves. It does not automatically infer that this is the best or only way of laying out settlements, or mean that they would be able to achieve the results desired. However, the existence of a consensus regarding the broad principles of public transport orientation should allow attention to focus on the detail of how to achieve designs which accord with the shared aims of sustainable development and sustainable mobility.

Although there appears to be consistency of the basic principles of public transport orientation, these may be realized in a variety of forms. These include not only examples whose public transport orientation has been consciously devised, but traditional urban areas whose physical forms – as well as their socioeconomic characteristics – happen to suit public transport orientation.

Key to public transport-orientated urban design is the conception of an integrated public transport–pedestrian system, where much of the focus of the attention will be on the detailed design of pedestrian access. Moreover, given that walking is more than a mode of transport but an urban activity in its own right – interfacing with other urban activities – the access issue must also be seen in the wider context of urban functions and land use in general. The physical solution implied is therefore as much to do with the creation of urban public space as it is to do with the abstract patterns made by the public transport system itself.

Public transport orientation, then, is not simply about 'beads on a string'.

For a start, while the general principle of loci based on stops is sound enough, the translation to a rigid pattern based on this schema is not inevitably the best solution, or even necessarily a good one in every case. Designs should allow for flexibility of layouts to meet local circumstances. This applies equally to the suggestions proposed in this chapter.

In fact, the suggestions proposed are effectively developments of existing public transport-orientated layouts, retaining the underlying principles of accessibility common to the familiar exemplars, while attempting to break free from formulaic 'beads on a string' formats.

For example, grid forms allow good pedestrian permeability, and create rectilinear plots suitable for development while allowing access to the public transport stop from a variety of directions. The use of 'tartan' grids can allow a mix of corridor types (mode and density) and types of node (for example, 'A'-, 'B'- or 'C'-type locations). This type of grid also allows continuity of pedestrian routes and corridors such as 'string of high streets' with street-running public transport. At the same time, they can also accommodate segregated public transport and traffic routes.

A key to these proposals is the use of a more flexible hierarchy of route types and their permissible combination in different types of network. A flexible hierarchy can permit and encourage routes which mix public transport and pedestrian access in a judicious way, matching points of greatest accessibility and connectivity in each network.

The use of a more flexible and differentiated hierarchy can in fact assist all of the other suggested possibilities for public transport orientation. These all imply a switch away from rigid 'linear' hierarchies and associated layouts which tend to separate public transport from the pedestrian domain, which tend to promote 'tree-like' layouts where only the main roads for through-vehicular traffic are sufficiently connective, and which relegate 'streets' (that is, access roads permitting associated building frontages) to a relatively subordinate and disjointed position in the system. If isolated 'public transport-orientated' features are simply tacked on to such a system – which apart from anything else continues to accommodate car use – it is not surprising if their results are ineffectual.

Effectively, public transport-orientated urban design must imply the prioritization of the public transport and pedestrian routes, independent of their position in the conventional traffic hierarchy, and the promotion of streets which integrate buildings, pedestrian space and public transport routes and interfaces. This is in addition to the familiar concerns of directness of route and clustering of activities around public transport stops. To ensure that all these conditions can be facilitated, a hierarchy that is geared to the needs of the public transport–pedestrian system is required. Without such a hierarchy, efforts are likely to be undermined.

As stated previously, to take forward the ideas developed here would require further empirical research and testing. This would involve identification of examples on the ground which exhibit the various characteristics of public transport orientation – for example, the eight principles, individually and in combination – to allow empirical validation or testing of the relationships between these forms and actual travel behaviour. It would also imply taking forward the seven suggested 'possibilities' for public transport orientation, again, by identification and analysis of cases which matched these characteristics. From there, it would be possible to further develop the ideas.

In addition to matching travel behaviour with different patterns of urban form and layout, there is also a need to consider wider user preferences for mobility and urbanity. This would need to take into account the actual preferences for living in compact, corridor-based settlements as opposed to suburban and exurban locations.

It should be noted that most of the considerations discussed here have related to a scale intermediate between that of individual block (or public transport stop) and the city as a whole. Public transport orientation at the settlement scale is yet to be resolved. In one sense, this is to do with ensuring that public transport provision serves places where people want to go, and increases the probability that both trip ends of any particular journey are well served by public transport. It also requires consideration of what happens when public transport-orientated enclaves such as those found in inner cities are transplanted to new sites on the periphery of cities. These issues are as much to do with land-use planning as they are to do with transport. For the sustainable city, it would appear that an integrated approach is required.

Bearing these points in mind, it should be possible to set a course towards further understanding of the relationships between public transport orientation, urban design, urban activities and travel behaviour and hence allow the development of design solutions which can more closely meet the objectives of sustainable mobility and urbanity. The concept of public transport orientation is well enough established. Further development of the concept can lead us beyond the aspiration of 'orientation' to achieve a working realization of public transport *sustainable* urban design.

REFERENCES

Baker, R.C. (1977), 'Future urban transport technology', in R. Cresswell (ed.), *Passenger Transport and the Environment: The Integration of Public Passenger Transport with the Urban Environment*, London: Leonard Hill, pp. 191–206.

Banister, D. and J. Berechman (2000), *Transport Investment and Economic Development*, London: UCL Press.

Banister, D. and S. Marshall (eds) (2000), *Encouraging Transport Alternatives: Good Practice in Reducing Travel*, London: HMSO.

Barton, H., G. Davis and R. Guise (1995), *Sustainable Settlements: A Guide for Planners, Designers and Developers*, Bristol: University of the West of England and Local Government Management Board.

Beimborn, E. and H. Rabinowitz (1991), *Guidelines for Transit – Sensitive Suburban Land Use Design*, Washington, DC: US Department of Transportation.

Bendixson, T. and J. Platt (1992), *Milton Keynes: Image and Reality*, Cambridge: Granta Editions.

Berman, M.A. (1996), 'The transportation effects of neo-traditional development', *Journal of Planning Literature*, **10** (4), 347–63.

Bernick, M. and R. Cervero (1996), *Transit Villages in the 21st Century*, New York: McGraw-Hill.

Calthorpe, P. (1989), 'The pedestrian pocket', in R.T. LeGates and F. Stout (eds), *The City Reader*, London and New York: Routledge, pp. 468–74.

Calthorpe, P. (1993), *The Next American Metropolis: Ecology, Community and the American Dream*, New York: Princeton Architectural Press.

Cervero, R. (1994), 'Transit villages: from idea to implementation', *Access*, no. 5, Fall, 8–13.

Cervero, R. (1998), *The Transit Metropolis. A Global Inquiry*, Washington, DC: Island Press.

Cervero, R. and R. Gorham (1995), 'Commuting in transit versus automobile neighborhoods', *Journal of the American Planning Association*, **61** (2), 210–25.

Confederation of British Road Passenger Transport (CBRPT) (1981), *Urban Planning and Design for Road Public Transport*, London: CBRPT.

Department of the Environment/Department of Transport (DoE/DoT) (1995), *PPG13: Guide to Better Practice – Reducing the Need to Travel Through Planning*, London: HMSO.

Department of the Environment, Transport and the Regions (DETR) (1998a), *A New Deal for Transport – Better for Everyone*, London: HMSO.

Department of the Environment, Transport and the Regions (DETR) (1998b), *Places, Streets and Movement. A Companion Guide to Design Bulletin 32, Residential Roads and Footpaths*, London: DETR.

Department of the Environment, Transport and the Regions (DETR) (1998c), *Planning for Sustainable Development*, London: HMSO.

Ewing, R. (1996), *Pedestrian- and Transit-friendly Design*, Report prepared for the Public Transit Office, Miami: Florida Department of Transportation.

Garbrecht, D. (1997), 'Walking and public transport: two sides of the same coin', in R. Tolley (ed.), *The Greening of Urban Transport*, Chichester: John Wiley & Sons, pp. 207–12.

Hall, P. (1992) 'East Thames corridor: the second golden age of the garden suburb', *Urban Design Quarterly*, **43**, 2–9.

Hall, P. and C. Ward (1998), *Sociable Cities: The Legacy of Ebenezer Howard*, Chichester: John Wiley & Sons.

Hanna, J. (1997), 'Putting people at the centre of planning in Britain: from "Feet First" to "Streets for People" ', in R. Tolley (ed.), *The Greening of Urban Transport*, Chichester: John Wiley & Sons, pp. 275–85.

Hillier, B. (1996), *Space is the Machine*, Cambridge: Cambridge University Press.

Houghton, G. and C. Hunter (1994), *Sustainable Cities*, London: Jessica Kingsley.

Houghton-Evans, W. (1975), *Planning Cities: Legacy and Portent*, London: Lawrence & Wishart.

Howard, E. (1904), *Tomorrow: A Peaceful Path to Real Reform*, reprinted as Vol. 2 of R. LeGates and F. Stout (eds) (1998), Early Urban Planning series, London: Routledge/Thoemmes Press.

Institution of Highways and Transportation (IHT) (1999), *Guidelines for Public Transport in Developments*, London: IHT.

Irvine Development Corporation (IDC) (1971), *Irvine New Town Plan*, Irvine: IDC.

Kraay, J.H. (1996), 'Dutch approaches to surviving with traffic and transport', *Transport Reviews*, **16** (4), 323–43.

Lemberg, K. (1977), 'Passenger transport as an urban element', in R. Cresswell (ed.), *Passenger Transport and the Environment: The Integration of Public Passenger Transport with the Urban Environment*, London: Leonard Hill, pp. 3–34.

Llewelyn-Davies, R. (1968), 'Town design', in D. Lewis (ed.), *Architects' Year Book 12: Urban Structure*, London: Paul Elek, pp. 44–8.

Loukaitou-Sideris, A. (1993), 'Retrofit of urban corridors: land use policies and design guidelines for transit-friendly environments', University of California Transportation Center Working Paper no. 180.

Lynch, K. (1991), in T. Banerjee and M. Southworth (eds), *City Sense and City Design: Writings and Projects of Kevin Lynch*, Cambridge, MA: MIT Press.

Maat, K. (2000), 'Travel reduction "built in": the role of land use planning', in D. Banister and S. Marshall (eds), *Encouraging Transport Alternatives: Good Practice in Reducing Travel*, London: HMSO.

MacCormac, R. (1996), 'An anatomy of London', *Built Environment*, **22** (4), 306–11.

Marshall, S (1998), 'Towards the integration of urban transport networks and urban design', 8th World Conference on Transport Research, Antwerp, July.

Marshall, S. (2001), 'Transport and the Design of Urban Structure', PhD thesis, Bartlett School of Planning, University College London.

Milton Keynes Development Corporation (MKDC) (1970), *The Plan for Milton Keynes*, Volume 2, Milton Keynes: MKDC.

Morris, W. and J.A. Kaufman (1998), 'The new urbanism: an introduction to the movement and its potential impact on travel demand with an outline of its application in Western Australia', *Proceedings of Seminar B, Policy, Planning and Sustainability (Vol. 1)*, PTRC European Transport Conference, Loughborough University, September, pp. 199–222.

Owers, D. (1996), 'The quarter within the mesh: urban theory territory', *Built Environment*, **22** (4), 283–99.

Pickrell, D. (1992), 'A desire named streetcar', *Journal of the American Planning Association*, **58** (2), 158–76.

Punter, J. and M. Carmona (1997), *The Design Dimension of Planning*, London: E & FN Spon.

Rapoport, A. (1987), 'Pedestrian street use: culture and perception', in A.V. Moudon (ed.), *Public Streets for Public Use*, New York: Van Nostrand Reinhold.

Richards, B. (1969), *New Movement in Cities*, London: Studio Vista.

Richmond, J.E. (1998), 'The mythical conception of rail transit in Los Angeles', *Journal of Architectural and Planning Research*, **15** (4), 294–320 (forthcoming as book, University of Akron Press).

Risemberg, R. (1997), 'Bicycling and the multiple main street model', *The Sustainable Urban Neighbourhood*, Issue 4: Spring/Summer, 8.

Runcorn Development Corporation (RDC) (1967), *Runcorn New Town*, Runcorn: RDC.

Simmonds, R. (1993), 'The built form of the new regional city: a "radical" view', in R. Hayward and S. McGlynn (eds), *Making Better Places: Urban Design Now*, Oxford: Butterworth Architecture, pp. 95–102.

Southworth, M. and E. Ben-Joseph (1997), *Streets and the Shaping of Towns and Cities*, New York: McGraw-Hill.

Stead, D. (1999), 'Planning for less travel – identifying land use characteristics associated with more sustainable travel patterns', PhD thesis, Bartlett School of Planning, University College London.

Stead, D. and S. Marshall (1998), 'The relationship between urban form and travel patterns: an international review and evaluation', 8th World Congress of Transport Research, Antwerp, July.

Sustainable Urban Neighbourhood Initiative (SUNI) (1997), 'The model sustainable urban neighbourhood', *The Sustainable Urban Neighbourhood*, Issue 4: Spring/Summer, 4.

Transportation Research Board (TRB) (1996), *TCRP Report 16: Transit and Urban Form*, Washington, DC: National Academy Press.

Transport Research Laboratory (TRL) (1997), *Urban Design Considerations in Transport Planning: A Guide for Planners and Engineers*, Crowthorne: TRL.

Turner, T. (1996), *City as Landscape. A Post-postmodern View of Design and Planning*, London: E & FN Spon.

Walmsley, D. and K. Perrett (1992), *The Effects of Rapid Transit on Public Transport and Urban Development*, London: HMSO.

White, P. (1976), *Planning for Public Transport*, London: Hutchinson & Co.

White, P. (1995), *Public Transport: Its Planning, Management and Operation*, 3rd edn, London: UCL Press.

Williams, K., E. Burton and M. Jenks (eds) (2000), *Achieving Sustainable Form*, London: E & FN Spon.

10. Effects of the Dutch compact city policy on travel behaviour

Kees Maat

INTRODUCTION

The turbulent growth of mobility in most countries is now a matter of fact. Roads are backed up more often and over longer distances, while attempts to prevent traffic jams are less effective. The economic core areas in and around the cities are increasingly difficult to reach. All in all, the use of the car is growing at the expense of liveability. The problem is that more people travel (somewhat) more frequently over longer distances. Moreover, they take the car much more often rather than sustainable forms of transport.

For a long time, authorities have responded to the rising demand for mobility by investing in infrastructure. Specifically, the government has built new roads, widened existing ones, and increased road capacity in some other ways. The motorway system in the Netherlands, measured as the combined length of all individual lanes, is now twice as extensive as in 1970. Gradually, policy makers have come to realize that any improvement is just temporary, as it generates more traffic. At places, for instance in the cities, where capacity is not increased fast enough, traffic gets tied up. At other places, there is no way to increase capacity. This realization prompted a new response to the insatiable demand for mobility, namely by attempting to cap the growth of car mobility. This objective may be broken down into the following three strategies:

1. *Limiting car use*:   by way of a shift from the car to more sustainable modes of transport. This involves discouraging driving (push policy) and promoting use of the bicycle and public transport.
2. *Limiting the distance travelled*:   by locating housing, jobs and services closer together, people will not have to travel as far.
3. *Limiting the number of trips*:   by linking trips, people will not travel as frequently. Teleworking, for instance, may make certain trips altogether unnecessary.

Since the spatial structure of housing, employment and services forms the context within which people travel, and since suburbanization and mobility have gone hand in hand in the Netherlands (and no doubt elsewhere too), it seems self-evident that policy makers would try to reverse the growth in mobility by making spatial development more compact (second section). Potentially, compact urbanization could give the three strategies mentioned above a better chance of success. The concept would foster improvement in three areas: first, a broader base for the bicycle and public transport; second, shorter trips, thereby reducing overall mobility; and third, the potential for linking trips, by locating work and services close to each other (third section).

The aim of reducing mobility in the Netherlands is increasingly pursued through instruments of spatial policy. Clearly, in the past decade, the compact city concept has become a basic principle of spatial planning in the Netherlands. However, although the compact city seems to be a promising concept, it should be operationalized with great care. Its implementation calls for a major policy commitment, as the ambition is to reverse the direction of a spontaneous development. For that reason, it is useful to carry out empirical evaluations after a few years of compact urbanization policy to see whether the concept is effective and works as expected. Two such studies are described in the fourth section. As we shall see, the outcomes are modest and do not support the compact city concept convincingly. It is unfortunate that the effects of compact urbanization on mobility do not meet expectations. The effects may also be insufficient since compact city principles have not been sufficiently realized. This is because the compact city concept itself conflicts with planning objectives in other areas, such as housing and the urban economy (fifth section).

Although Dutch practice is often held up as a model for other countries, using 'progressive' solutions while other countries are merely proposing them, the chapter draws attention to the mixed results of these solutions.

SPATIAL PLANNING IN THE NETHERLANDS

The increase in car mobility over the past decades is the result of a complex process with various factors reinforcing one another. One of the key determinants of car use is car ownership. Car ownership per capita has been growing continuously since 1946. The most explosive growth occurred in the 1960s and 1970s. Between 1960 and 1998, the number of cars in the Netherlands rose from roughly half a million to almost six million (Figure 10.1), and the number of cars is still growing by more than 100,000 per year. The two factors that have contributed most to that increase are population growth (mainly due to the post-war baby boom) and rising prosperity. As people became more

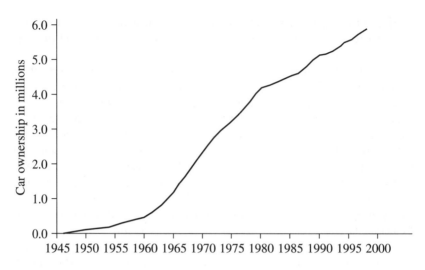

Source: CBS.

Figure 10.1   Car ownership in the Netherlands between 1946 and 1998

affluent, they were able to buy a car, and more and more people did just that. In particular, the combination of these two developments had a strong effect on mobility by generating a huge demographic wave, a high rate of car owner- ship, and a high level of car accessibility (MV&W, 1997).

Owning a car gave people the opportunity to change their travel behaviour. First of all, they were able to cover longer distances (see Figure 10.2); many soon moved to residential areas that were farther away from their place of work. Between 1978 and 1995, the average trip length to work increased by 43 per cent. Moreover, people were able to make the entire trip, from door to door, in one vehicle; there was no need to transfer. Since drivers could travel in a criss-cross pattern, their home, their work and the services they used could lie in scattered and far-flung places.

The availability of the car made an enormous suburbanization process possible, starting in the 1960s. Many households who could afford it moved out of the cities to live in rural settings nestled in between built-up areas. They preferred living in a house with a yard in a green village to the alternative, which was a flat in a new district on the outskirts of the city. Moreover, small developments in villages could meet the demand for housing relatively quickly and cheaply, in contrast to urban developments.

The influence of urbanization on mobility was recognized at an early stage. In 1967, the Second Report on Spatial Planning was published by the Spatial Planning Agency (Department of the Ministry of Housing, Spatial Planning

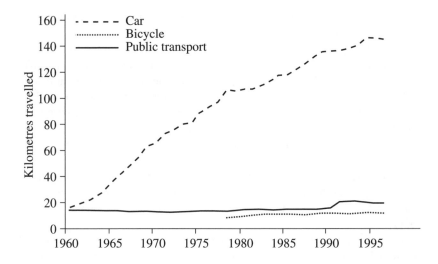

Source: CBS.

Figure 10.2   Annual kilometres travelled in the Netherlands between 1960 and 1998

and Environment), outlining the government's standpoint on the impending effects. In the early 1960s, when the Netherlands had 12.5 million inhabitants, the government projected a population of 21 million by the year 2000 (the 1998 population is just over 15.5 million). The authorities foresaw that this population growth would lead to enormous congestion in the western part of the country unless they did something to curb the unbridled urbanization. Thus, the Second Report proposed deflecting the growth towards other parts of the country. In order to prevent amorphous development, the government formulated a policy known as 'concentrated deconcentration' in growth centres, which was to control the urbanization. They also tried to keep the cities accessible by putting in a very extensive system of motorways. On the drawing boards, not even the Green Heart was spared. This area, which separates the cities that make up the Randstad conurbation and even back then was supposed to be kept open and rural, was to be given ample coverage by motorways. Nevertheless, not all of them were actually built.

A decade later, the Third Report on Spatial Planning no longer put the emphasis on dispersal. Instead, the growth centres were supposed to absorb the population overspill from the big cities. Some of these centres were optimally located with respect to their mother cities. Zoetermeer, for instance, was close to The Hague and well connected by public transport. Other growth centres, however, were too far away (Hoorn was too far from Amsterdam) or did not have rail links (Hellevoetsluis, near Rotterdam).

The car surged into the inner cities too, tying up traffic on the feeder roads leading into the city centre, and once there, the cars took up precious urban space for parking. The ensuing congestion made the city centres less attractive and less accessible, prompting the suburbanization of services and employment: furniture stores congregated at the edge of the city, which customers could easily reach by car; offices moved to sites along the motorways and the hotels in the city centre met stiff competition from motels on the outskirts (de Boer, 1996).

Meanwhile, the city was thinning out and the rural areas were becoming built up. The resulting spatial form favoured the car; the distances were too great for bicycle use and the densities too low for attractive public transport supply.

The Structure Sketch for Urban Areas, presented in 1983, marked the end of the policy of concentrated deconcentration and the beginning of an era of urban concentration. Planners took the concept of the compact city as their guiding light. The current policy was set forth in the Fourth Report on Spatial Planning (MVROM, 1987) and in the extension, the Fourth Report on Spatial Planning Extra (MVROM, 1991), known by its acronym Vinex. That document elaborated on the concept. Most of the housing construction programme, roughly half a million dwellings, is supposed to be implemented at urban development areas called Vinex locations. The aim of the Vinex policy is to allow residential, employment and service functions to operate at the level of the city region. The policy would provide the critical mass for services on a scale conducive to cycling and public transport while limiting the growth in mobility. At the same time, this policy would discourage further urbanization in rural areas. In the Vinex plan, proximity takes priority over accessibility. New housing development areas have to be sited within, adjacent to, or in the vicinity of the big cities, preferably along the axes of public transport lines. Furthermore, economic activities with many employees or functions that draw many visitors are to be established in areas that are easily accessible by public transport – on condition that those activities do not pose a nuisance to people living and working in the city.

In Updating Vinex (MVROM, 1996), the compact city policy was extended beyond the mobility goals related to the 'distance' between residential, employment and service locations. The 'design' of the Vinex locations also had to be amenable to bicycle and public transport use.

It had been a long time since the Ministry of Transport and Public Works had used spatial policy as an instrument of governance. That changed in 1995, with the publication of Vision on Urbanization and Mobility (MV&W, 1995). This document revealed the ministry's commitment to diverse principles allied with the compact city concept. For instance, the ministry considers itself a proponent of concentration, mixed-use development, and higher densities around public transport stops. Furthermore, the document emphatically advocates the connection of new locations with the main infrastructure of public transport. In fact, the ministry attaches greater importance to accessibility by public transport than to proximity. In the Randstad, locating new developments 'between' city regions but on public transport lines might have priority over proximity to one single city; a location with those features allows for multiple orientations.

In preparing for the upcoming Fifth Report, the Ministry of Housing, Spatial Planning and Environment has opened up the discussion by introducing a preference towards corridors and network cities. Both forms of development can make optimal use of existing infrastructure. Just like the preference of the Ministry of Transport, this option emphasizes accessibility over proximity. Moreover, the network option breaks with the compact city policy (MVROM, 1999). In any event, compact cities or networks, the mobility problem will play an increasingly important role in spatial policy.

THE COMPACT CITY CONCEPT

Defining the Concept

In the previous section, we noted that the dispersal of urban functions that had taken place over the past few decades had laid the foundations for a spatial form facilitating car traffic at the expense of the bicycle and public transport. It would seem plausible to assume that this relation can be turned around. The appeal of that assumption lies primarily in its simplicity. The train of thought is straightforward: increasing urban density and reducing the travel distances will surely cut back on the need to travel, especially by car. The aim of compact urbanization is thus two-pronged. It seeks to reduce the travel distances in order to achieve an overall reduction in mobility. At the same time, it seeks to improve the base for public transport and the bicycle in order to promote a modal shift.

The concept of compact urbanization has been receiving attention in the last decade, since the publication of the studies conducted by Newman and Kenworthy (1989). In the Netherlands, the compact city concept has become a cornerstone of spatial policy. The European Commission's Green Paper on the Urban Environment reveals the EC to be a strong proponent of the compact city. The EC sees the implementation of this concept as a means to make urban areas more environmentally sustainable and improve the quality of life there (Breheny, 1992). In the United States as well, New Urbanism is a strong movement in favour of the compact city as a weapon in the battle against urban sprawl (Handy, 1996). However, while the ideas of the New Urbanism concerns the level of neighbourhoods, the compact city policy concerns not only neighbourhoods, but also the level of urban regions.

What, precisely, do we mean by compact urbanization? The term 'compact' implies concentration and high densities. Yet, other features are generally associated with the compact city too. The following items describe these principles of urbanization as they are applied in the Netherlands.

- *Concentration* Instead of a dispersed urbanization pattern, whereby small locations are developed (often through a more or less market-driven process), locations that are directly adjacent to the cities or in their immediate vicinity should be developed (MVROM, 1991). This would allow a more direct use of existing amenities and public transport (PT) lines that are already in service (MV&W, 1995). This might seem self-evident. Nevertheless, in the recent past, completely new growth centres have been built very far from the central city.
- *Urban containment policy* is the complement of concentration. This policy prohibits building outside the existing urbanized area (MVROM, 1991).
- *Mixed-use development* The integration of housing, employment and services at the scale of the city region reduces the need to travel long distances. By mixed use, it is possible to live close to work and take the bicycle to go shopping nearby. It is especially the Ministry of Transport and Public Works (MV&W, 1995) that strongly favours this principle.
- *High density* The essence of compactness is high density, which means building more dwellings per hectare. The main goal is to increase the population base for public transport. Higher densities are imperative near the stops; this might call for multifamily structures. Compactness also reduces the distance between urban activities, which is also in favour of bicycles (MVROM, 1991).
- *Form* The critical mass for public transport is not only related to density but also to the layout of the district. For example, mid-rise or high-rise structures should be built near public transport stops; and a park or pond that separates the dwellings from the public transport routes forms an obstacle.
- *Development at public transport nodes* Any industries, offices or services that have a high intensity of use by personnel or visitors should be established at locations that are easily accessible by public transport. Moreover, those areas should be subject to a highly regulated parking policy. In the Netherlands this policy is called 'business location policy' (MVROM, 1991).

Table 10.1 shows the assumed effects of urbanization factors on mobility.

Table 10.1   *Assumed effects of urbanization factors on mobility*

Urbanization principles	Effects on Travel Behaviour			
	Reduce trip length	Population base PT	Connection existing PT infrastructure	Activity and trip linking
Concentration	•	•	•	○
High densities	•	•		○
Mixed use	•	•		•
Development at PT nodes	○	•	•	•
Urban form	○	•	○	○

Note: • Major effects   ○ Minor effects.

Studies in other countries reveal a few additional features that generally receive less attention in Dutch policy documents. One such feature is the size and structure of the city. The discussion about structure is mainly concerned with whether a highly centralized form is preferable to a multi-nucleated form (Anderson et al., 1996). In the Netherlands, the structure of the growth centre of Houten, near the city of Utrecht, is an innovative urban form. The residential neighbourhoods are connected by a network of bicycle paths. These paths also link the neighbourhoods directly with the town centre and the railway station. Car traffic is always led around the built-up area. Not surprisingly, the use of the bicycle and public transport is exceptionally high in Houten.

Effectiveness of Compact City Policy

The compact city is a theoretical concept, based on several, at first glance, plausible assumptions. Yet it is conceivable that travel behaviour will not comply with those assumptions. Other factors may intervene, disrupting the effect of the concept (see the concluding section, below). Moreover, the policy to implement compact urbanization calls for drastic measures. People tend to seek more space, whereas compact urbanization requires the opposite, namely concentration. Since the policy runs counter to the current of spontaneous development, more effort is required to implement it. That is why it is so important to find out whether or not the concept actually works.

As noted earlier, the compact city concept is firmly rooted in Dutch spatial planning. That concept may even play a more prominent role in the Netherlands than elsewhere. Thus, its effectiveness should be most evident in this country, whereby the Netherlands would be fertile ground for empirical testing of the concept. However, hardly any studies have been carried out along these lines thus far.

Most of the insights that are currently being put into practice in the Netherlands are derived from scenario studies based on simulation models (for example, Clerx and Verroen, 1992). Those models formalize people's travel behaviour in several mathematical equations. In most cases, these are estimated on the basis of cross-sectional data. The variables of distance and/or travel time and cost per mode of transport are used frequently. So are access to a car and the present and future infrastructure quality of roads and public transport. The area covered by the study is divided into zones. Each zone is associated with its population size and the number of jobs there. With the aid of a traffic model, the differences in mobility and choice of mode of transport are calculated for each of the scenarios. Such studies are extremely useful for *ex ante* research. In particular, they reveal the sensitivity of variants with respect to the parameters that are included (for instance, the spatial form and the available infrastructure). Consider the study carried out by van Wee and van der Hoorn (1997) in which they analyse diverse scenarios. According to their findings, all of the reviewed *ex ante* studies indicate that the influence of spatial structure on mobility is strong. Furthermore, those studies show that elements of compact urbanization are important. However, some studies indicate that construction along transport axes between cities, or even in the Green Heart, leads to a lower rate of growth in mobility, especially by car. Even so, the authors mention that the models might tend to overestimate the influence of spatial form.

That caveat is in line with the findings reported by Handy (1996). She analysed recent studies on urbanization and mobility and found that the degree of empirical evidence varied mainly according to the research method that was used. Model studies scored markedly better than aggregate analysis. In contrast, estimates of individual choice behaviour expressed the most reservations about the impact of compact urbanization on travel behaviour.

In fact, many empirical evaluation studies have been conducted in other countries. The results have been mixed. Some authors find a relation between compact city variables and lower rates of car mobility. For instance, Frank and Pivo (1994) found strong correlations between density and mode choice, and some weaker correlations with mixed land use. Others are more cautious in their interpretations. A very solid study has been done by Cervero and Kockelman (1997). They found that density, land-use diversity and pedestrian-orientated designs generally reduce trip rates and encourage non-auto travel. Nevertheless, they conclude that the results must be interpreted as being associative rather than causal, and that the influences of the built environment on travel are modest. Kitamura et al. (1997) also prove a relationship between urbanization and travel behaviour; but they also conclude that people's attitudes are more strongly associated with travel than with land-use characteristics. Banister et al. (1997) suggest that spatial planning *may help* (my italics) reduce the need to travel. Breheny (1992, pp. 156–7), writing about the compact city, states that

> [T]he relationship between urban form and environmental improvement may not be as direct as planners would like. Complex political, economic and social factors determine the relationship as well as urban form. However, there is little doubt that they do have an effect, and that planning can contribute.

To summarize, compact city policy seems plausible. For some years now, policy in the Netherlands has been steeped in the concept of compact urbanization. The time was ripe to evaluate that policy by carrying out an empirical study. Several studies performed to test the effectiveness of this concept are described in the next sections.

COMMUTING PATTERNS IN NEW RESIDENTIAL AREAS

Several investigations have been conducted by the OTB Research Institute for Housing, Urban and Mobility Studies to measure the mobility effects of new housing programmes emanating from the compact city concept. These studies are largely comparable (see also Kruythoff, 1998). One of them was commissioned by the Ministry of Housing, Spatial Planning and the Environment to test the effect of new housing built according to the principle of proximity at four new residential development areas in the Randstad (den Hollander et al., 1996). For the province of Noord-Brabant, the mobility effects of siting and urban density were checked at 25 new residential locations (Konings et al., 1996). Both investigations focused exclusively on commuting behaviour. They were carried out by interviewing people who had recently moved to new areas. For both locations, the respondent and his/her domestic partner were asked about their present and previous housing situation, the employment situation and the journey to work (specifically, mode of transport and distance travelled). The questionnaires also covered demographic characteristics, car ownership and income level. The average rate of response for the Randstad was 59 per cent, which means that about 325 interviews were held at each location. In Noord-Brabant, the response was 61 per cent, making a total of 909 interviews there.

The decision to interview households who had recently moved in was made to allow measurement of any change in commuting that may have occurred. The rationale was that major long-term decisions that people make, such as the choice of or change in the place of residence and place of work, determine the context in which mobility will take place (for instance, by setting the commuting distance) in the longer term. Deliberate long-term decisions such as these induce people to re-evaluate their travel behaviour, including the choice of mode of transport (Salomon and Ben-Akiva, 1983).

A few brief remarks should be made about these studies. They were limited to commuting trips and to people living in new residential locations. The Dutch policy focuses chiefly on commuting, because the journey to work causes most traffic congestion, due to its concentration in place and time (yet it accounts for a mere 20 per cent of the total volume of mobility). The choice to focus the study on the behaviour of people living in these new developments has policy implications, since more than half a million dwellings still have to be built over the coming years.

The Randstad Case Study

At the time the investigation was being carried out in the Randstad, no Vinex locations had been developed. Nevertheless, the four study areas that were

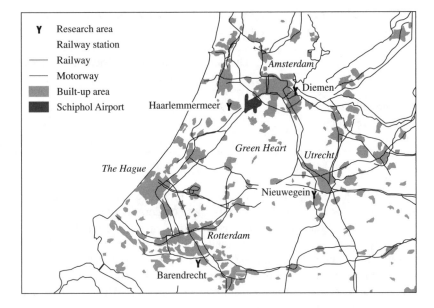

Source: OTB.

Figure 10.3   Map of the case-study locations in the Randstad

selected had been recently built in accordance with the principles of the
compact city. All lie on the outskirts of pre-existing cities. All are well located
with respect to employment and services. All are accessible by high-quality
public transport. And all were built at relatively high densities. The selected
districts are Nieuweland in the municipality of Barendrecht, which is close to
Rotterdam; Diemen-Noord, near Amsterdam; Toolenburg in the municipality
of Haarlemmermeer, which is near Amsterdam's Schiphol Airport; and
Galecop in the town of Nieuwegein, just outside Utrecht (see Figure 10.3).

The supply of dwellings in the districts shows a clear bias in favour of
single-family houses in the owner-occupied sector. Representing 65 per cent
of the supply, this reflects the current housing demand. The profile of the residents is also clear. The majority are households that move from one house to
another, half of whom have moved out of a single-family house. Regarding
employment, very few households are inactive and nearly 65 per cent are dual-
income families. Moreover, most people have a full-time job: 90 per cent of
the breadwinners and over half of their domestic partners work more than 32
hours a week.

The study shows that the move to the new developments shortened the
average commuting distance per household by 16 kilometres per week. This

Table 10.2   Effect of the move on the number of kilometres travelled per week for each location (Randstad case study)

	Baren-drecht	Diemen	Haarlem-mermeer	Nieuwe-gein	Total
Average reduction in kilometres per family	–4.0	–20.9	–27.4	–7.5	–15.7

Source: Den Hollander et al. (1996).

comes down to a reduction of 8 per cent for the breadwinners and 5 per cent for their partners. As Table 10.2 reveals, these outcomes differ from one location to the next. None the less, it is interesting to note that the reduction may be largely attributed to a relatively small group (15 per cent) of long-distance movers. These households moved specifically to shorten their journey to work. And indeed, the move reduced the commuting distance in every instance of a long-distance move. But the rest of the movers showed a hefty increase in their average commuting distance!

The move has had a minor effect on the mode of transport used for the journey to work (see Table 10.3). The car remains the most frequently used mode. Nearly 70 per cent of the breadwinners and over 60 per cent of their partners continue to use the car after the move. This represents a slight increase among the breadwinners. Along with the decline in average commuting distance, the number of kilometres driven also declined somewhat. A comparison of the locations reveals that people tend to use the car and public transport less in Nieuwegein, in favour of the bicycle. This is largely explained by the shorter distances between home and work in Nieuwegein.

Table 10.3   Modal share in the journey to work by location (Randstad case study)

	Baren-drecht	Diemen	Haarlem-mermeer	Nieuwe-gein	Total
Cyclist, pedestrian	23	18	18	32	23
Car	61	64	68	55	62
Public transport	15	13	13	10	14
Other	1	1	1	1	1
Total	100	100	100	100	100

Source: Den Hollander et al. (1996).

The Province of Noord-Brabant Case Study

Unlike the study in the Randstad, the Brabant study was not limited to a few select locations. Instead, the study covered a large number of new residential development areas spread throughout the province. The selected locations were distinguished according to urbanization type and housing density, making it possible to compare the outcomes across location types.

Three types of urbanization have been distinguished. These are inner-city locations; urban extension areas, on the edge of the built-up area; and locations in rural areas. Likewise, housing density is classified in three levels: low (less than 20 units per hectare); intermediate (21–30 units per hectare); and high (more than 30 units per hectare). The minimum density for Vinex locations is set at 30 dwellings per hectare. But in the context of the more or less rural character of Brabant, this is a fairly high density. When the three urbanization types are combined with the three density classes, nine location types can be distinguished in principle. A few of these types seldom occur in practice, however; 'high-density rural development' is a case in point. Actually, five location types are used here (see Figure 10.4).

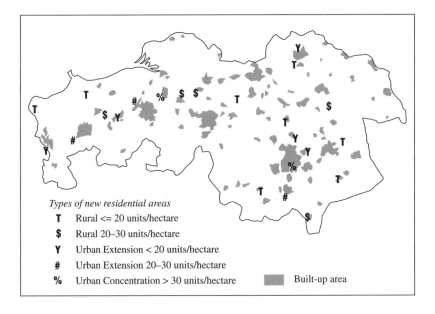

Types of new residential areas
T	Rural <= 20 units/hectare
$	Rural 20–30 units/hectare
Y	Urban Extension < 20 units/hectare
#	Urban Extension 20–30 units/hectare
%	Urban Concentration > 30 units/hectare

Built-up area

Source: OTB.

Figure 10.4   Locations of the new residential areas in the Brabant case study

Both the dwellings and their inhabitants resemble those described above for districts in the Randstad case study. The predominance of single-family owner-occupied houses is somewhat stronger in Noord-Brabant, though, at 83 per cent. The distribution by location type is shown in Table 10.4. The more urbanized a location becomes, the higher its proportion of dwellings in multi-family structures. Dwellings in rural areas are almost exclusively single-family houses. Typical for Brabant is the predominance of single-family houses, even at infill developments within the urban regions. Here too, most households are filtering. As many as 70 per cent have moved out of a single-family house. Few of the residents are out of work (and most of those individuals are retirees). Nearly 60 per cent of the households are dual-income families, the majority working full-time.

The study reveals no significant differences between the location types with regard to the number of kilometres driven weekly per household. At infill development areas within the urban regions, where densities are high, many households (25 per cent) do not drive to work. But their contribution to reduced mobility is virtually wiped out by a group with a long way to commute by car. The differences in number of car-kilometres are chiefly explained by the variables of car ownership and household composition. A two-car family will drive at least twice as many kilometres as a one-car household. Dual-income families drive more kilometres than one-income households. One-income households with children drive more than those without children; however, the opposite applies to dual-income households: those with children drive less than those without children.

Car ownership is higher in Noord-Brabant than anywhere else in the Netherlands. On top of that plateau, the new residential districts studied here form even higher peaks: 67 per cent of these households have one car and 26 per cent have two or more vehicles. Most households (69 per cent) choose to drive to work. There is a slight but significant correlation with housing density: driving decreases somewhat at higher densities. A respectable share of the commuting (25 per cent) is done by cycling or walking, however. Interestingly, in rural areas especially, the bicycle plays a specific role. Public transport is scantily used, though its use rises in tandem with higher densities. (See Table 10.5.)

The move to a new residential location has had virtually no effect on the choice of mode of transport for the journey to work. On average, there has been a slight reduction in the number of kilometres travelled to work. However, that decline may be explained by one member of the household ceasing to work. As found in the Randstad study, most of the reduction in kilometres may be attributed to the households that have moved over a long distance; the rest of the newcomers actually travel more kilometres than previously (see Table 10.6 and Figure 10.5).

Table 10.4   *Distribution of dwellings by location type (%) (Brabant case study)*

	Rural ≤ 20	Rural 20–30	Urban ext. ≤ 20	Urban ext. 20–30	Urban concentr. > 30	Total
Single-family dwelling	97	97	82	76	64	83
Multifamily dwelling	3	3	18	24	36	17
	100	100	100	100	100	100

Source: Konings et al. (1996).

Table 10.5   *Share of mode of transport in the journey to work by location type (%) (Brabant case study)*

	Rural ≤ 20	Rural 20–30	Urban ext. ≤ 20	Urban ext. 20–30	Urban concentr. > 30	Total
Cyclist, pedestrian	24	31	21	23	27	25
Car	74	66	76	67	61	69
Public transport	2	3	3	10	12	6
Total	100	100	100	100	100	100

Source: Konings et al. (1996).

223

Table 10.6 Increase and decrease in the distance to work due to the move (per moving distance class) (Brabant case study)

Moving distance to the new location	Breadwinner			Partner		
	No.	Mean (km)	Sum (km)	No.	Mean (km)	Sum (km)
< 5 km	254	2.6	654	179	0.3	55
5–10 km	48	3.7	179	35	1.7	58
10–20 km	37	2.4	89	30	2.6	77
20–30 km	12	7.8	93	9	5.0	45
30–40 km	6	0.5	3	5	–18.8	–94
40–50 km	6	6.0	36	5	20.6	103
50–60 km	5	–66.6	–333	1	50.0	50
60–70 km	5	–33.2	–166	2	39.0	78
70–80 km	5	–59.0	–295	1	77.0	77
80–90 km	3	–34.7	–104	2	2.0	4
90–100 km	3	–64.3	–193	2	51.5	103
> 100 km	10	–62.2	–622	5	–27.6	–138

Source: OTB survey (1999).

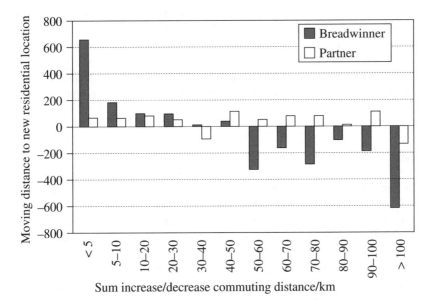

Sum increase/decrease commuting distance/km

Source: OTB   Survey (1996).

Figure 10.5   Total increase or decrease in the distance to work due to the move (per moving distance class) (Brabant case study)

Implications

Both investigations have tested the influence of compact urbanization princi-ples on commuting. In the Randstad study, the test concerned whether or not moving to a location that complies with the concentration principle actually reduces mobility in general and driving in particular. The Brabant study compared the siting of residential development areas with respect to the built-up urbanized area and in terms of their housing density. That study also tested the effect of the move on mobility.

Both studies indicate that the influence of the compact urbanization princi-ples (namely, proximity and housing density) has been very limited. In the Randstad, a modest reduction in commuting distance was found, leading to a decline in the number of kilometres driven per week. However, that decline can only be explained by the contribution of a small number of long-distance movers. In fact, those households whose previous dwelling was not as far away proved to drive more kilometres than they used to. In Noord-Brabant, there is absolutely no evidence that the move has led to a decline in commuting distance or in the number of kilometres driven. The car continues to predominate, both in the Randstad and in Noord-Brabant.

The choice to drive to work remains virtually unchanged in both studies. Travel behaviour proves to be persistent, even after a move. Although the use of public transport increases at higher densities, it remains disappointingly low. The use of the bicycle proves to have some potential for shorter commuting distances.

IMPLEMENTATION PROBLEMS

The previous section showed that the effect of the compact urbanization principles is very limited. The effect may be insufficient for another reason: compact urbanization itself has not been sufficiently realized. It takes a major policy effort to build compact cities. That is because the policy goes against the grain of market-driven developments. Moreover, there is tension between this policy and other policy areas. In the following paragraphs, two examples of tension are described. One concerns the preferences of housing consumers, and the other concerns the urban economy.

Example of Housing Preferences

The construction programme of roughly half a million dwellings to be built in the Netherlands over the coming years will have to take place primarily at the Vinex locations. The government has stipulated that a large share will have to be private-sector housing. Half of these private-sector units will be within the built-up area of the cities, while 70 per cent will be constructed in urban extension areas. As the developers and financiers observe, the greatest demand is for single-family houses in a green suburban environment that is easily accessible by car. No wonder that the plans for the Vinex urban extension areas call for more than 80 per cent of the dwellings to be built as single-family houses in densities ranging from 30 to 35 units per hectare. The minimum Vinex densities have become almost the maximum, and there is no sign that higher densities are being considered.

In addition, the dwellings in question are in higher price classes. Almost all of the residents have one or two cars. The low densities and the correspondingly greater distances are not conducive to bicycle use. Moreover, good public transport service is being provided only incidentally. What is the problem? The Ministry of Transport and Public Works has made a commitment to finance the effort to make the Vinex locations accessible by high-quality public transport. At the same time, the ministry made its financing conditional upon a cost-effective operation of the lines. Specifically, revenues from the public transport system would have to cover half of the operating costs. Consequently, the density and layout of the developments will have to ensure a sufficient number of passengers. In short, the financial arrangements make compact urbanization imperative. As a result of the production of suburban housing by the private sector, however, many developments do not comply sufficiently with this condition. For that reason, accessibility by high-quality public transport remains deficient or absent; in some cases the introduction of service is postponed. Thus, the aim of building a sufficient number of dwellings, particularly in the private sector, does not run parallel to the aim of compact urbanization (Priemus and Maat, 1998).

Example of the Urban Economy

The location policy for companies and services sets conditions on where places of business can be established in order to control mobility. The main tenet of the policy is to put the right company at the right place. Companies with a high intensity of use by employees and/or visitors are supposed to establish premises at locations that are easily accessible by public transport. Moreover, the parking capacity is highly regulated at these locations; the policy restricts the number of parking spaces that can be provided. In the light of that policy, companies that depend on road transport should look for locations with good road connections. Type A locations are particularly well accessed by public transport and are subject to tight restrictions on parking (one space for every ten employees in the Randstad). Type B locations are well connected by road as well as by the public transport system and the parking restrictions are moderate. The only practical way to reach type C locations is by road; parking is thus not restricted there. However, no offices are allowed at these locations.

The effect of the so-called 'ABC formula' on mobility may be outlined as follows. Companies prefer a place of business at car-friendly locations, which is obviously conducive to more frequent trips by car. Type B locations are very appealing to municipalities, as that type of location will attract businesses. In contrast to type C locations, offices are welcome at type B locations, since offices have a large number of employees and do not cause any environmental nuisance. The appeal of type B locations is enhanced by their excellent accessibility by car and their less stringent parking regulations than at type A sites. For these reasons, it is clear why local authorities try to obtain a type B status for locations within their territory (either by upgrading a type C or downgrading a type A certification). The municipalities attach most importance to the economic advantages that companies can provide, such as employment, revenues from land development and local taxes. As a tradeoff, they are willing to live with the mobility effects. In reality, the municipalities

have more pressing issues to deal with than the problem of clogged up hinterland connections (Priemus and Maat, 1998).

CONCLUSIONS

The relationship between suburbanization and mobility, as described in the
second section, above, is undeniably strong. However, the assumption that it
can be reversed by means of compact urbanization is not convincingly
supported by evidence from the Randstad and Brabant studies. Moreover, the
implementation of the compact city policy has its difficulties.

Various developments complicate the compact city policy. The theory
assumes that concentration and mixed-use development will ensure that
people will be able to live, work and use services at the level of the city region.
However, there are several reasons why this convergence occurs less than
anticipated. Let us consider some examples. An increasing degree of specialization in the workforce extends the spatial boundaries for a job search.
Meanwhile, job mobility is increasing. However, this does not necessarily
mean that people will look for a home close to work every time they change
jobs. People prefer to be reasonably accessible to all potential jobs (global
accessibility) rather than being very accessible to their own existing job (local
accessibility). One of the reasons for that is that the housing market cannot
meet the demand, in a qualitative sense. Thus, a longer journey to work is
often the tradeoff for being able to live in a nice home. As the studies show,
people prefer to live in suburban residential areas with low-density housing.

Dual-income families obviously make more commuting trips. Moreover,
their trips are often longer, since these households are orientated towards two
places of work. They have to choose which one of the two partners will live
close to work (or else find a location midway between the two places). All
these developments might show that the compact city concept (as painted in
Table 10.1) is less plausible than often has been assumed. The concept con-
centrates on compact morphological urbanization (such as buildings and
roads), and assumes, as a consequence, a compact 'activity' pattern, too.

Furthermore, the aim of increasing the use of public transport remains
problematic. Dual-income families increasingly combine diverse destinations
in a single chain trip (for instance, from their house to the childcare centre and
on to work, returning by way of the supermarket). Complex trips are only efficient with individualized transport, which in most cases will be a car (Gordon
et al., 1988; Dijst, 1995).

All these points could be summarized as the 'notion of a compact city with
a greater diversity and people living close to their workplaces simplifies the
complexity of life-styles' (Banister, 1992, p. 180). The developments do not

entirely preclude a spatial form that reduces the need to travel, but they do demonstrate that the problem is very complex. It is evident that a relationship exists between spatial form and mobility. For one thing, the process of suburbanization spurs mobility. Yet, this observation does not prove that a different travel behaviour could be achieved by reversing the deconcentration process. Many other factors enter into the equation. Mobility is also, or perhaps chiefly, influenced by social, demographic, economic and administrative conditions.

Furthermore, it is conceivable that urbanization form does not 'influence' people's travel behaviour, but that households with different travel behaviour or attitude 'choose' a specific urbanization type. People who want to cycle or drive or travel by public transport seek neighbourhoods where they can do that (for instance, public transport-orientated households might choose to live in compact cities). In that case, urbanization form only selects the type of inhabitants, and that pattern results in various patterns of travel behaviour.

Thus, future research must go beyond the question of which urbanization factors affect the need to travel. It is essential to study the conditions under which such factors do or do not exert that influence.

REFERENCES

Anderson, W.P., P.S. Kanaroglou and E.J. Miller (1996), 'Urban form, energy and the environment: a review of issues, evidence and policy', *Urban Studies*, **33**, 7–35.

Banister, D. (1992), 'Energy use, transport and settlement patterns', in M.J. Breheny (eds), *Sustainable Development and Urban Form*, London: Pion, pp. 160–181.

Banister, D., S. Watson and C. Wood (1997), 'Sustainable cities: transport, energy and urban form', *Environment and Planning B: Planning and Design*, **24**, 125–43.

Breheny, M. (1992), 'The contradictions of the compact city', in M.J. Breheny (ed.), *Sustainable Development and Urban Form*, London: Pion, pp. 138–59.

Cervero, R. and K. Kockelman (1997), 'Travel demand and the 3 Ds: density, diversity and design', *Transportation Research D*, **2**, 199–219.

Clerx, W.C.G. and E.J. Verroen (1992), *Ruimtelijke inrichtingsvarianten voor Nederland, vervoerspatronen en milieuconsequenties* (Alternatives of Spatial Organisation for the Netherlands, Travel Patterns and Environmental Implications), Delft: Inro-TNO.

de Boer, N. (1996), *De Randstad bestaat niet. De onmacht tot grootstedelijk beleid* (The Randstad Does not Exist. Inability for Metropolitan Policies), Rotterdam: NAi Uitgevers.

den Hollander, B., H. Kruythoff and R. Teule (1996), *Woningbouw op Vinex-locaties: effect op het woonwerk-verkeer in de Randstad* (Housing at Vinex locations: Effects on Commuting in the Randstad), Delft: Delft University Press.

Dijst, M.J. (1995), *Het elliptisch leven: actieruimte als integrale maat voor bereik en mobiliteit – modelontwikkeling met als voorbeeld twee-verdieners met kinderen in Houten en Utrecht* (The Elliptical Life: Action Space as an Integral Measure for Reach and Mobility – Model Development with Double-earning Households with Children living in Houten and Utrecht as Example), Delft: TU Delft.

Frank, L.D. and G. Pivo (1994), 'Impacts of mixed use and density on utilization of three modes of travel: single-occupant vehicle, transit and walking', *Transportation Research Record*, **1466**, 44–52.

Gordon, P., A. Kumar and H. Richardson (1988), 'Beyond the journey to work', *Transportation Research A*, **22**, 419–26.

Handy, S. (1996), 'Methodologies for exploring the link between urban form and travel behavior', *Transportation Research D*, **1**, 151–65.

Kitamura, R., P. Mokhtarian and L. Laidet (1997), 'A micro-analysis of land-use and travel in five neighbourhoods in the San Francisco Bay area', *Transportation*, **24**, 125–58.

Konings, J.W., H.M. Kruythoff and C. Maat (1996), *Woningdichtheid en mobiliteit. Woon-werkverkeer op nieuwbouwlocaties in de provincie Noord-Brabant* (Housing Densities and Mobility: Commuting on New Residential Areas in the Province of North-Brabant), Delft: Delft University Press.

Kruythoff, H.M (1998), 'Nieuwe woongebieden: ligging, woningdichtheid en woon-werkmobiliteit' (New residential areas: location, housing densities and commuting), in M.J. Dijst and L.L. Kapoen (eds), *Op weg naar steden van morgen* (On the Way to Cities of Tomorrow), Assen: Van Gorcum, pp. 39–55.

Ministry of Housing, Spatial Planning and the Environment (MVROM) (1987), *Vierde Nota over de Ruimtelijke Ordening* (Fourth report on spatial planning), Den Haag: MVROM.

Ministry of Housing, Spatial Planning and the Environment (MVROM) (1991), *Vierde Nota over de Ruimtelijke Ordening Extra* (Fourth Report on spatial planning extra), Den Haag: MVROM.

Ministry of Housing, Spatial Planning and the Environment (MVROM) (1996), *Actualisering Vierde Nota over de Ruimtelijke Ordening Extra* (Updating fourth report on spatial planning extra), Den Haag: Sdu Uitgevers.

Ministry of Housing and Spatial Planning and the Environment (MVROM) (1999), *De ruimte van Nederland. Startnota ruimtelijke ordening 1999* (The Space of the Netherlands. Starting report on Spatial Organisation), Den Haag: Sdu Uitgevers.

Ministry of Transportation and Water Management (MV&W) (1995), *Visie op verstedelijking en mobiliteit* (Vision on urbanization and mobility), Den Haag: MV&W.

Ministry of Transportation and Water Management (MV&W) (1997), *Zeven trends. Mobiliteit in veranderend Nederland* (Seven trends. Mobility in the changing Netherlands), Rotterdam: Adviesdienst Verkeer en Vervoer.

Newman, P.W.G. and J.R. Kenworthy (1989), 'Gasoline consumption and cities. A comparison of US cities with a global survey', *Journal of the American Planning Association*, **55** (1), 24–37.

Priemus, H. and C. Maat (1998), *Ruimtelijk en mobiliteitsbeleid: interactie van rijksinstrumenten* (Spatial and Mobility Policies: interaction of instruments of the national government), Delft: Delft University Press.

Salomon, I. and M. Ben-Akiva (1983), 'The use of life-style concept in travel demand models', *Environment and Planning A*, **15**, 623–38.

van Wee, B. and T. van der Hoorn (1997), 'De invloed van ruimtelijke ordening op verkeer en vervoer: scenariostudies vergeleken' (Land-use impacts on traffic and transport: a comparison of scenario studies), *Tijdschrift Vervoerswetenschap*, **33** (1), 43–61.

11. Land-use impacts on passenger transport: a comparison of Dutch scenario studies

Bert van Wee and Toon van der Hoorn

INTRODUCTION

Land use has several impacts on transport. For example, long (average) distances between residential areas and retail locations result in relatively long travelling distances for shopping, a significant discrepancy between the number of jobs for the working population and the number and/or quality of jobs available in a town or countryside, which will force many people to commute over longer distances. Land-use impacts on transport, the subject of studies for many years, have been investigated using several methods. Handy (1996) distinguishes five categories: (i) model simulation studies, (ii) aggregate analysis, (iii) disaggregate analysis, (iv) choice models and (v) activity-based analyses. A distinction within category (i) can be made on a spatial scale basis: urban or regional versus supraregional. For a review of urban/regional simulation models we refer to Wegener (1998). Our chapter will focus on Dutch model simulation studies carried out for the supraregional scale since the mid-1980s, as reported in van Wee (1993, 1997) and van Wee and van der Hoorn (1997). The study described here aimed at showing the possible effects of land-use policies on passenger transport in all geographical areas from the so-called 'Randstad' to the Netherlands as a whole. Furthermore, the two following questions required an answer: (i) are the indicators used in the studies adequate and (ii) how well do state-of-the-art models estimate effects of land-use scenarios?

The next section describes the relationships between transport, land use and the environment. The third section then presents a conceptual model for the relationship between land use and transport, while the fourth section briefly describes the models used in the simulation studies. The fifth section reviews the simulation studies and the sixth section compares the studies and their results. The seventh section focuses on the transferability of the results to other countries and the eighth section on the indicators used to describe the possible impact of land use on transport. The ninth section answers the question of how well the state-of-the-art models estimate the effects of land-use scenarios. The tenth section suggests further research and the final section summarizes the main conclusions.

TRANSPORT, LAND USE AND THE ENVIRONMENT

Transport contributes to many environmental problems such as climate change, acidification and noise nuisance. Emissions from motor vehicles (for example, CO, fine particulate, NO_x) cause or contribute to a wide range of health effects (see Walsh, 1990, for a general view). Whitelegg et al. (1993) conclude that living on streets with heavy traffic increases illness significantly. Table 11.1 shows the share of cars, total road transport and total transport in the emissions of several pollutants for the Netherlands.

The CO_2 figures do not include emissions due to international transport by ship and aircraft. Of the total Dutch population, 28 per cent are inconvenienced by noise nuisance of road traffic, 18 per cent by noise from aircraft and 5 per cent by noise from rail traffic (RIVM, 1997). The standards for maximum concentrations of one or more pollutants are exceeded along some 200 kilometres of road (RIVM, 1998). In many streets children can no longer play due to parked and moving vehicles. Many children have to be brought to school because the roads are not safe.

To reduce environmental impacts of transport, several objectives and instruments can be chosen. An 'objective' in this chapter refers to what is wanted (for example, a shift from car use to public transport, the use of cleaner technology) and an 'instrument' refers to how this is to be achieved (for example, changes in prices, regulations). The environmental impact of traffic and transport (and the congestion level) can be influenced by several

Table 11.1   Share of transport in Dutch emissions, 1997

	Cars	Road transport	Total transport
CO_2	10	17	18
NO_x	21	44	64
VOC	24	38	42
CO	43	54	59
PM10	9	21	38

Source: Van den Brink and Annema (1999) and RIVM (1998) based on data from Statistics Netherlands.

Table 11.2   Relationships between instruments and objectives

	Volume	Modal split	Technology	Efficiency	Behaviour
Infrastructure	*	*	*	*	*
Information and organization		*		*	
Marketing		*			
Land-use planning	*	*		*	*
Pricing	*	*	*	*	*
Restrictions	*	*	*	*	*

Source: Blok and van Wee (1994).

kinds of objectives related to the total volumes (for example, less mobility or less car use), the modal split (for example, a shift from car to public transport), the techniques used (for example, the use of three-way catalytic converters), the efficiency of vehicle use (for example, fuller lorries, higher occupancy rates of cars) and the way vehicles are used (behaviour, for example, the driving speed of cars). Table 11.2 shows how these instruments can contribute to the objectives, thereby changing the environmental impact of traffic and transport.

The table shows that land-use policies can influence traffic volumes, modal split, efficiency and behaviour: for example, due to shorter distances between relevant locations the volume may be reduced. Building new residential areas and offices close to railway stations may increase the share of public transport. Because of higher densities in residential areas it may be easier to find others willing to participate in a carpool to get to work. The way of urbanization may (in combination with infrastructure policy) influence the share of intraurban, motorway and other road traffic. Besides, land-use policies can contribute to open-space conservation, especially in the case of compact building and concentrating urbanization in relatively few areas. Because land-use policies may potentially have a lot of influence on the environmental impact of transport, it is understandable that in official Dutch land-use plans the relationships between land use and transport have been emphasized explicitly. The Dutch land-use plans focus mainly on passenger transport and aim to reduce the growth in car use. In the Netherlands, car use between 1980 and 1997 increased by 52 per cent. Assuming current policy and three long-term scenarios, future growth in car use may vary between 30 and 50 per cent (Geurs et al., 1998). The Dutch government tries to reduce the growth in car use. Land-use policies should contribute to this reduction in growth.

A CONCEPTUAL MODEL FOR THE RELATIONSHIPS BETWEEN LAND USE AND TRANSPORT

Given the overall population size and demographic characteristics, the total volume of passenger transport and the split between transport modes depends on the locations of human activities, the needs and desires of people and the transport resistances (generalized transport costs). Locations are related to such activities as living, working, shopping, recreation and education. The needs and desires of people are related to socioeconomic and cultural factors. Income is an important determinant, but not the only one. Availability of cultural facilities such as museums within a short distance, might stimulate people to think about wanting to visit them. Transport resistances (generalized as transport costs) are dependent on monetary factors, travel times, comfort and reliability of all alternatives. Figure 11.1 illustrates the relationships between these determinant categories.

The figure shows that all three categories are influential in all directions. Changes occurring in one of the three categories of determinants, could have an impact on the complete system. Changes in land-use patterns might change transport resistance between certain locations. For example, the suburbanization of offices in the Netherlands in the 1980s resulted in longer travel times using public transport and more congestion on motorways. It also increased the benefits of car ownership because of the poor public transport accessibility of the new office locations. More air connections and decreasing air fares made it possible to equip remote locations with recreational facilities. This development stimulated people's interest in holidays at such locations.

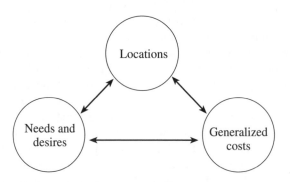

Source: Van Wee (1997).

Figure 11.1   Relationships between activity locations, needs and desires, transport resistances and passenger transport

Growing car ownership levels decreased travel times by car and encouraged suburbanization. Partly because of growing car ownership levels and car use, most Western countries have expanded the motorway network, resulting in shorter travel times, more car use and dispersed land-use patterns.

The current situation can be considered as a kind of continuously changing equilibrium (or maybe better: disequilibrium). This is because changes occur long before the long-term equilibrium becomes a fact.

THE MODELS USED IN THE SIMULATION STUDIES

All studies reviewed in this chapter use a more-or-less traditional transport model, including modules for production/attraction, distribution, modal split and network assignment. The models are cross-sectionally based and calculate the long-term equilibrium directly. The years in which changes, such as the development of new residential, working, shopping or recreational areas, occur, and the changes in level of service per mode, have no impact on the final results.

The models simultaneously estimate the distribution and modal split. This is particularly important if land-use alternatives are simulated because if the level of service varies between the scenarios, for example, not only does the modal split change, but also the origin–destination pattern. For instance, an improvement in the railway system (more railway lines, faster trains, higher frequencies) not only leads to a higher share of rail transport, but also to longer distances between home and work for rail-based home–work travel.

A REVIEW OF THE SIMULATION STUDIES

In this section, four studies on possible transport impacts of land-use scenarios will be reviewed. The studies are: the Randstad Strategic Study; a study of the EROMOBIL Working Group, also focusing on the Randstad area; a TNO study for the Netherlands as a whole, which we shall call 'land-use scenarios'; and another TNO study, 'Model calculations of Randstad scenarios', focusing on the Randstad and connection areas. The studies reviewed were all carried out to give policy makers insight into possible mobility effects of strategic policy options for land use at the regional or supraregional level. As far as we know, these are all the scenario studies of this type that were carried out in the Netherlands in the 1986–95 period.

Randstad Strategic Study

This study focuses on the Randstad area, with 1982 as the base year and 2000 as the forecasting year (De Jong et al., 1986). Scenarios are related to:

Table 11.3   Car and public transport use for four urbanization concepts

Urbanization concept	Car use (vehicle-km)	Public transport use (passenger-km)	Public transport/ car use
Base year	100	100	100
Concentration	109	114	105
Ring	112	117	102
Growth inside ring	121	126	104
Growth outside ring	130	148	114

1. urbanization concepts for new housing areas;
2. the spatial distribution of new employment opportunities;
3. commuting between local municipalities; and
4. networks for car and public transport.

Urbanization concepts for new housing areas
The four urbanization scenarios below were developed for new housing areas:

- *Concentration*:   in the bigger cities and towns, as well as some towns where fast growth is stimulated.
- *Ring*:   at the so-called ring of the Randstad (the axes between the main cities and towns, forming a ring-shaped structure); no urbanization within the ring area.
- *Growth inside ring*:   within the Randstad ring.
- *Growth outside ring*:   outside the Randstad ring.

Table 11.3 summarizes the results. The table shows that mobility is highly influenced by the urbanization concept. In the scenario with the highest level of car use, this is 19 per cent higher than in the scenario with the lowest level of car use. The difference for public transport is 30 per cent.

The spatial distribution of new employment
Apart from default distribution (current policy at that time/business as usual), three scenarios were developed:

- *Follow*:   (new) places of employment 'follow' the residential locations of the working population.
- *Concentration*:   (new) places of employment will be located more or less in/near the new housing areas, as in the ring scenario for urbanization
- *Suburbanization*:   suburbanization of (new) employment areas in/near the new housing areas.

These spatial distributions were combined with specific scenarios for new housing areas. Table 11.4 shows the combinations and mobility results. The table shows that mobility is much less influenced by the assumed distributions of employment than by the distribution of new housing areas. This is not surprising if we realize that many more trips are private (that is, from home to home) than employment-location based. Again, differences in public transport use are larger than differences in car use.

Commuting between local municipalities

Based on the 'ring' scenario for housing, three scenarios for commuting between local communities were developed. In one of the scenarios it is assumed that people work and live as much as possible in the same community. Intercommunity commuting therefore only exists when the number of jobs is not equal to the number of the working population. In this scenario, car use is less than half of the ring-scenario car use. The use of public transport is about 45 per cent lower. This should be emphasized as a hypothetical scenario, in which behaviour (with respect to residential and working locations) is not assumed to be derived empirically. The scenario shows a huge potential reduction in mobility resulting from people working and living in the same community as much as possible.[1]

Networks for car and public transport

Based on the housing scenarios 'ring' and 'growth inside ring', the following three network scenarios were developed:

* extension of the road network;
* extension of the public transport network; and
* extension of both the road and public transport networks.

Table 11.5 gives the results. The margins within each cell reflect differences between urbanization scenarios. The small differences recorded in the table show the relatively minor importance of the urbanization scenarios for the effects of infrastructural changes on mobility. The impact of the assumed extension of the road network on car use is relatively high. However, public transport improvements hardly seem to affect the level of car use.

Overall conclusion

The researchers conclude here that land-use developments can largely influence mobility. The study also shows that extension of the road network will lead to more car use, whereas extension of the public transport network hardly influences car-use levels.

Table 11.4 Car and public transport use in scenarios for the distribution of new employment opportunities

Employment locations	Urbanization concept	Car use	Car use compared to default distribution of employment (%)	Public transport use	Public transport use compared to default distribution of employment (%)
Follow	Concentration	112	+3	109	−5
Follow	Ring	114	+2	109	−8
Concentration	Ring	111	−1	119	+2
Suburbanization	Ring	113	+1	121	+9
Follow	Growth outside ring	116	−5	106	−20

Note: The +3% for the first scenario means, for example, that car use is 3% higher if employment is distributed as in the 'follow' scenario compared to default distribution.

Table 11.5   Car and public transport use for infrastructural scenarios

	Difference in car use compared to default network (%)	Difference in public transport use compared to default network (%)
Extension of the road network	+22 to +24	−27 to −28
Extension of the public transport network	−1 to −2	+31 to +32
Extension of both the road and public transport networks	+21 to +22	−4

EROMOBIL Working Group

The study done by this working group in 1989, with 2010 as the scenario year, compares four urbanization scenarios for the Randstad:

- *The 'point scenario'*: 'perfect' core-to-core rail connections between cities and towns, future urbanization close to main railway stations in the four main cities and some urbanization close to other railway stations in the agglomerations of the four big cities.
- *The 'lob scenario'*: urbanization at the edges of the big cities with emphasis on regional public transport.
- *The 'axes scenario[2]'*: accent on short-distance rail transport, with new housing areas located along the rail axes between the four big cities in the Randstad (Amsterdam, Rotterdam, The Hague, Utrecht); new employment areas located in the centre of the four big cities.
- *The 'central scenario'*: urbanization in the so-called 'Green Heart' of the Randstad.

The scenarios were compared with the so-called 'unchanged policy scenario' as described in the Second Transport Structure Plan (TSP-II, 1990). Although road networks in all scenarios are the same, public transport networks are adapted to the urbanization scenarios. Assumptions on densities of housing and employment also differ. Table 11.6 gives the main results as indices (1986 = 100).

The maximum reduction in car use compared to the 'unchanged policy scenario' is 10 index points (6 per cent). The possible impact on the use of public transport varies much more, the differences reaching to 73 index points

Table 11.6   Car and public transport use for the EROMOBIL Working Group (index, 1986 = 100)

Scenario	Car use (vehicle-km)	Public transport use (passenger-km)	Public transport/ car use
Unchanged policy	170	155	91
Point	165	199	121
Lob	166	212	128
Axes	165	228	138
Central	160	166	104

(47 per cent). The central scenario leads to the lowest level of car use without a sharp increase in the use of public transport. However, the authors conclude that this scenario should be rejected because of the socioeconomic consequences for the large agglomerations, the land-use implications for the Green Heart of the Randstad[3] and its lack of realism. The main conclusion of the study is that combined land-use and transport policies could influence car-use levels significantly.

Land-use Scenarios

Clerx and Verroen (1992) used the Netherlands as a whole as study area for the period up to 2015, separating it into two spatial levels: (a) the parts of the country showing the most urbanization and (b) the manner in which urbanization comes about in these parts. Three urbanization types were developed on level (a):

- accent on the Randstad;
- accent on the intermediate zone;[4]
- a deconcentrated regional development in all parts of the Netherlands ('regions on their own').

Four urbanization types were developed on level (b):

- *The compact city*:   urbanization within the cities and lobs at their edges.
- *'Top locations'*:   future residential areas at locations highly preferred as living areas.
- *Axes*:   new housing areas located along railways and main motorways; new employment areas located near cities and towns, and along the railway and motorway axes.
- *'Sprawl'*:   urbanization mainly outside the bigger cities and towns in areas where the market pressure will be high.

Table 11.7   Car and public transport use and land-use scenarios (index 1990 = 100)

First spatial level (a)	Second spatial level (b)	Car use	Public transport use	Public transport/ car use
FRSP	FRSP	138	120	87
Accent on the Randstad	Compact city	160	191	120
Accent on the Randstad	Top locations	163	188	115
Accent on the intermediate zone	Axes	129	111	86
Regions on their own	Sprawl	137	125	91

Only four of the 4 × 3 possible combinations of levels (a) and (b) were worked out.

Table 11.7 gives the main results and compares them to the policy of the Fourth Report on Spatial Planning Extra (FRSP, 1990). The table shows the compact city scenario to have a relatively high level of car use. The authors explain this by the relatively long home–work distances, although many short trips within cities are made. The authors cite mobility and environmental impacts as varying significantly between land-use scenarios. The main cause of differences in mobility is the (im)balance between population and employment within agglomerations. The authors also conclude that scenarios with relatively low levels of car use will need a huge policy effort to answer to market forces, which the scenarios do not.

Model Calculations of Randstad Scenarios

The fourth study described covers the Randstad area and connection areas: it also focuses on land-use alternatives for the period from 2005 to 2015 (Verroen and Hilbers, 1995).[5] The basis for this scenario study was a study on so-called 'critical design dimensions', used to find the most 'mobility-friendly' forms of urbanization, that is:

- *Single-core as opposed to multicore orientation*:   further urbanization through the development of separate metropolitan areas or assuming the development of networks of cities with the idea of spreading the daily patterns of activities out over several metropolitan areas.

- *Near as opposed to far*:   urbanization linked directly to existing urban areas/zones or further away.
- *Connected as opposed to unconnected to the main public transport infrastructure*:   locations either close to stations or stops of high-quality public transport or not.
- *Clustered as opposed to dispersed*:   development of large-scale, urban extensions with emphasis on the main infrastructure versus a development of small-scale urban extensions with emphasis on the secondary infrastructure.
- *Mixing as opposed to separating*:   mixed land-use versus separating functions, such as living, working and shopping within neighbourhoods.

Scenarios based on only three of these design criteria were developed. The scenarios do not differ with respect to the other two criteria. For example, in all scenarios further urbanization is assumed to take place near high-quality public transport and existing urban areas/zones because it is clear that this results in 'mobility-friendly' forms of urbanization. Table 11.8 gives an overview. The study not only gives kilometres per mode but also total time spent on travel and an accessibility indicator, the so-called 'potential accessibility' (the average number of activities that can be reached within a certain time).

The study shows that mixed land use results in 1 per cent less car use and 3 per cent fewer public transport passenger-kilometres. However, potential accessibility is better (3 per cent). Concentrating future urbanization in relatively few locations (areas with more than 25,000 to 40,000 homes and jobs) leads to slightly less car use but a significantly better accessibility. Public transport use increases by 2 to 3 per cent. Positive effects of this concentration

Table 11.8   Promising urbanization options tested

Clustering principle	Mixing principle	Orientation	
		Single core	Multicore
Clustering	Separate functions	Compact city 'separated'	New cities along axes, 'separated'
	Mixed functions	Compact city, 'mixed'	New cities along axes 'mixed'
Dispersing	Separate functions	Incremental city 'separated'	Belt cities 'separated'
	Mixed functions	Incremental city 'mixed'	Belt cities 'mixed'

are felt mainly outside the Randstad area because prospects are better there. In the Randstad, urbanization is so far advanced that hardly any non-urbanized areas qualifying for further urbanization could be found.

Single-core locations have a lower level of car use if they are located closer to the centre of the closest metropolitan district, if there is less urbanization outside the central metropolitan district and if the multicore proximity is better, that is, the more these locations are found closer to the centres of other metropolitan districts.

At a certain point, single-core locations further away from the centre of the closest metropolitan district lead to more car use than multicore locations, especially in the Randstad (where the four big cities are located). The main reason is that travel distances to the central urban areas are too far for these single-core locations.

Although the differences in mobility might seem small, only 6 per cent of all the locations of homes and only 12 per cent of all job locations show variations between the scenarios.

A COMPARISON OF THE STUDIES

It is hard to compare the studies for several reasons. For example, the time horizons differ, and the percentage of homes or places of employment that have different locations in the scenarios differ; some studies show only differences within regions (parts of the study area), whereas others also show differences between regions; some studies focus on the Randstad area only, while others also focus on the national level; some show variation only in home locations and others also show it in place of employment; in some studies only the locations of activities vary whereas in others the transport networks also vary (see Table 11.9 for a comparison of some characteristics). In spite of all these differences, several scenarios are to a certain extent comparable.

First, one of the Strategic Study Randstad scenarios is more-or-less comparable to one of the scenarios of the working group, EROMOBIL. The 'growth inside ring' scenario of the Randstad Strategic Study (for home locations) combined with the scenario in which places of employment follow the labour force (see Table 11.4) assumes a growth in the Green Heart of the Randstad of both homes and places of employment. The main scenario of the working group EROMOBIL has more or less the same assumptions. Both scenarios have a relatively low level of both car and public transport use. This conclusion is especially relevant considering the never-ending debate in the Netherlands about the position of the Green Heart (see note 2). Because it is beyond the scope of this chapter to focus on the discussions, we can only state that policy decisions should not merely be based on transportation effects.

Table 11.9 A comparison of the studies

	Randstad strategic study	EROMOBIL	Land-use scenarios	Model calculations
Area	Randstad	Randstad	The Netherlands	Randstad and connecting areas
Basic year	1982	1986	1990	1990
Reference year	2000	2010	2015	2020
Reference scenario	No reference scenario	'Unchanged policy' scenario of TSP-II	FRSP	FRSP, situation 2005
Variables in the urbanization scenarios	Inhabitants	Inhabitants, employment locations	Inhabitants, employment locations	Inhabitants, employment locations
Character of urbanization scenarios	Within Randstad area at meso level	Within Randstad area at meso level	Within the Netherlands	Within Randstand and connection area; meso and micro levels (micro level: mixed land use)

Second, the 'axes' scenario of the working group EROMOBIL is comparable with the ring scenario of the Randstad Strategic Study and the 'New towns–mixed-land-use' scenario of the Randstad Model calculations. All three scenarios have a relatively low level of car use.

These comparisons show that further urbanization within the Green Heart of the Randstad and along the axes of the Randstad (which connect the four big cities in this area) will result in a low level of car use.

Other, more general, conclusions are:

- Potential influence of land-use planning alternatives on mobility is large. The differences in car use between the scenarios can be more than 20 per cent when related to homes and employment locations with different locations in the scenarios.
- Differences in mobility between these alternatives are mainly due to the extent to which there is a balance between working and living in regions.
- The alternatives leading to the lowest level of car use differ greatly from the situation resulting from the Dutch policy of the past 20 years. A strong governmental policy is therefore required to arrive at a land-use situation where there is a relatively low level of car use. Such a policy will result in strong opposition from some of the relevant 'actors', such as companies, municipalities, consumers' organizations and real estate developers.

We shall use the study of Verroen and Hilbers (1995) to demonstrate the possible impact of land use on transport. Although only 6 per cent of the homes have different locations in the scenarios of 2015, the difference in car use is 2 per cent. This difference is not the largest possible: scenarios seen as 'undesirable' (for example, scenarios with a very diffuse pattern for new urbanization or those where the urbanized areas lack proper public transport) were not considered. So, relatively speaking, the possible impact of land use on car use is very large.

THE TRANSFERABILITY OF THE RESULTS OF OTHER COUNTRIES

The question of transferability to other countries is very relevant: will the possible impact of land-use policies be roughly the same in other countries or not? Before answering the question we consider it relevant to find the mechanisms between land use (in combination with infrastructure), on the one hand, and mobility on the other. According to literature the impacts of land use on mobility are related to key variables such as densities, the degree of mixing of locations of jobs, houses, facilities and so on, shape of the city, city size, and the locations of urban areas relative to different kinds of infrastructure (for car, public transport, slow modes) (see Martens et al., 1998). Considering these indicators we think there are similarities between the Netherlands and other countries, and also differences.

First, the similarities: since the results are partly related to the impact of densities and to the relationships between residential and working locations, on the one hand, and infrastructure (locations of railway stations, locations of motorway access points) on the other, in many countries building in higher densities may influence mobility (see Anderson et al., 1996). In most countries, urbanization close to railway stations will increase the share of public transport, compared to urbanization in areas far from railway stations.

The first difference is that cycling is much more popular in the Netherlands than in many other countries. With a share of 7 per cent in total passenger-kilometres by 'surface modes', only a few other countries are comparable. In many countries, the car and public transport (rail, bus) are supposed to be major competitors for local trips;[6] in the Netherlands the bicycle competes with public transport. Second, the urban structure of countries very often differs. For instance, the Netherlands lacks a big city such as London or Paris. Urbanization near to big metropolitan regions may have other impacts on transport than urbanization next to a medium-sized town (see Martens et al., 1998), for example, because distance to the centre varies significantly and because heavy rail very often is available in big cities but less or not at all in medium-sized cities and towns. Third, imbalance between jobs and the employment force on a local or regional scale may vary significantly between countries (and even regions within countries). Fourth, the quality of the inter-local rail system in the Netherlands is relatively high, giving public transport a better potential market share, especially for intercity trips. Therefore the impact of alternative urbanization concepts of modal choice may be greater in the Netherlands than in countries with a less-developed rail system.

It is very difficult to say to what extent the conclusions of this chapter are valid for other countries. We think that the direction of differences in mobility due to alternative urbanization concepts may be the same in many countries. But the level of impact may vary significantly between countries. We think that the only way a decent answer can be given is by modelling.

THE INDICATORS USED TO DESCRIBE THE POSSIBLE IMPACT OF LAND USE ON TRANSPORT

The first three scenarios described use only 'traditional' indicators such as car use and public transport use. The general line of thought shows a preference for a lower level of car use. Some people think a higher level of public transport use is 'better' than a lower level, while others prefer a lower level, arguing that public transport also uses energy, emits pollutants (exhaust emissions or electric traction at power plants) and is responsible for noise nuisance.

If the scenarios have to be evaluated for general policy reasons, making it possible to draw conclusions on the overall desirability of the scenarios, we believe that these indicators should not be the only ones for comparing land-use scenarios (or infrastructural scenarios, or, more generally speaking, all transport scenarios). We think that alternatives for the traffic and transport system should be judged using a broader set of indicators for both the costs and the benefits. Van Wee (1995) distinguishes three categories of costs: direct costs, related to the production, maintenance and use of infrastructure and vehicles; other costs within the transport system, for example, related to transport being unsafe and travel times (congestion); and external costs outside the transport system such as environmental costs, for example, related to noise, local air pollution, acidification and climate change.

Although several methods have been developed to calculate these cost categories, there is still much discussion about the methods and values of external costs. It is even harder to calculate the benefits. The number of passenger-kilometres or total travel times are poor indicators. The benefits should be partly expressed in accessibility indicators: to what extent does the land-use/transport system provide possibilities for people to carry out activities at different places? The consumer surplus of trips should also be included, as well as indicators for the reliability of the transport system (in other words: not only travel times but also the *chance* of encountering congestion) and the option value, where people might, for example, acknowledge the *availability* of public transport without even using it. The development of indicators for the performance of the transport system is recommended.

HOW WELL DO STATE-OF-THE-ART MODELS ESTIMATE THE EFFECTS OF LAND-USE SCENARIOS?

We think that state-of-the art models (models as used in the studies reviewed; these are traditional four-stage traffic models using cross-section data, or slightly improved versions of them) overestimate effects of land-use scenarios for the following five reasons, mainly expressed as kilometres per mode (see van Wee and van der Hoorn, 1998).

1. Most traditional models do not use fixed time budgets. Therefore total time spent on travelling may vary between land-use scenarios. However, from several studies we know that on aggregate, people have a more-or-less

constant travel time budget (see Kraan, 1996, for an overview). Therefore traditional models may overestimate the variation in mobility between land-use (and other) scenarios.

2. State-of-the-art models do distinguish between household or individual classes, but within a single class people are assumed to be homogeneous. Mobility differences between land-use and transport scenarios are mainly the result of differences in generalized travel costs (time, money) between modes. However, a spatial bias is possible. Especially in the case of a coarse zoning system, people within household classes may vary with respect to their preferences in travel mode and therefore with respect to their residential location. People who prefer to travel by train may prefer a residential location close to a railway station. People without a car will not consider a residential location that is not accessible by public transport (Pickup and Town, 1983). This spatial bias might lead to an overestimation of variation in mobility between land-use and transport scenarios.

3. Traditional models calculating the long-term equilibrium do not consider the incremental character of changes. The timing of changes may influence long-term effects: for example, if public transport is implemented in new residential areas long after the first residents have moved in, fewer people may travel by public transport than if it had been available right from the beginning. Travel behaviour has a strong habitual component (van Vugt, 1996). Feedbacks as assumed in system dynamics models do not play a role in traditional models. Panel databased models sometimes show that effects of changes may be smaller than cross-section-based models predict (Meurs, 1991).

4. Traditional models assume a long-term equilibrium. Whether this long-term equilibrium will ever be reached is arguable, especially in the case of land-use and transport scenarios that differ greatly from the current situation or trend. For example, differences in employment data per zone between the base and forecasting years implicitly assume company/firm relocations. As shown in this study, the situation differs strongly from the long-term equilibrium five years after an office relocation. Most people do not move and do not change jobs, making average home–work distances longer than according to the long-term equilibrium.

5. Part of total travel is intrazonal and thus occurs over short distances. Short-distance travel is less sensitive to measures than other forms of travel. Especially if zones are relatively large, models may overestimate the effects of measures/changes.

We find the differences cited between land-use scenarios in the above five points and calculated with traditional models to be a step in the right direction, but the differences themselves are overestimated. Besides these five points there are two other factors that may be important, although we do not know a priori whether differences will be over- or underestimated. These two factors are described below as additional reasons:

6. The interaction between transport and land use is not incorporated into traditional models. These interactions may both lead to overestimation and underestimation of differences in mobility between land-use scenarios.
7. The second is the fact that mobility chains are normally not included in traditional models. People sometimes combine trips. From time–space literature we know that the home–work axis influences total mobility strongly. Land-use scenarios very often differ with respect to residential and employment locations. The influence of such land-use scenarios on total travel may be larger than calculated.

SUGGESTIONS FOR FURTHER RESEARCH

Partly based on the discussion in the section on the transferability of results to other countries, and suggestions made by Wegener (1998) and Kitamura et al. (1997), we think that simulation studies on the impact of land use on transport can be improved in several ways. First, dynamics should be incorporated to a greater extent than at present, using panel databased models. Second, the time path for changes in infrastructure and land use should be incorporated, especially for the medium-term or not very long-term effects (less than 20 years, for instance). An example to demonstrate the importance of this was a study carried out by van Wee (1997) on the effects on passenger mobility of office relocations to public transport nodal points. He assumes a scenario in which about 12 per cent of Dutch office employment in 2015, sited at locations that are poorly accessed by public transport, will be relocated to railway station areas. The long-term equilibrium model calculates a reduction in car use of about 30 per cent of the employees whose jobs are relocated, whereas the combination of this long-term equilibrium model with special models for medium-term reactions of employees to office relocations calculates a reduction in car use of only 10 per cent. Third, activity-based models (instead of trip-based models) might both be conceptually more satisfying and give better results. Fourth, the interaction between transport and land use (and not only the impact of land use on transport) should be incorporated, especially if land-use implications of (changes in) the transport system can be expected. For a review of urban models for the land-use/transport link, see Wegener (1998). Fifth, we think that time budgets for transport (related to activities) should be included, and sixth, that within the so-called homogeneous population groups, behaviour with respect to the residential location might not be the same. People who prefer to travel by public transport will not even consider a residential location far away from a public transport nodal point (Pickup and Town, 1983). Seventh, the use of more spatial disaggregated data (smaller zones: Geographic Information System (GIS) techniques) might improve the results.

The eighth method (related to the seventh) is that micro-simulations might give better results, but will be hard to develop and implement for studies at the supraregional level (for example, for the Netherlands as a whole).

The question remaining is: are such improvements worth the effort? Some of the improvements will make the model much more expensive because, for example, much more data are required. It is hard to draw general conclusions on which improvements will be worth the effort. Our impression is that improvements which can be relatively easily incorporated into state-of-the-art models may be more cost-effective than others. However, in the long term, we think that traditional models will have to be replaced by dynamic activity-based models using GIS techniques, and maybe micro simulations.

CONCLUSIONS

We shall summarize our findings in four categories of conclusions: the relationships between transport, land use and the environment, impacts of urbanization, influence of land use on mobility and methodological conclusions.

Transport, Land Use and the Environment

1. Transport has a large share in several enivironmental problems. In the Netherlands the share of transport in emissions of CO_2, NO_x, VOC, CO and PM10 varies between almost 20 per cent to more than 60 per cent. The share of cars in total emissions of these components varies from almost 10 per cent to more than 40 per cent.
2. To reduce the environmental impact of transport, several instruments are available. Land-use policies can influence traffic volumes, modal split, transport efficiency and traffic behaviour.

Impacts on Mobility of Urbanization in the Netherlands

1. Further urbanization of the so-called 'Green Heart' of the Netherlands can be beneficial from a transport point of view (for example, a lower level of car use) but has several other (negative) impacts.
2. Urbanization on the Ring of the Randstad and along the axes results in a relatively low level of car use, especially in the case of mixed land use.

Influence of Land Use on Mobility

1. Potential influence of land-use planning alternatives on traffic and passenger transport is large. The differences in car use between the scenarios can be as much as 30 per cent when related to the number of homes and jobs with different locations in the scenarios.
2. Differences in mobility between these alternatives are caused mainly by the extent to which there is a balance between working and living in regions.
3. The alternatives that result in the lowest level of car use differ greatly from the situation resulting from the Dutch policy of the past 20 years. A strong governmental policy will therefore be required to reach a land-use situation where there is a relatively low level of car use. Such a policy will also lead to strong opposition from some of the relevant 'actors'.

Methodological Conclusions

1. Most scenario studies use only 'traditional' indicators to compare scenarios, such as car-kilometres and public transport passenger-kilometres. Only one study quantifies the accessibility of the land-use scenarios. The studies do not use indicators for the total 'costs' (including external costs) and the 'benefits' of the transport system.
2. State-of-the art models overestimate the effects of land-use scenarios.
3. Model improvements that can be relatively easily incorporated into state-of-the-art models may be more cost-effective than others. However, in the long term we think that traditional models will have to be replaced by dynamic activity-based models using GIS techniques and maybe making use of micro simulations.

NOTES

1. For literature on excess commuting due to this imbalance, see Hamilton (1982, 1989); Cropper and Gordon (1991); Small and Song (1992); Giuliano and Small (1993); White (1988); Scott et al. (1997).
2. The 'corridor concept' for urbanization has been recently introduced in the Netherlands. As in the axes scenario, corridors also represent the areas between the main cities. However, in the axes scenario, urbanization only takes place along the rail axes between the four big cities in the Randstad, whereas in the corridor concept road axes and axes outside the Randstad area are mentioned as being possible urbanization areas.
3. In the Netherlands there is an ongoing discussion about the desirability of urbanizing the Green Heart. Should it remain as it is (mainly meadows, with limitations on urbanization except at a few locations)? Should further urbanization be allowed, and if so, should it be of high or low density? Should more recreational facilities be developed, for example, more forests? For several decades there has been a policy of heavy restrictions on further

urbanization in this area, partly because of the benefits of having non-urbanized areas in the immediate proximity of the big cities.
4. The intermediate zone is the area between the Randstad (which is in the western part of the country), Belgium to the south and Germany to the east. The rest of the Netherlands comprises the southwest, north and two regions in the east.
5. See Verroen and Hilbers (1996) for an English-language version of this study.
6. However, in the SESAME project (SESAME, 1998; see also Martens et al., 1998) it was found that the car and the non-motorized modes compete more than the car and public transport.

REFERENCES

Anderson, N.P., P.S. Kanaroglou and E.J. Miller (1996), 'Urban form, energy and the enivronment: a review of issues, evidence and policy', _Urban Studies_, **33** (1), 7–35.
Blok, P.M. and G.P. van Wee (1994), 'The traffic question', in F. Dietz, W. Hafkamp and J. van der Straaten, _Handbook of Environmental Economics_, Amsterdam/Meppel: Boom, pp. 216–34 (in Dutch).
Clerx, W.C.G. and E.J. Verroen (1992), _Land-use Scenarios for the Netherlands: Travel Patterns and Environmental Impacts_ (Main report and appendices), Delft: INRO-TNO (in Dutch).
Cropper, M. and P.L. Gordon (1991), 'Wasteful commuting: a re-examination', _Journal of Urban Economics_, **29**, 2–13.
De Jong, M.A., L.H. Immers, J.W. Houtman and C.W.W. van Lohuizen (1986), _Strategic Study Randstad_, Delft: TNO (in Dutch).
Fourth Report on Spatial Planning Extra (FRSP) (1990), The Hague: SDU uitgeverij (in Dutch).
Geurs, K.T., R.M.M. van den Brink, J.A. Annema and G.P. van Wee (1998), _Traffic and Transport in the National Environmental Outlook 4_, Report no. 773002011, Bilthoven: National Institute of Public Health and the Environment (RIVM) (in Dutch).
Giuliano, G. and K.A. Small (1993), 'Is the journey to work explained by urban structure?', _Urban Studies_, **30**, 1485–500.
Hamilton, B.W. (1982), 'Wasteful commuting', _Journal of Political Economy_, **90**, 1035–53.
Hamilton, B.W. (1989), 'Wasteful commuting again', _Journal of Political Economy_, **97**, 1497–504.
Handy, S. (1996), 'Methodologies for exploring the link between urban form and travel behavior', _Transportation Research D_, **1** (2), 151–65.
Kitamura, R., S. Fujii and E.I. Pas (1997), 'Time-use data, analysis and modeling: toward the next generation of transportation planning methodologies', _Transport Policy_, **4** (4), 225–35.
Kraan, M. (1996), _Time to Travel? A Model for the Allocation of Time and Money_, Enschede, The Netherlands: University of Twente.
Martens, M.J., E.J. Verroen, N.J. Paulley and K. Skarman (1998), _Urban Form and Mobility_, SESAME Report D4: Report on analysis of relationships, Report for the European Communities.
Meurs, H.J. (1991), _A Panel Data Analysis of Travel Demand_, Groningen, The Netherlands: Groningen University.
Pickup, I. and S.W. Town (1983), 'Commuting patterns in Europe, an overview of the

literature', in *TRRL Supplementary Report 796*, Berkshire: Transport and Road Research Laboratory.

RIVM (1997), *Background Document for the Environmental Balance 1997*, Alphen aan den Rijn: Samson H.D. Tjeenk Willink (in Dutch).

RIVM (1998), *Environmental Balance 1998*, Alphen aan den Rijn: Samson H.D. Tjeenk Willink (in Dutch).

Scott, D.M., P.S. Kanaroglou and W.P. Anderson (1997), 'Impacts of commuting efficiency on congestion and emission: case of the Hamilton CMA, Canada', *Transportation Research D*, **2** (4), 245–57.

Second Transport Structure Plan (TSP-II) (1990), The Hague: Sdu Uitgeverij (in Dutch).

SESAME (1998), *Interactions between Land Use, Transport Supply and Travel Demand*, Final Report, Report for the European Communities.

Small, K.A. and S. Song (1992), ' "Wasteful" commuting: a resolution', *Journal of Political Economy*, **100**, 888–98.

van den Brink, R.M.M. and J.A. Annema (1999), *Traffic and Transport in the Environmental Balance 1998*, Bilthoven: National Institute of Public Health and the Environment (in Dutch).

van Vugt, M. (1996), *Social Dilemmas and Transportation Decisions*, Southampton: University of Southampton Design and Print Centre.

van Wee, G.P. (1993), *Location Policy and Land Use: The Effects on Traffic and Transport*, Bilthoven: National Institute of Public Health and the Environment, Report 251701010 (in Dutch).

van Wee G.P. (1995), 'Pricing instruments for transport policy', in F.J. Dietz, H.R.J. Vollebergh and J.L. de Vries, *Environment, Incentives and the Common Market*, Dordrecht/Boston: Kluwer Academic Publishers, pp. 97–124.

van Wee, G.P. (1997), *Office to the Station. The Influence of Firm Relocations to Public Transport Nodal Points on Passenger Transport*, Bilthoven/Amsterdam: National Institute of Public Health and the Environment/PhD Thesis, University of Amsterdam (in Dutch).

van Wee, B. and T. van der Hoorn (1997), 'The influence of land use on traffic and transport: a comparison of scenario studies', *Tijdschrift Vervoerswetenschap*, **1**/97, 43–61 (in Dutch).

van Wee, B. and T. van der Hoorn (1998), 'Effects of office relocations on public transport nodal points on passenger mobility', Paper prepared for the Network on European Communications and Transport Activities Research (NECTAR), Tel Aviv, 19–23 April.

Verroen, E.J. and H.D. Hilbers (1995), *Model Test of the Randstad Vision: The Results*, Delft: INRO-TNO (in Dutch).

Verroen, E.J. and H.D. Hilbers (1996), 'Promising mobility friendly urbanisation strategies: time for a paradigm shift?', Paper presented in *European Transport Forum*, Proceedings of Seminar B Transport Policy and its Implementation, Uxbridge (London) UK.

Walsh, M.P. (1990), 'The impact of transport on health and the environment', Paper prepared for the World Health Organization, Commission on Health and the Environment.

Wegener, M. (1998), 'Applied models of urban land use, transport and environment: state of the art and future developments. Network infrastructure and the urban environment', in L. Lundquist, L.-G. Mattson and T.J. Kim (eds), *Network Infrastructure and the Urban Environment*, Stockholm, pp. 245–67.

Werkgroep EROMOBIL (1990), *Interaction between Land Use and Mobility in the Randstad: The Exploration of a New Approach* (main report + 3 appendices) (in Dutch).

White, M.J. (1988), 'Urban commuting journeys are not "wasteful" ', *Journal of Political Economy*, **96** (5), 1097–110.

Whitelegg, J., A. Gatrell and P. Naumann (1993), *Traffic and Health*, Lancaster: Environmental Epidemiology Research Unit, University of Lancaster.

12. International transport and the environment: an assessment of trends and driving forces

Daniëlle B. van Veen-Groot and Peter Nijkamp

INTRODUCTION

The world-wide liberalization trends have created the conditions for the internationalization of our economies. These internationalization trends may have large impacts on the transport system and the global environment. In particular, the rise in greenhouse effects is a major environmental problem. There is a growing concern that emissions of carbon dioxide and other greenhouse gases resulting from human activities might cause an increase in the earth's surface temperature, and change the climate of the earth by means of an enhanced greenhouse effect (IPCC, 1995). For example, carbon dioxide has been responsible for 55 per cent of the enhanced greenhouse effect in the past, and is likely to remain so in the future. Other important greenhouse gases are water vapour and ozone (IPCC, 1992).

Transport is a significant contributor to the greenhouse effect. World-wide, transport causes 20 per cent of the problem, while agriculture and deforestation cause 25 per cent and power generation 25 per cent. Although other sectors also contribute considerably to the emission of greenhouse gases, the contribution of the transportation sector is expected to increase drastically. Several trends indicate a steady growth of goods as well as of passenger transport. On the other hand, the development of new transportation technologies may reduce the negative environmental consequences of transport (for a detailed overview, see Nijkamp et al., 1998).

The relation between globalization, international transport and the global environment involves a large number of processes and interactions. Many factors influence future economic developments and the introduction of new transportation technologies. The transport sector is interrelated with social and economic developments, and is subject to numerous political and institutional constraints. The future developments of globalization, transportation and the environmental consequences are uncertain. How will the globalization process develop? What will be the impacts on the use of international transport and the development of new technologies? How will this affect global environmental quality?

Reliable and complete information about these future developments is a necessary condition for making 'right' choices. Unfortunately, existing information is often incomplete and sometimes not reliable. The lack of information and the long time scales lead to a significant amount of uncertainty. To reduce these uncertainties, decision makers need decision support tools. One way to deal with uncertainty is to construct various scenarios and examine the way different (policy) options perform in each of them. In this context, a scenario is a description of a hypothetical future state of the world, including a consideration of major uncertainties encountered in moving far into the future. Scenarios are not predictions or forecasts about the future; nor do they represent the most likely future developments. Scenarios do not tell us what will happen in the future; rather they tell us what can happen (RAND, 1997).

An important phase in scenario construction is the assessment of present and future trends and driving forces (Bood and Postma, 1998). Therefore, in this chapter we shall introduce a framework for analysing the implications of globalization via international transport on the global environment. The purpose of this chapter is to assess the driving forces behind globalization and the trends in globalization, spatial organization, transport and the environment, which are relevant for the construction of scenarios. We shall focus mainly on the effects of internationalization on CO_2 emissions caused by transportation. It should be added that changes in trade or environmental policy will be left out of consideration.

The outline is as follows. The next section is dedicated to the effects of internationalization on transport and the environment. Attention is given to the characteristics and indicators of internationalization and the relationship with transport. Furthermore, a framework for analysing the implications of globalization via international transport on the global environment is presented. A first step in scenario analysis is a description of present trends. According to the framework presented here, we shall make a distinction between driving forces behind internationalization and the trends as a result of this. In the third section, the driving forces behind internationalization are described, while trends in spatial organization, transport and environmental pressure are assessed in the fourth section. An evaluation as well as concluding remarks are offered in the final section.

THE EFFECTS OF INTERNATIONALIZATION ON TRANSPORT AND THE ENVIRONMENT

Pathways Towards Internationalization

Internationalization tendencies impact on economic markets, technologies and communication patterns, resulting in an increasing mutual dependency between economies. International trade has risen steadily since the beginning of the twentieth century. Sharp cuts in tariffs and non-tariff barriers, together with continued falls in transportation and communication costs, stimulated international trade even more than the sharp decline in the ratio of trade to GDP that had occurred in the interwar period (OECD, 1997b). Although globalization is a main issue at the moment, it is not a new phenomenon, since economic internationalization has been the foundation of capitalism since the sixteenth century. For the industrializing nations, the ratio of international trade to production was 14.3 per cent in 1993, but it was already 12.9 per cent in 1913. However, three new developments of the pattern and degree of internationalization can be mentioned, which make present internationalization different from former internationalization trends.

First, an increasing part of the world and a larger number of independent countries are participating in the world economy (IMF, 1997). A new phenomenon, dating back to the 1970s, is the competition from the emerging economies of Asia and Latin America (Courier, 1997). The emergence of these economies opens up new possibilities on new economic markets.

Second, the internationalization of industry has evolved from plain export and import strategies to more complex industrial linkages. The number of interfirm collaboration agreements increased from 120 in the 1980–84 period to 220 in the 1990–92 period (see Table 12.1). A large share of reported agreements are between firms from OECD countries, while a very small share do not involve firms from Europe, North America or Japan. Agreements are most common between firms within the European Community (EC), next between the EC and North American firms, and finally between the EC and Japanese firms.

Third, internationalization has emerged from global competition in labour-intensive sectors to competition in the capital-intensive and service sector. During the 1960s, new competitors emerged in labour-intensive sectors such as the textile industry, particularly from newly industrializing countries. During the 1970s, globalization tendencies are reflected in the increase in international competition of the more capital-intensive sectors such as the shipping and car industries. Since then, a global market has also emerged in high-tech sectors such as the computer industry and consumer electronics. More recently, a large share of interfirm agreements has been set up to develop

Table 12.1 Collaboration agreements, 1980–1992 (%)

Number per year		Main regions*		Main industries*		Main purpose	
1980–84	120	Europe/Europe	30	Automotive	21	Development	31
1985–89	240	Europe/North America	23	Electronics	17	Production	25
1990–92	220	Europe/Japan	15	Aerospace	15	Marketing	13
		North America/Japan	11	Telecommunications	14	Mixed	30
		North America/North America	10	Computers	13		
		Other	10	Other	20		
		Total	99	Total	100	Total	99

Note: * Including agreements before 1980.

Source: OECD (1996).

258

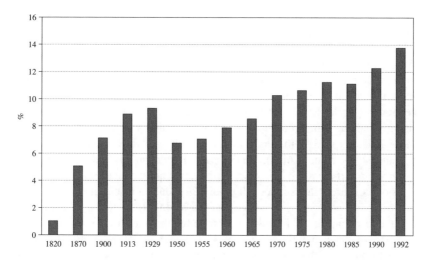

Source: OECD (1997b).

Figure 12.1   World exports as a percentage of GDP (1990 $)

new technologies and tend to be clustered in R&D-intensive industries. Sectors most commonly involved include the automotive sector as well as high-technology sectors such as electronics, aerospace, telecommunications and computers. Furthermore, globalization also affects the service sector, including the financial sector, transport and the media (van Esch, 1994).

Indicators for internationalization are international trade and international foreign investment related to GDP. The first indicator is the ratio of international trade to GDP. World exports have risen from 7 per cent in 1950 to about 14 per cent in 1992 (see Figure 12.1). Furthermore, these ratios increased strongly in some regions in the past ten years, but fell in Sub-Saharan Africa, were flat in the Middle East and North Africa, and barely edged in South Asia. The high increase of trade ratios for East Asia and Latin America and the Caribbean in the last decade is remarkable. In general, a tendency towards an increase in international trade can be observed. It should be noted that a large part of international trade is intraregional trade. Intraregional trade – as part of overall trade – in Europe climbed from about 55 per cent in the mid-1960s to 70 per cent in 1989. Asian intraregional trade doubled its share of Asian trade, to more than 40 per cent at the end of the 1980s, while in North America (Canada and the United States), intraregional imports fell from about 40 to 30 per cent. Intraregional trade is a large part of total trade, especially in Europe, but is of decreasing importance in other regions.

A second indicator for internationalization is the ratio of foreign direct

investment (FDI) to GDP. As with trade, FDI is a significant indicator for globalization because of its potential for diffusing technologies and skills. Regions
with particularly low ratios of FDI to GDP include South Asia, Sub-Saharan
Africa, and the Middle East and North Africa. The large increase in FDI in
high-income countries underscores the fact that these countries, already the
most integrated, are continuing to deepen their interaction with the world
economy (World Bank, 1996a). The share of international investments is
rising in all high-income countries, which implies that these countries are
more linked to world markets. In the rapidly growing economies in Asia
(Southeast Asia and China), in the past decade an investment boom has
occurred. Apart from this, the share of the developing countries and regions in
the stock of direct investment fell as of 1991, due to instability, poor market
prospects in Latin America, Africa and the Middle East. It can be concluded
that the vast majority of FDI is concentrated in the industrialized world, at the
expense of investments in the less-developed countries (OECD, 1996).
Furthermore, as with trade, intraregional investment is important. The development of intraregional investment shows that for the main investing and host
countries in the European Community, intraregional investment became more
important over the 1980s and early 1990s. For North America, it became less
important. We can thus conclude that intraregional investment is important in
Europe and of lower importance for North America.

Effects of Internationalization on Transport and Environment:
A Framework

Internationalization may have a large impact on transport and the environment. The conceptual framework presented in Figure 12.2 describes the implications of internationalization on transport and the environment. The first part
of the conceptual framework represents the driving forces behind globalization. Insight into these driving forces is important to understand the complex
relationship between international transport and the global environment. The
five main categories of driving forces behind internationalization are changes
in the macroeconomic situation, the population, the political situation, the
resource use and technological change. Consumer preferences and firm strategies are not really driving forces in the same sense at the other five, because
both firms and individuals react as 'actors' to situations presented by the external driving forces. Changes in these factors creates the condition for the internationalization of the world economy.

The effects of the emergence of world markets has given rise to a vivid
debate among scientists and policy makers. In general, viewed at the world
level, internationalization may enhance efficiency by making the international
division of labour, economies of scale and competition more efficient. This

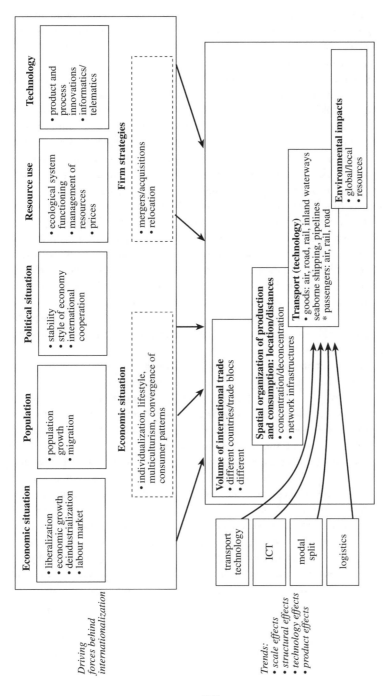

Figure 12.2 A multilayer approach for tracing the effects of internationalization

261

will allow world output to expand, in the form of additional economic growth. The OECD (1997a) distinguishes four effects of globalization on the economy, namely *scale, structural, technology* and *product* effects. These effects also have consequences for transport and the environment.

The second part of the conceptual framework represents the volume and spatial effects of internationalization and the effects on transport and the environment, by making a distinction between four interacting layers. The first layer represents changes in the volume of international trade flows. Globalization will lead to larger world outputs: the so-called *scale effects* of globalization. An increase in the volume of production and consumption may lead to an increase in the volume of transported goods and the number of trips made by passengers. However, expanding world output may be caused by a higher share of services, which have low volumes.

The second layer represents changes in the spatial organization of production and consumption activities. Due to specialization patterns, resulting from comparative advantages and scale economies, international trade will take place. Globalization will then lead to shifts in the composition and location of production and consumption activities, that is, the *structural effects* of globalization. In other words, structural effects involve changes in the country of origin and destination of goods. If internationalization leads to the transportation of goods and passengers over a longer distance, the effects on the environment are negative.

The third layer includes all sorts of transport activities and infrastructure development. The volume and nature of transport depends on the state of transport technology, the use of information and communication technology, the modal split and logistics. The *technology effects* refer to the innovation and dissemination of technologies on a global scale. In regard to the transport sector, this reflects changes in transportation technologies, the use of information and communication technologies, logistic systems and so on. Positive environmental effects may occur as a reduction in emissions per tonne/km or in passenger/km as a result of these new technologies. Finally, the composition of the product mix – or *product effects* – determine, to a large extent, not only the volume of the transported goods but also the transport mode which will be used.

Then, the fourth layer refers to the environmental effects of these transport activities such as noise and air pollution. Apparently, the implications of globalization on transport and the environment depend on the scale, structural, technological and product effects. These effects are mutually dependent. An increase in the volume of transported goods or the number of passenger-kilometres does not merely imply an increase in CO_2 emissions. This increase can be compensated by changes in the modal split in favour of less environmentally damaging transport modes or the development of cleaner transport technologies.

It is clear that several linkages between the different levels exist. Therefore, it seems necessary to identify the driving forces behind internationalization and trends in order to examine whether this phenomenon has a positive or negative effect on transport and the environment. In the next section, we shall describe the driving forces behind globalization, while subsequently the main trends in spatial organization, transport and the environment will be considered.

DRIVING FORCES BEHIND INTERNATIONALIZATION

The globalization of economic markets, technologies and communication patterns is driven by several factors. In this section the driving forces behind internationalization will be dealt with. Attention will be given to economic, demographic, political, technological and resource-use driving forces, as well as to consumer preferences and firm strategies. The first four engines of change (that is, economy, demography, policy structures and technology) are at a global level of course also interrelated, but will be treated here as distinct forces for the sake of simplicity.

Economic Driving Forces

The world economy has exhibited drastic changes since the beginning of the twentieth century. Four important driving forces behind internationalization are the liberalization of trade and finance, high economic growth rates, continuing deindustrialization and rising inequalities on the labour market.

An important economic development is the liberalization of trade. The Bretton Woods institutions, the OECD and the General Agreement on Tariffs and Trade (GATT) (now the World Trade Organization: WTO) have played pivotal roles in encouraging a growing number of countries to adopt open, market-based economic systems. Countries have lowered barriers to the movement of goods, services and capital (IMF, 1997). Sharp cuts in tariffs and non-tariff barriers have stimulated international trade. Despite the trends towards trade liberalization, there are still large differences in the extent of liberalization and the levels of protection remaining in the developing countries (South Asia, Africa, Latin America). Among OECD countries, international financial movements have also been liberalized. Although the dismantling of financial barriers began later than in the case of goods trade, it has been more complete and there are now no significant barriers to financial flows in almost all OECD countries (OECD, 1997a). However, there are large differences in the level of financial protection in other countries.

This trade liberalization has had a large influence on the development of

GDP. Absolute levels of per capita income have increased very substantially. Maddison (1989) has analysed that 'world' GDP rose thirteenfold between 1900 and 1987; a compound growth of 3 per cent per year (see Table 12.2). Aggregate growth in the OECD countries was 3 per cent a year. Asia showed the least progress with a rise of 2.7 per cent a year. Absolute levels of per capita income were more than three times bigger in Asia, on average, in 1987 than in 1900, and nearly five times as high as in Latin America. In OECD countries they rose nearly sixfold, and in the former Soviet Union more than sevenfold.

Furthermore, 'world' economic growth decreased from 5.1 per cent in 1966–73 to 1.5 in 1991–94, whereas a GDP growth of 3.5 per cent is expected in the 1996–2005 period (World Bank, 1996a). The transition economies – the countries of Central and Eastern Europe and the former Soviet Union – are expected to consolidate their recovery and to achieve higher growth than all other developing regions except East and South Asia. Although all developing regions are projected to match or exceed their growth performance of the past decade, the disparities among them will remain large, with Sub-Saharan Africa and the Middle East and North Africa registering only modest increases in per capita incomes (World Bank, 1996a).

In spite of an improvement of economic growth, an increasing polarization between the developed and developing countries can be observed. Growth patterns over recent decades show that many developing countries are diverging away from advanced economies measured in per capita income levels. In the developing countries, real per capita income has risen substantially in the past thirty years. The newly industrialized economies have improved their living standard dramatically. However, there are large differences between countries. In relative terms, most developing countries have failed to raise their per capita income towards that of the industrial countries.

The growth process has been accompanied by major structural changes. Manufacturing employment as a share of total employment has declined continuously since the beginning of the 1990s. This phenomenon is often referred to as deindustrialization. As incomes rise, the relative demand for food drops, and the increase in consumer demand is directed more strongly to the products of other sectors. For the advanced economies as a whole, the share of manufacturing employment declined from about 28 per cent in 1970 to about 18 per cent in 1994. Deindustrialization began first in the United States. The trend of deindustrialization in the countries of the European Union started around 1970. Manufacturing employment fell from 30 per cent in 1970 to 20 per cent in 1994. Finally, in Japan the trend of deindustrialization began later and was less steep than in the US and the EU. In some East Asian economies, the process of deindustrialization has just recently started (IMF, 1997).

Table 12.2 The 'world' economy and its components, 1980–1987

	16 OECD countries	9 Asian countries	6 Latin American countries	former Soviet Union	32 country total
GDP in billion 'international' dollars at 1980 prices					
1900	603.1	303.5	30.3	98.0	1,035.0
1987	7,759.3	3,203.1	982.2	1,683.8	13,628.5
Per capita GDP in 'international' dollars at 1980 prices					
1900	1,946.0	405.0	645.0	797.0	3,793.0
1987	11,073.0	1,332.0	3,107.0	5,948.0	21,460.0
Rate of growth of GDP					
1900–87	3.0	2.7	4.1	3.3	3.0
Rate of growth of per capita GDP					
1900–1950	1.1	-0.2	1.5	2.1	1.1
1950–1987	3.3	3.5	2.2	2.6	2.5
1900–1987	2.0	1.4	1.8	2.3	1.7

Source: Maddison (1989).

Furthermore, in the advanced economies, there is a trend towards increasing wage inequalities between the more skilled and less skilled, and a rise in unemployment among the less skilled (IMF, 1997). The increase in wage inequality can be explained by a labour demand shift towards skilled workers. First, demand for labour has shifted across industries: the share of output produced by industries that intensively employ low-skilled workers has fallen and that produced by more skill-intensive industries has risen. Second, a change in skilled demand within industries has occurred, as firms have shifted away from unskilled towards skilled workers. This shift in demand has raised the relative wages of these workers, which increases inequality between low- and high-skilled workers.

Demographic Driving Forces

A second category of driving forces behind the process of internationalization is composed of demographic driving forces. Important factors are the increase in world population, ageing in the developed countries and a large share of young people in the developing countries, and migration.

First, the increase in world population will be considered. The development of the world population is dependent on fertility rates and life expectancy. The World Bank (1997) maintains that in many countries a tendency to smaller families is experienced, while in some countries fertility remains high and the differences per region are high (Bos et al., 1994). In 1994, the total fertility rate for the world as a whole is just above three children per woman. However, large differences exist between different world regions. The average household size of Europe and North America is among the lowest in the world, namely between 2.2 to 2.8, but within Asia there are marked differences between the higher-income countries and those which are at a lower level of development; for instance, the average household size is 3.1 for Japan, whereas for Indonesia it is 4.9 (Euro-CASE, 1996). Furthermore, the World Bank suggests a long-term trend towards longer life, since mortality levels in all continents have decreased in the last decade. Current life expectancy is estimated to be 66 years for the world in 1994. However, the discrepancies among different continents are large: in East and West Africa life expectancy at birth is only 52, whereas it is 77 in Northern America and 74 in Europe.

Due to increasing life expectancy and high fertility rates in some countries, the world population is projected to reach 6 billion before the end of the century (see Table 12.3). The World Bank expects that a billion people will be added each 12 years until 2023, after which the increase in world population will decline slightly due to a rapid decline in birth rate (Bos et al., 1994). World population will double in the year 2100. Asia will be responsible for the largest part of the world population, whereas Africa will be growing the fastest

Table 12.3   World population growth: years to next billion

Year	Population (bn)	Years to next billion
1800	1	125
1925	2	35
1960	3	14
1974	4	13
1987	5	12
1999	6	12
2011	7	12
2023	8	16
2039	9	21
2060	10	43
2130	11	–

Note: Population projected to stay below 12 billion.

Source: Bos et al. (1994).

Table 12.4   Population projection by region

	Population (m)					
Region	1990	2000	2025	2050	2075	2100
World	*5,266*	*6,114*	*8,121*	*9,578*	*10,481*	*10,958*
Africa	627	821	1,431	1,999	2,419	2,643
North America	280	310	362	374	381	384
Latin America	435	512	686	804	859	883
Asia	3,174	3,703	4,860	5,638	6,070	6,289
Europe	723	737	744	721	708	714
Oceania	27	31	38	42	44	45

Source: Bos et al. (1994).

(see Table 12.4). Europe is the only continent projected to have fewer people in 2100 than in 1990. Africa's share of world population is expected to double from 12 to 24 per cent from 1990 to 2100. The share of Europe will decline from about 14 per cent in 1990 to 7 per cent in the year 2100. All other continents will contain a smaller share of the world's population than today.

The difference in age structure between the low-income countries and the high-income countries will diverge considerably in the next time period. Population pyramids show that the very rapid growth of the population in the low-income countries is responsible for the extremely large share of young people in the total population of these countries; the pyramid becomes increasingly rectangular. In contrast, the high-income countries will be confronted with an increasing percentage of people aged 65 or over in the population; by 2025 the largest cohort will be that of 75 years and older (Bos et al., 1994). So, a trend towards ageing in developed countries can be observed, whereas in developing countries the share of young people in total population is increasing.

Furthermore, increasing international migration has a large influence on the global economy. A distinction can be made between: (i) the increasing economic migration from rural to urban regions, (ii) the increasing economic migration from underdeveloped to developed countries and (iii) the increasing number of political refugees. First, people are moving from rural to urban areas, a tendency which is related to the emergence of megaconurbations. Second, migration flows to areas with high income and/or with high economic growth rates are increasing. These flows are continental as well as global (this migration will partially compensate the increasing age of the original population in those areas). Finally, the increasing violations of human rights in many countries will lead to a rapidly increasing number of political refugees. These increasing international migration effects will have impacts on the economy, social values and so on.

Political Driving Forces

Political driving forces behind the globalization process are the establishment of more democratic nations, the renewed appreciation of market forces and the increasing attempts of international economic and environmental cooperation.

First, a renewed focus on the state's role has been inspired by the changes in the global economy, which have changed the environment in which states operate. The globalization of markets, technologies and communication patterns has meant new and different roles for government – no longer as sole provider but as facilitator and regulator (World Bank, 1997). Although the role of the state is different in the various world regions, some general tendencies can be identified. It seems that democracy is gaining ground, especially outside the developed countries: in Central Europe, in the republics of the former Soviet Union, in Latin America and also in various countries in Africa and Asia (CPB, 1992).

Second, in the past decade, free market principles have been adopted by a wide range of countries, which has spurred their economic growth and integration in the global economy (OECD, 1997b). The former centrally planned economies (including Russia) have now made progress in moving towards a market system, and China has emerged as the world's fastest-growing economy.

Indonesia has transformed itself from a heavily resource-dependent economy in the early 1980s to a major exporter of light manufactures. Brazil and many other Latin American countries have made progress in stabilizing, reforming and restructuring their economies. In Western and Eastern Europe as well as in North America, a renewed appreciation of market forces and a much more critical attitude towards government intervention than was the case about 15–20 years ago can be observed (CPB, 1992). As a result of the renewed appreciation of market forces, in many countries a trend towards deregulation and privatization can be observed in different sectors of the economy such as the energy, agriculture and the transport sector.

Third, economic cooperation is gaining ground in Europe, by the establishment of the European Union. The idea of European unification has been accepted throughout Europe as decisive for the evolution of Europe towards international competitiveness, economic and technological leadership at the global level, and internal cohesiveness and cooperation. The completion of the single European market of all EC member countries will mean the emergence of a unified market of some 300 million customers (Nijkamp et al., 1994). A number of countries, particularly the Baltics and the countries of Central and Eastern Europe, are moving rapidly towards relatively liberal trade regimes. New regional free trade areas have been formed, including the Central Europe Free Trade Area (CEFTA), composed of the Czech Republic, Hungary, Poland, the Slovak Republic and Slovenia, and the Baltic Free Trade Area (BFTA), which comprises the three Baltic countries. Several of these Central and East European countries see the necessity of joining the European Union to share the development of the single market with other countries. Furthermore, since the revolutions of 1989, trade between the East European countries and the EFTA countries (European Free Trade Association) has swelled at double-digit rates, due to the geographical situation and historical connections of many EFTA countries with Central and East European countries (Baldwin, 1993).

The formation of the EU has also had a stimulating effect on debates about economic cooperation in other regions. Therefore, in other parts of the world we also see the emergence of free trade areas, for example, NAFTA compromising the USA together with Canada and Mexico. Also in the dynamic Asian economies (Korea, Taiwan, Thailand, Hong Kong, Singapore and Malaysia) there are increasingly open regimes of trade. Furthermore, the formation of the Asia-Pacific Economic Cooperation Council (APEC) has stimulated an increase in capital inflows of developing APEC countries. For example, in 1993 capital inflows to the APEC countries accounted for about 85 per cent of the capital that went to developing countries (Khan and Reinhart, 1995).

Finally, global integration also gives rise to demands for states to cooperate to combat international threats such as global warming. Although economic, cultural and other differences between countries can make such cooperation difficult, stronger cooperation is needed for concerns that transcend national borders (World Bank, 1997). Among other things the following new areas for international cooperation can be mentioned:

- *Managing regional crises* The end of the cold war has given way to many smaller conflicts. No solid international framework exists of managing these conflicts or helping to avoid them.
- *Promoting global economic stability* Concern has been growing about the potentially destabilizing effects of large and rapid flows of portfolio capital, particularly when a crisis in one country can spill over into other markets.
- *Protecting the environment* International collective action can help to solve urgent global environmental issues including climate change, loss of biodiversity and so on through better coordination, greater public awareness, more effective technological transfer and better national and local practices. However, progress in international cooperation has been slow.

Technological Driving Forces

Innovation and diffusion of new technologies are a basic element of the globalization process. Two important driving forces behind globalization are the introduction of new clusters of technologies and the growing importance of multinationals in technology transfer.

First, the introduction of new technologies contributes to expanding production possibilities and opportunities for economic growth. Four main categories of clusters of technologies which have provided technological opportunities can be distinguished, namely: (i) information and communication technology, (ii) biotechnology, (iii) new materials, and (iv) environmental or energy-linked technology. These 'key or base technologies' result in the innovation of many new products, influence production processes, are applicable in many sectors in the economy and may lead to a decrease of problems in the economic system (Tuininga, 1989). The boundaries between the different technology clusters are not so clear-cut; many links and much coherence exists between these base technologies.

The introduction and dissemination of information and transportation technology has had a main influence on the globalization process. These technologies have reduced transportation, telecommunication and computation cost (see Table 12.5). As a result, economic distances have shrunk and coordination problems have diminished to such an extent that in many cases it has become an efficient method of industrial organization for a firm to locate

Table 12.5   Costs of air transportation, telephone calls and computer price deflator (in 1990 $US unless otherwise indicated)

Year	Average air transportation revenue per passenger mile	Cost of a three-minute call, New York to London	US Department of Commerce computer price deflator (1990 = 1000)
1930	0.68	244.65	–
1940	0.46	188.51	–
1950	0.30	53.20	–
1960	0.24	45.86	125,000
1970	0.16	31.58	19,474
1980	0.10	4.80	3,620
1990	0.11	3.32	1,000

Source: IMF (1997).

different phases of production in different parts of the world (IMF, 1997). These information and communications technnologies are helping to over-come the barriers of physical distance and are therefore an important driving force behind globalization.

However, large differences between the developed and the developing countries exist. Johnstone (1997) concludes that differences in factor endow-ments and technological capacity between nations indicates a potential for bifurcation, with some countries converging at the technological frontier and others being left behind. OECD countries have benefited most from global-ization in terms of the incorporation of new technologies, whereas developing countries are lagging behind. However, some newly industrialized countries have also managed to benefit from international flows in knowledge and tech-nology. In general, technology transfer to developed countries is increasing. Developing countries are lagging behind.

Finally, multinationals play an important role in technology transfer. Garrod (1997) gives two main reasons for this. First, in a highly competitive global economic environment, corporate success depends largely on a company's ability to optimize access to, and use of, resources, while at the same time minimizing production and bureaucratic constraints. This depends on the company making the most of any technological opportunities that arise. Second, multinationals tend to diffuse technology more rapidly than their national counterparts, because of their international linkages with other firms in terms of strategic alliances and joint ventures.

Resource Use

Driving forces related to resource use are the functioning of the ecological system (disruptive events), the management of material and energy resources (energy conservation, dematerialization), material and energy prices and the use of alternative sources.

The use of natural resources plays an important role within the global economic system. Natural resources can be divided into (i) renewable resources, such as the natural environment; and (ii) non-renewable resources, especially fossil resources. Possible disruptive events influencing the functioning of the ecological system can have a large impact on the global economic system. The supply of raw materials and energy (type, structure, quantities) and the stability in availability of fossil fuels are a condition for globalization. The increasing frequency and severity of natural disasters (floods, droughts, hurricanes and so on), possible disruptive events such as a major ecological disaster or a severe energy crisis give rise to discussions about the dramatic effects of these disruptive events on the global economy.

At the moment, our economic systems are largely based on the use of fossil fuels, responsible for the emission of CO_2, and the extraction of large quantities of matter from the environment. In recent years, particular concern is given to climate changes caused by the emission of greenhouse gases. There is growing awareness that concentrations of carbon dioxide and other greenhouse gases in the atmosphere were a result of human activities and would cause global temperatures to rise, with accompanying climatic changes (IPCC, 1992).

Use of fossil energy sources is one of the major causes of the greenhouse effect. Energy conservation is considered as an important strategy to reduce carbon dioxide emissions. Energy conservation or improvement of energy intensity covers many different activities and processes, which can be divided into two main categories: improvement of energy-efficiency of activities, and a structural change towards less energy-intensive activities. Before 1973 and after 1985, the energy efficiency of products and production processes generally improved, but the growing share of energy-intensive activities in the economy (transport, long-distance tourism, use of materials) was the reason why this improvement did not show up in the figure of energy intensity of the economy as a whole (Becht and van Soest, 1997). Next to energy conservation, another possibility for reducing carbon dioxide emissions is the use of alternative energy sources such as wind, water and solar energy, biomass and hydrogen, which use electricity primarily as an energy carrier. The contribution of alternative energy sources to the total energy supply is limited, but will become more important in due course.

Furthermore, in recent years, the closing of material cycles and a further increase in the efficiency in material flows and waste flows has become an important issue in environmental economics. Dematerialization is an important strategy for raising the productivity of material resources (Ayres and Ayres, 1996). The 'Factor 10 Club' calls for an increase in the current resource productivity in industrialized countries by an average of 'factor 10' during the next 30 to 50 years (Factor 10 Club, 1994). Von Weizsacker et al. (1997) give many examples of raising the material and energy productivity with a 'factor four'; for the transport sector several technological and logistical options have been suggested to increase the material and energy productivity. Dematerialization is becoming an important strategy to reduce environmental problems.

Consumer Preferences

Consumer preferences are largely influenced by social and cultural changes. The main driving forces related to consumer preferences are: (i) changing lifestyles as a result of individualization, a reduction in gender inequality and an increase of leisure time, and (ii) a convergence of consumer patterns.

First, especially in the developed countries several tendencies towards different lifestyles can be distinguished. Within the developed countries a tendency towards individualization can be observed. There are a number of trends related to this. A slow but steady decline of male–female inequality can be observed. In the less-developed countries there has been remarkable progress towards more equality in the educational field. In most other areas many inequalities still exist. Within the developed countries, gender gaps are generally much narrower, although inequalities still exist, for example, with respect to labour force participation and equal pay (CPB, 1992). Furthermore, during the last century, in the developing countries working hours have been reduced. Whereas in the last century the common working week consisted of approximately 50 hours, nowadays the working week has 36–40 hours. Furthermore, general housekeeping tasks have become less time-consuming due to electric household appliances. This has resulted in an increase in leisure time (Nijkamp et al., 1994/1995).

Second, changing consumption patterns, leading to product standardization or the 'hamburger economy', is an important phenomenon in the age of globalization. The same products are available all over the world. Not only are McDonald's and Coca-Cola found throughout the world, but more and more stores, brands and products aim at the world market. This results in more competition and a search for market niches in a globalizing market economy by entrepreneurs.

Firm Strategies

Finally, the internationalization of firm strategies is a driving force behind globalization. In the 1950s and 1960, trade between nations expanded rapidly as tariffs and quotas were reduced through multilateral agreements. The 1970s were marked by an emphasis on foreign investments. Shifts in patterns of international economic activity and competition between multi-national corporations were main issues in the internationalization process. The third phase of internationalization, after 1980, emerged largely due to the influence of technology. The ability to innovate and to adapt and implement technologies became necessary to industrial competitiveness. To compete globally, companies increasingly needed technological sophistication, maximum flexibility, customized products and extensive supplier networks. This phase is characterized by new patterns of industrial linkages. Corporations interact on a global scale through a wide range of external alliances such as joint ventures, subcontracting, licensing and interfirm agreements (OECD, 1992).

Firms show a tendency to execute their activities in the most cost-effective and productive way. With the increasing internationalization and possibilities for faster and cheaper transport, the world becomes smaller and smaller. Distance is no longer an insurmountable barrier. Companies can choose a location where specific production factors are available, important for their production process. As a consequence, firms can produce their goods in a cost-effective and productive way at different locations. Increasing competition forces firms to concentrate more and more on their core activities. Other activities are outsourced, sometimes in the home country, but also world-wide.

It should be clear that internationalization is driven by a multitude of factors. Among other things, the liberalization of trade and finance, continuing economic growth, the increase of world population, the establishment of more democratic nations and the adoption of more market based-systems, the innovation and dissemination of new technologies, a convergence of consumption patterns and internationalization of firms' strategies have led to the globalization of the world economy. These changes will have scale, structural, technology and product effects which are related to transport and the environment. In the next section, the main trends as a result of a world-wide focus will be presented.

EXPECTED TRENDS AS A RESULT OF INTERNATIONALIZATION

This section presents the main trends as a result of globalization. Attention will be given to trends in spatial organization (structural effects), trends in goods as well as transport (scale, structural, technology and product effects) and the resulting environmental consequences.

Trends in Spatial Organization

The orientation towards world markets can lead to changes in the spatial organization, that is, the composition and location of production and consumption activities (structural effects). Globalization of industry will in principle result in a more appropriate location of firm activities and greater efficiency in production of intermediate inputs and components (OECD, 1996). In a globalization strategy, labour-intensive production of components will be situated in low-wage areas, whereas the production of high-technology and high-value added parts or services requires a well-developed infrastructure. This means that for individual countries and firms, relocation of firm activities could also imply drastic changes in terms of economic performance, employment and so on.

A phenomenon that is accompanying the current globalization is the trend towards a network economy at all levels: local, regional, national and global. Industrial interdependencies are emerging in an attempt to minimize costs in a mature industrial economy, in particular outsourcing. The fierce competition in mature markets leads to a trend towards concentration on core activities, with a strong emphasis on a logistic organization of production. Physical production may then become more fragmented with a loss of integrated chain production within the firm, while assembling and distribution gain in importance. The emerging component industry is based on worldwide trading and transport (Lagendijk, 1993). The new information and communication technology (ICT) sector allows for a sufficient and efficient coordination of dispersed production patterns. Production also tends to become more footloose, due to the integrating potential of the ICT sector. Global networks are supporting this phenomenon, not only in terms of industrial linkages, but also in terms of infrastructure networks. Such networks which are based on high mobility are thus becoming the vehicles for intensive global competition.

In a networked economy, nodal centres play a strategic role. Hubs are then able to acquire a dominant position. Such nodal centres refer to industrial power concentration in the form of global oligopolies controlling a significant part of the world market, but they refer also to mainports and gateways in international infrastructure networks. There is no doubt that proximity effects – through their intense communication possibilities – offer many scale advantages. Although the ICT sector may suggest a 'death of distance', the fact is that geographical agglomeration forces are becoming increasingly important for the complex ramification of an industrial network economy. Thus scale economies of all kind seem to favour concentration and agglomeration, while at the same time the ICT sector allows for a spatial spread of production.

Trends in (International) Goods Transport

The scale, structural, technology and product effects of globalization have effects on international goods transport. The *scale* effects of globalization refer to a larger scale of production and consumption. Because the demand for freight transport is commonly referred to as a derived demand; that is, it derives from a more basic demand – a location-specific demand for a product that results in a need to ship the product to that location – the most basic influence on total freight demand is the volume of products produced and consumed. Because globalization has led to larger production and consumption, the general trend over the past centuries of goods transport has been growth. The demand for freight transport shows a considerable rise in the last decade.

Furthermore, a shift from the use of slower modes to the use of faster modes can be observed. A study of the modal split of freight transport of 12 European countries shows that road transport expanded from 47.8 per cent in 1975 to 69.0 per cent in 1992, principally at the expense of rail whose share declined from 44.4 per cent in 1975 to 25.2 per cent in 1992 (see Table 12.6).

Furthermore, the use of inland waterways also decreased slightly from 7.7 per cent in 1975 to 5.8 per cent in 1992 (ECMT, 1997). It is expected that the bulk of the expected increase in demand for freight transport will be for road transport. At a global level, in the maritime sector, the trans-Pacific and trans-Atlantic routes will remain important, but movement within Asia will grow most rapidly, and significant increases in movement between Asia and Europe can be expected. Inland waterway transport has a long tradition in countries with extensive river systems (for example, Brazil, China, Russia and Vietnam). In these countries and in several others in South America and West Africa, further development of inland waterway transport is likely. Rail transport will continue to play a very important role in China, India and some smaller countries with substantial bulk freight movements. The absolute decline in rail transport that has occurred in Central and Eastern European

Table 12.6   Modal split of freight transport in 12 European countries (tonne-km %)

	1975	1985	1992
Inland waterways	7.7	6.6	5.8
Rail	44.4	36.4	25.2
Road	47.8	57.0	69.0

Source: ECMT (1997).

countries in the past five years has reached a bottom line in some countries, and traffic should recover with economic growth. Nevertheless, the share of rail transport in transition and developing countries may decline (World Bank, 1996b). In general, a tendency towards the use of faster modes can be observed.

The *structural effects* of globalization refer to changes in the composition and location of production and consumption activities. Changes in the country of origin and destination of goods are largely influenced by new information and communication technology which in general has led to an increase in transport distance. Advances in information processing and telecommunications give rise to new possibilities for complex logistic systems including multimode transport (Masser et al., 1992). The success of road transport is mainly due to its advantage in door-to-door speed, flexibility and reliability. Logistic systems linking procurement, production and distribution processes replace warehousing functions by 'just-in-time' delivery of small shipment sizes and hence often rely on flexible small and medium-sized vehicles. The introduction of new logistic concepts has led to a reduction in order cycle times, which is leading firms to seek suppliers who can offer faster delivery times, even though they are located further away. Partly due to changes in the relative costs of sea and road transport, a growth in international sourcing can be noticed (Euro-CASE, 1996). In Table 12.7 this tendency is expressed; the table shows a gradual switch from local to national and then international sourcing in European countries. This increase of international sourcing may lead to an increase in average distance travelled.

The *technology effects* of globalization refers in this case to the innovation and dissemination of both vehicle and infrastructure technology and to information and communication technology. There are high expectations that the environmental impacts of transportation will be reduced by the innovation and diffusion of new transportation technologies. Three categories of new transportation technologies can be distinguished, namely (i) improvement of existing modes, (ii) development of new transport modes, and (iii) development of new fuels. In the case of freight transport, it is expected that the use of ICT will increase efficiency. Many improvements to transport efficiency could be

Table 12.7   European supply sourcing (%)

	Local	National	International
1987	18	51	31
1992	14	42	44

Source: Euro-CASE (1996).

made, if better information on the state of the network were available to planners and users. The application of ICT can improve the functioning of all transport modes as well as the integration of these modes, for example, systems for monitoring and data processing, and information dissemination.

Trends in (International) Passenger Transport

Globalization in terms of the previously mentioned scale, structural, technology and product effects also influences international passenger transport. The *scale effects* in passenger transport seems to be a persistent growth. Passenger transport, like goods transport, is a derived activity: it is derived from the demand for other activities such as work, shopping, business, education, leisure and so on. Personal mobility has become a central value of modern society, and the freedom to move with ease between home, work, service and leisure has become a characteristic feature of a modern lifestyle (Masser et al., 1992).

The general trend over the past decades of the demand for passenger transport has been one of growth. Table 12.8 shows a considerable rise in passenger air transport with a rise of 300 to 700 per cent of passenger-kilometres between 1970 and 1995. The bulk of the expected increase in demand will be for road transport. The world-wide fleet of road motor vehicles is expected to grow 34 per cent between 1989 and 2000, from 557 million to 745 million. This rapid growth will occur particularly in countries that are on the threshold of industrialization. For example, a tripling of the vehicle fleet is expected in China in the decade 1990–2000. The number of car miles travelled tends to grow even faster than the number of cars owned (World Bank, 1996b).

The *structural effects* of globalization, regarding the transport sector, are related to the average transport distance. Schafer and Victor (1997) argue that people devote on average a constant fraction of their daily time to travel; the travel-time budget. If people hold their time for travel constant, but also if demand for mobility increases because incomes rise, they must select faster modes of transport to cover more distance in the same time. Schafer and Victor conclude that the data from every region are consistent with that expectation. At low incomes (below $5000 per capita), motorized travel is dominated by buses and low-speed trains. As income rises, slower public transport modes are replaced by automobiles, high-speed trains and aircraft. This means that in general a trend towards faster modes and increasing distance can be observed.

Considering the *technology effect* of globalization, the innovation and diffusion of new transportation technologies is an interesting option for achieving a more sustainable transport system. Three categories of new transportation technologies can be distinguished, namely (i) improvement of

Table 12.8 Passenger air transport (passenger-km; monthly averages; 1970 = 100)

		Base year	1970	1980	1990	1995
N. America	USA	17,664	100	184	295	405
	Canada	1,283	100	215	300	322
	Mexico	245	100	472	625	573
W. Europe	France	1,132	100	251	319	365
	Germany	688	100	255	511	748
	Netherlands	481	100	246	491	–
	Norway	163	100	208	324	294
	Sweden	204	100	183	297	351
	Switzerland	368	100	245	359	–
S. Europe	Greece	688	100	238	365	372
	Italy	700	100	148	271	378
	Portugal	191	100	150	299	337
	Spain	490	100	264	376	411
E. Europe	Poland	46	100	427	632	769
Asia	Japan	1,369	100	312	374	784
Australasia	Australia	772	100	275	299	–
	New Zealand	140	100	337	631	–

Source: UN (several years).

existing modes, (ii) the development of new (collective) transport modes, and (iii) development of new fuels. An increase in energy efficiency is an example of an improvement of existing modes. It is expected that the energy consumption of conventional fuel cars may decrease by 15–22 per cent per kilometre in the 1990–2000 period, after which a 25 per cent autonomous efficiency improvement is expected up to 2030. The development of new collective modes includes people movers, light-rail systems, subterranean transport systems, Maglev high-speed trains and so on. The third category involves the development of alternative fuels, which is still in an early stage of development. However, there are high expectations for their application because these alternative fuels reduce greenhouse gas emission, while the existing car and air transport system can still be used (Nijkamp et al., 1994/1995). In general, the development of new transportation technologies offers a high potential for reducing environmental effects of transportation.

However, the availability of, especially, new telecommunication and information technologies has led to new 'transportation' alternatives to many actors within the global economy. Both consumers and producers might alter or restructure their respective consumption and production patterns, given the emerging options. Some travel might be replaced by other means of transportation. However, new travel via so-called 'traditional' means might also be generated as a consequence of the impetus that these new technologies provide to economic activity or of information on other attractive places (for example, international tourism).

Trends in Environmental Pressure

The general trend in transportation seems to be a persistent growth in volume, distance and speed. The increasing globalization of our economies induced transportation as a result of a rise in consumption and production, accompanied by a shift in the location of production and consumption, the emergence of new (transportation) technologies and a shift in the product mix. Consequently, mobility world-wide has increased. These increased mobility patterns cause severe environmental problems.

As described in the introduction, transport is a significant contributor to the greenhouse effect (global warming). Global warming is primarily a result of the levels of industrialization and motorization in the industrial countries. However, if current trends continue, by 2010 developing countries could be the largest source of emissions of carbon dioxide and methane. Figure 12.3 shows the expectation that CO_2 emissions caused by transport will significantly increase in 2010. The contribution of CO_2 emissions will be the highest for Central and Eastern Europe and the former Soviet Union, China and centrally planned Asia and other developing countries.

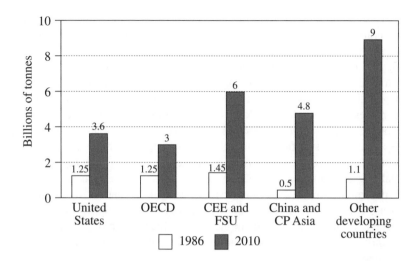

Note: CEE, Central and Eastern Europe; FSU, Former Soviet Union; CP Asia, Centrally Planned Asia.

Source: World Bank (1996b; from Faiz, 1993).

Figure 12.3 Transport and the global environment: carbon dioxide emissions, 1986 and projected for 2010

It is evident that the rise in international transport will generate a wide variety of environmental costs caused by a rise in air pollutants, greenhouse gases, waste, depletion of natural resources, and negative landscape changes. In Nijkamp et al. (1998) an extensive review of the various emissions is given. It seems plausible that there is no single policy trajectory which would ensure a sustainable transport development. Therefore, policy makers would have to resort to portfolios of measures incorporating technological, behavioural, industrial and land-use options, supported by market-based incentives.

EVALUATION AND FUTURE RESEARCH

The world economy faces important changes. The increasing globalization of the world economy may have large impacts on the transport system. The environmental problems caused by the transport sector, especially the emission of greenhouse gases effect, is a major concern. Because the future developments of globalization, transportation and the environmental consequences are very uncertain, scenarios can help to explore these uncertain developments.

Scenarios can be a useful tool for analysing possible futures and the impacts of several policy packages, especially as far as multiple actors and different time horizons are concerned.

In this chapter the driving forces and trends – an important step in scenario construction – are assessed. For describing the effects of globalization on transport and the environment, a conceptual framework is presented. The first part represents the driving forces behind globalization which include economic, demographic, technological, political and resource-use driving forces and changes in firm strategies and consumer preferences. The second part of the framework consists of four interacting layers, which represent the spatial effects of internationalization and the subsequent effects on transport and the environment. The increasing internationalization of economic markets, consumer preferences and technologies have implications for the global environment via changes in the spatial organization of production and consumption and the transportation needed for the movement of goods and passengers.

Worrying trends are – *inter alia* – the increasing volume of goods as well as passenger transport and the use of faster and less environmentally benign modes resulting in more CO_2 emissions. New opportunities are available via the development of new transportation technologies, the use of information and telecommunication technologies, the use of alternative energy sources and dematerialization.

However, the interactions between this multitude of driving forces and trends are very complicated, and the resulting effects for the global environment rather uncertain. Therefore, much additional and thorough research is needed. It may be useful to elaborate the above presented framework in more detail, *inter alia* by giving attention to several linkages between globalization, spatial organization, transport and the environment. Also relations within each subsystem can be analysed. Furthermore, the assessment of trends and driving forces can be used for the construction of international transport scenarios. In these scenarios the consequences of globalization via transport on the global environment have to be mapped out. Finally, in a strategic policy assessment the impact of government policy and changing firm strategies need to be analysed.

REFERENCES

Ayres, R.U. and L.W. Ayres (1996), *Industrial Ecology: Towards Closing the Materials Cycle*, Cheltenham, UK and Brookfield, USA: Edward Elgar.

Baldwin, R. (1993), 'The potential for trade between the countries of EFTA and Central and Eastern Europe', Discussion Paper series no. 853, London: Centre for Economic Policy Research.

Becht, H.Y. and J.P. van Soest (1997), 'Energy conservation for a long term, sustainable energy policy', in P.A. Okken, R.J. Swart and S. Zwerver (eds), *Climate and Energy: The Feasibility of Controlling CO$_2$ Emissions*, Dordrecht/Boston/London: Kluwer Academic Publishers, pp. 267 ff.

Bood, R.P. and T.J.B.M. Postma (1998), *Scenario Analysis as a Strategic Management Tool*, Groningen, The Netherlands: Graduate School/Research Institute Systems, Organization and Management.

Bos, E., M.T. Vu, E. Massiah and R.A. Bulatao (1994), *World Population Projections: Estimates and Projections with Related Demographic Statistics*, Baltimore, MD and London: Johns Hopkins University Press.

Courier, T. (1997), 'Globalisation: some key questions', *Africa – Caribbean – Pacific*, no. 164, 50–84.

Central Planning Bureau (CPB) (1992), *Scanning the Future: A Long-term Scenario Study of the World Economy 1990–2015*, The Hague: Sdu Publishers.

Euro-CASE (1996), *Mobility, Transport and Traffic*, Paris: European Council of Applied Sciences and Engineering.

European Conference of Ministers of Transport (ECMT) (1997), *Trends in the Transport Sector, 1970–1995*, Paris: OECD.

Factor 10 Club (1994), *Carnoules Declaration*, Friedrich Schmidt-Bleek, Wuppertal: Wuppertal Institute.

Garrod, B. (1997), 'Business strategies, globalization, and environment', in OECD, *Globalisation and Environment: Preliminary Perspectives*, Paris: OECD, pp. 11–23.

International Monetary Fund (IMF) (1997), *World Economic Outlook: Globalization: Opportunities and Challenges*, Washington, DC: IMF.

International Panel on Climate Change (IPCC) (1992), *The IPCC 1990 and 1992 Assessment*, IPCC: Canada.

International Panel on Climate Change (IPCC) (1995), *Report on Climate Change*, IPCC: Canada.

Johnstone, N. (1997), 'Globalisation, technology and environment', in OECD, *Globalisation and Environment: Preliminary Perspectives*, Paris: OECD, pp. 24–39.

Khan, M.S. and C.M. Reinhart (eds) (1995), 'Capital flows in the APEC region', Occasional Paper, Washington, DC: International Monetary Fund.

Lagendijk, A. (1993), *The Internationalization of the Spanish Automobile Industry and its Regional Impact. The Emergence of a Growth Periphery*, Amsterdam, The Netherlands: Thesis Publishers.

Maddison, A. (1989), *The World Economy in the 20th Century*, Paris: OECD.

Masser, I., O. Sviden and M. Wegener (1992), *The Geography of Europe's Futures*, London and New York: Belhaven Press.

Nijkamp, P., S.A. Rienstra and J.M. Vleugel (1994/1995), *Comparative Analysis of Options of Sustainable Transport and Traffic Systems in the 21st Century; Phase 1: State of the Art and Phase 2: Scenarios for a Sustainable Transport System*, Bilthoven: National Research Programme Office.

Nijkamp, P., S.A. Rienstra and J.M. Vleugel (1998), *Transportation Planning and the Future*, Chichester/New York: John Wiley.

Nijkamp, P., J.M. Vleugel, R. Maggi and I. Masser (eds) (1994), *Missing Transport Networks*, Aldershot, UK: Avebury.

Organization for Economic Cooperation and Development (OECD) (1992), *Globalisation of Industrial Activities: Four Case Studies*, Paris: OECD.

Organization for Economic Cooperation and Development (OECD) (1996), *Globalisation of Industry: Overview and Sector Report*, Paris: OECD.

Organization for Economic Cooperation and Development (OECD) (1997a), *Economic Globalisation and the Environment*, Paris: OECD.

Organization for Economic Cooperation and Development (OECD) (1997b), *Towards a New Global Age: Challenges and Opportunities: Policy Report*, Paris: OECD.

RAND (1997), *Scenarios for Examining Civil Aviation Infrastructure Options in the Netherlands*, Delft, The Netherlands: European-American Center for Policy Analysis.

Schafer, A. and D. Victor (1997), 'The past and future of global mobility', *Scientific American*, October, 41–3.

Tuininga, E.J. (1989), 'Nieuwe Basistechnologieen: Oplossing of Probleem voor het Milieu?', in H. Vollebergh (ed.), *Milieu en Innovatie*.

United Nations (UN) (various years), *Monthly Bulletin of Statistics*, New York: United Nations.

van Esch, R. (1994), *Globalisation and European Economies: from Brazilian Dialersquads to Irish Teleworkers*, The Hague: Ministry of Economic Affairs.

von Weizsacker, E., A.B. Lovins and L.H. Lovins (1997), *Factor Four: Doubling Wealth, Halving Resource Use*, London: Earthscan Publications Ltd.

World Bank (1996a), *Global Economic Prospects and the Developing Countries*, Washington, DC: International Bank for Reconstruction and Development.

World Bank (1996b), *Sustainable Transport: Priorities for Policy Reform*, Washington, DC: World Bank.

World Bank (1997), *World Development Report 1997: The State in a Changing World*, New York: Oxford University Press.

Index